Elements of Programming with Perl

Elements of
Programming with Perl

Andrew L. Johnson

MANNING

Greenwich
(74° w. long.)

For Susanna, Joseph, and Thomas

For electronic browsing and ordering of this and other Manning books,
visit http://www.manning.com. The publisher offers discounts on this book
when ordered in quantity. For more information, please contact:

Special Sales Department
Manning Publications Co.
32 Lafayette Place   Fax: (203) 661-9018
Greenwich, CT 06830   email: orders@manning.com

Library of Congress Cataloging-in-Publication Data
Johnson, Andrew L., 1963–
  Elements of Programming with Perl / Andrew L. Johnson.
    p. cm.
  Includes bibliographical references and index. (p. 348).
  ISBN 1-884777-80-5 (alk. paper)
   1. Perl (Computer program language) I. Title.
 QA76.73.P22J644 1999
 005.13'3—dc21   99-42510
            CIP

Manning Publications Co.   Production services: TIPS Technical Publishing
32 Lafayette Place   Copyeditor: Adrianne Harun
Greenwich, CT 06830   Typesetter: Lorraine B. Elder
            Cover designer: Leslie Haimes

Printed in the United States of America
1 2 3 4 5 6 7 8 9 19 – CM – 02 01 00 02

contents

v

Part III Practical elements

preface

The Norse God Odin had two ravens, Hugin and Munin (Thought and Memory). He would send them out each day to fly to the corners of the earth. At night, they would return and tell him all their secrets. Odin knew how to manage his resources. Thought and memory, cogitation and recall, processing and storage—as a programmer, these are the important resources you too must tame. This book aims to be your guide in this endeavor. By the time you finish this book, you should have the skills to manage your own Hugin and Munin. In other words, you will be able to write your own `hugin` Perl program to scour the web for interesting information, as well as a `munin` program to manage and query the database of information you collect.

There are a lot of books about Perl on the market today, and some of them I recommend highly. (See Appendix C, "Additional resources.") However, many authors of these other Perl books assume readers are already familiar with programming. Other authors take the *side-effect* approach, teaching readers the vocabulary and syntax of the language but offering few guidelines on how to use it effectively. I do not believe that the side-effect approach is an effective means of teaching programming.

This book instead presents the basic elements of programming using the context of the Perl language. I do not assume that you've programmed before, nor do I merely hammer you with syntax and function names. This book is designed to teach you both programming and Perl, from the basics to the more advanced skills you need to become an accomplished Perl programmer.

Audience

This book is intended for two types of readers: those approaching Perl as their first programming language and those who may have learned programming off the cuff but now want a more thorough grounding in programming in general, and Perl in particular.

More people than ever are learning Perl. Undoubtedly, Perl's widespread use for Common Gateway Interface (CGI) and web-client programming contributes to its popularity. Some people need Perl skills for their jobs, while others just think Perl programming is cool. Whatever your motivation, you need to understand up front that this book is *not* about using Perl for web-related programming, although an example or two illustrates that application of Perl. Instead, this book is about *learning how to program* using Perl. Once you have that knowledge under your belt, you can apply it to a multitude of problem domains.

This book does not assume that you know what variables, arrays, and loops are, or that you've programmed before. However, familiarity with basic mathematical concepts and logic will certainly be helpful. Readers with no prior programming experience should, of course, begin at the beginning and work their way through the first nine chapters in order. Chapters 10 through 15 are largely independent and can be read in any order. Chapters 16 through 19 introduce advanced Perl concepts. Each of these chapters lays a foundation for the following chapter, so read these four chapters in order.

If you are already familiar with elementary Perl programming, you may want to read chapters 2 and 3, and then pick and choose chapters that tackle areas in which you wish to improve. For example, chapters 6, 10, and 11 cover different aspects of regular expressions and matching operators. Chapter 8 covers references.

If you are a competent programmer in another language, this book may still be useful in demonstrating Perl's way of doing things. However, the discussions may not be as concise as you'd like, and the content is not organized as a reference book.

Organization

The book is organized in four main parts, starting with things to consider before you begin programming, followed by the essential aspects of programming with Perl. The third section explores a few of the more practical and Perl-specific areas. Finally, the later chapters introduce more advanced concepts, such as abstract data structures and object oriented-programming using Perl.

Introductory elements   The three chapters in this section provide elementary information on programming and the Perl language. Chapters 2 and 3 also delve into the basics of program structure and design. In chapter 3, we work through two examples, providing a whirlwind tour of the Perl language in the process.

Essential elements   Chapters 4 through 9 cover the essential concepts and structures you need to learn to program effectively. Here you will find everything from variables to loop control constructs to file input and output to basic regular expressions to subroutines to references and nested data structures. When you finish this section of the book, you will have all the tools you need to build real-world applications.

Practical elements   Chapters 10 through 15 take you into areas more specific to the Perl language, exploiting some of Perl's unique and powerful strengths. Here we explore regular expressions in more detail, string and list processing, more input and output techniques, using modules, and the Perl debugger.

Advanced elements   Chapters 16 through 19 provide an introduction to more advanced programming techniques, including building modules and abstract data structures. You are also introduced to object-oriented programming features in Perl. Chapter 20 mentions a few areas not covered in this book and suggests references for further study.

Appendices   The four short appendices cover command-line switches, special Perl variables, additional resources for readers, and a brief explanation of binary, octal, and hexadecimal numeric representation. Following the appendices is a small glossary of technical terms used in this book.

Source code, solutions, and errata

The source code for many of the example programs and modules presented in this book may be obtained from Manning's website. Point your browser to *http://www.manning.com/Johnson* for links to the online resources for the book, including source packages.

Many chapters have a small number of exercises at the end. There is no appendix of answers to these exercises. However, the web page mentioned above contains a link to a solutions page.

Finally, although we have strived to eliminate mistakes from the manuscript, some errors may have slipped through. The previously mentioned web page contains a link to an online errata listing corrections to errors discovered after the book was published. If you find any errors, please let us know so we can list them on the errata sheet and fix them in a later printing. The errata page lists an email address to which you can submit error reports.

Conventions

In this book, "Perl" (uppercase P) refers to the Perl programming language, while "perl" (lowercase p) refers to the perl compiler/interpreter or the perl distribution.

Filenames and URLs appear in *italics.* Code, program names, and any commands you might issue at the command line prompt appear in a `fixed-width` font. Some blocks of code are written using a form of literate programming (LP) syntax to break the code into smaller chunks for presentation (explained in chapters 3 and 9). In these cases, the real Perl code, or the pseudo-code, is in a plain `fixed-width` font, while the lines representing literate programming syntax are in an *`italic fixed-width`* font.

Many of the technical terms introduced in this book are defined in the glossary. When the terms first appear in the text, they are *italicized.*

You will also see the words `foo` and `bar` throughout this book. These are generic terms commonly used in syntax examples to represent the name of a variable or the contents of a string. They are used when the point of the example is not directly related to whatever is being called "foo." You might encounter these terms—and many similar "dummy" words, such as `foobar`, `baz`, `qux`, and `quux`—in publicly available articles and examples on programming.

Author online

Purchase of *Elements of Programming with Perl* includes free access to a private Internet forum where you can make comments about the book, ask technical questions, and receive help from the author and from other Perl users. To access the forum, point your web browser to *www.manning.com/Johnson.* There you will be able to subscribe to the forum. This site also provides information on how to access the forum once you are registered, what kind of help is available, and the rules of conduct on the forum.

acknowledgments

No author works in a vacuum, and I am certainly no exception. A large number of people deserve my gratitude for their help and support while I undertook this "little" project.

First I would like to thank Marjan Bace, the publisher, for taking a chance on my ideas, letting me run with them, and reining me in when necessary. He seems to take seriously the view that an author and publisher are partners, and it shows. His pleasant and personal style during our many phone conversations was always a welcome relief from the stresses and toils of making a living while writing a book.

Many other people at Manning contributed considerable efforts to make the book you now hold in your hands something of which I can be proud. I'd like to thank Brian Riley; Ben Kovitz, for his many insightful suggestions; Ted Kennedy, for managing the review process; Mary Piergies, for managing the production process; Syd Brown, for patiently testing the results of my script to convert the LaTeX chapters into MML format; Adrianne Harun, for her steadfast attention to detail in copyediting; and Robert Kern, Lynanne Fowle, and Lorraine Elder, for turning the manuscript into typeset pages.

A great many reviewers also caught embarrassing errors and glitches and provided helpful comments and suggestions. I would like thank Tad McClellan, Randy Kobes, Brad Fenwick, Jim Esten, Paul Holser, Dave Cross, Patrick Gardella, Mike Mullins, Michael Weinrich, Peter Murray, Richard Nilsson, Umesh Nair, Vasco Patricio, and Richard Kingston. My brother Brad Johnson also provided crucial advice at a couple of junctures in the book. All of these people are responsible for helping make this a better book. Any problems or errors that remain are my responsibility.

Parts of this book were written, or at least conceptualized, in my notebook while I was at Bellamy's, the local corner pub and restaurant, where I could almost always find one of my preferred beers on tap. Bellamy's offered a quiet table or booth when I needed to work, and a seat at the bar when I needed rejoin the living.

I'd like to thank Linda E., the bartender, for not only serving up good ale, but also being a cheerful friend.

Anyone who uses uses Perl and enjoys it as much as I do owes a serious debt of gratitude to Larry Wall for creating this gem and giving it to us so freely. Also, many thanks are due to Tom Christiansen, whose long and continued efforts have been instrumental in creating and maintaining a vast and informative documentation set that, in my opinion, remains unmatched in any other software documentation. Thanks are also due to the many and varied regular posters on comp.lang.perl.misc from whom I have learned much, the perl5-porters who continually work to improve Perl, and the rest of the Perl community who keep sharing code and ideas and taking Perl into new territory.

Lastly, but certainly not least, I'd like to thank my mother and three brothers who are always encouraging and never lacking in good advice whether you want it or not; my wife, Susanna, just for being who she is (and for putting up with my irregular hours and countless other faults...um, eccentricities); and my sons, Thomas and Joseph, for their patience and understanding when Dad disappeared into his office, and for continually keeping me in touch with the pleasant side of reality: playing games, reading stories, building snowmen, and other simple pleasures.

PART **I**

Introductory elements

CHAPTER 1

Introduction

To write a story, fiction or fact, one must grasp the basics of the language in use—enough at least so that one can make simple statements that may be understood by readers. One must also be able to string together a series of such statements in a manner that communicates meanings and events in relation to time and space. Stories also have certain compositional elements like a beginning, a middle, and an end, although the presentation need not proceed in that order.

Listen to writers talk about writing, and you'll find that writing is seldom the result of any "holistic inspiration" where the writer realizes the entire story at once in the mind and simply writes it down. Much more often, you'll find writers claiming that inspiration is rare and fleeting and usually comes during—and as a result of—the writing process, not the other way around.

Programming is similar in many ways to writing. One must know the basics of the language and how to string together a series of statements such that events and meaning are described in space and time. Structural elements—beginnings, middles, and ends—are also important in program composition. Finally, real inspiration generally occurs while immersed in the development process, not before.

Whether programming is an art or a science is often a subject of discussion. But programming is neither an art achievable only by innately talented right-brain visionaries, nor a strictly scientific left-brain logic of first principles. It is a craft, like writing, that can be learned, practiced, developed, and honed to a variety of skill levels and for a multitude of purposes.

Some writers write great literary novels, others write pulp fiction, and many people who are not writers by trade write all kinds of narratives from business reports to postcards to notes on little squares of adhesively backed yellow paper. Similarly, some programmers write elegant programs solving massively complex problems; others produce solid utilitarian code daily; and many, who are not programmers by trade, crank out all manner of tools and big and little programs and go on with their real jobs.

So, if programming is a craft like writing, and writing is about telling narratives, what is programming about? Programming is about solving problems.

1.1   On programming

Computers are mindless devices capable only of doing what they are told. Before we talk about the activities of programming we need to have a basic understanding of what a program is and the role it plays in turning an expensive piece of mindless hardware into a useful device.

Imagine the following scenario: You are taken to a room containing a desk and a chair. On the left of the desk is an "in-box" full of pages of numbers, and on the right is an empty "out-box." In between lies a manila envelope, a calculator, a pad of paper, and a stack of blank forms. You are told to open the envelope and follow the instructions you'll find inside. The simple and explicit instructions tell you to take the first page of numbers from the in-tray and perform certain simple arithmetic operations on particular sets of those numbers and to write the results of these calculations into certain numbered boxes on one of the blank forms. When you've completed one page of numbers, you must place the newly filled out form into the out-tray and begin again with the next page of numbers in the in-tray.

In this scenario, you are operating essentially as a mindless computing device: taking *input,* performing simple operations, and writing out the results. The instructions are simple and do not require "thought" or interpretation, merely that you can read in numbers, operate the calculator, temporarily store intermediate results on the pad of paper, and control the *output* device (pencil) to write out the results (see figure 1.1).

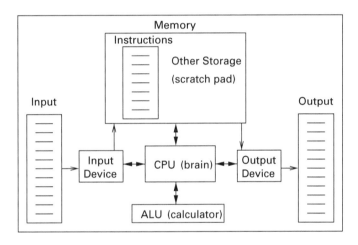

Figure 1.1   Processing data

An important point to note is that you have no idea about what you are doing in this scenario. You may be just one part of a team performing various steps in a complex encryption/decryption scheme, or you might simply be balancing my checkbook. At any rate, you would not likely enjoy this particular activity. In addition to being boring and repetitive—the usual definition of mindless—such activities nonetheless require attention to many small details. They occupy your brain, but don't absolutely free your mind. It would be hard to meditate while performing such a task.

The most important component in the above situation is the set of instructions. The mindless brain can be replaced by a mindless *central processing unit*

(CPU) controlling simple mechanical/electrical devices for input, output, arithmetic operations and temporary storage. However, it takes a mind to conceive a given set of instructions to control such a machine. Anyone who has stayed up late on Christmas Eve trying to put together a "some assembly required" toy for their child can appreciate the problems of working with incomplete, out of order, and badly written instructions.

I said programming is about solving problems, but that is not entirely accurate. You not only have to think of a way to solve a given problem, you also have to develop that solution into a complete step-by-step set of simple instructions for solving the problem. When a method for solving a problem is reduced to a series of simple, repeatable instructions, we call that set of instructions an *algorithm.*

An algorithm can be specified in any language, but regardless of how complex the algorithm might be, each step or instruction must be simple and not subject to interpretation or intuition. An algorithm must also always generate the same result. If each step is performed flawlessly, the outcome is guaranteed. Programming is about creating algorithms to perform simple or complex tasks and translating these algorithms into instructions that a computer can perform.

The particular instructions that a computer can execute are in a form known as "machine language" or simply "machine code." Machine code instructions consist of sequences of numbers, ultimately reduceable to zeros and ones (i.e., binary code). These instructions deal with low level operations such as storing a number into a particular memory location, reading a number out of a particular memory address, or adding a number into an accumulator. For example, the following snippet of machine code causes two numbers, which are stored in memory, to be added together and saved into another memory location for later use:

```
8B45FC 0345F8 8945F4
```

Of course, we humans have a hard time trying to formulate algorithms in a machine language so we soon developed a language consisting of abbreviated words to stand for the particular operations a given machine could perform. We could write programs out in this "assembly" language, then translate the language into the corresponding machine code using one machine instruction per each assembly instruction.

Assembly code was easier to write than the machine code it replaced, but because different machine architectures used different machine code, each had to be programmed in its own version of an assembly language. A program written for one machine type had to be rewritten to run on another machine type. Another problem with assembly languages is that they still dealt with the low level instructions of moving around bits of information.

Higher level languages were later developed to allow instructions to express higher level concepts. With a low level language like an assembly, one had to write individual instructions to place a number from a specific location in memory into a temporary holding area; add a number from a different memory location; and, finally, store the result of that operation in a third location in memory. With a high level language, one could write a single instruction that encapsulates the concept (see figure 1.2).

Machine Code	Assembler Code	High Level Code
8B45FC	movl a, %eax	
0345F8	addl b, %eax	c = a + b
8945F4	movl %eax, c	

Figure 1.2   Comparison of machine, assembly, and high level languages

Aside from the obvious advantage of making the instructions easier to read and write for humans, compilers were created that translated each high level statement down to the corresponding assembly and machine codes for different machines. This meant that one could a write a program once in the high level language and be able to run it on any machine that had a compiler for that language.

Early high level languages included Fortran, designed primarily for mathematical computing; COBOL, for business related programming; and BASIC and Pascal, intended initially as teaching languages. Today, a wealth of high level languages exist from which to choose, each with particular strengths and weaknesses. The remainder of this chapter is about the language that will be taught in this book.

1.2 On Perl

Perl was created by Larry Wall and initially released in 1987. Perl's inception is illustrative of its nature (and certainly says something about its creator as well). When Larry was faced with a problem that involved complex text processing and report generation exceeding the capabilities of what could be done easily with standard Unix tools like sed and awk he made a choice. Rather than restricting his viewpoint to solving this particular task, he saw that his problem was just one of a whole class of problems for which existing tools and languages provided no simple solutions. So, in the spirit of long-term laziness, Larry Wall created a new tool for solving such problems.

Perl did not simply fill a gap in the existing toolset. Perl incorporated the capabilities of existing tools and borrowed freely from other languages. It soon became the language of choice for getting things done in the Unix environment (and its usefulness soon spread to other operating systems and environments). Put another way, Perl didn't fill one particular gap in the toolset; it became *the* tool to use for filling gaps everywhere.

Designed not only for practical usefulness, but also for continued expansion, Perl has become a powerful general purpose programming language. In its current incarnation, it offers extremely powerful regular expression enhancements, object-oriented programming, a well defined module system, references, nested data structures, and quite a bit more.

Perhaps some, or even all, of the features I just mentioned don't mean a lot to you at the moment. You want to know what *you* can do with Perl. Telling you that you can write programs to do anything you want wouldn't be accurate, but it wouldn't be too far from the truth either. Perl isn't well suited for some kinds of programming: for example, writing operating systems, writing device drivers, and doing heavy numeric analysis. So what is Perl good for?

Perl excels at reading, processing, transforming, and writing plain text. Processing text may not seem like a big deal until you realize all the ways you might want a program to interact with textual data. Not only the plain text files you save on your hard drive, but the file and directory names themselves are representations of textual data. With Perl, you can easily write code that will read in directory listings, create new files or directories, rename files, delete (unlink) files, and more. Automating many kinds of system administration and backup tasks is but one common use of Perl.

Client-server interactions, such as the Structured Query Language (SQL) statements you send to a database server and the results it returns, or the HTTP requests you send to a webserver and the HTML pages it sends back, are all largely plain or simply encoded text. Similarly, communications between a webserver and external programs use a simple, encoded text protocol know as Common Gateway Interface (CGI). A significant portion of Internet sites that provide dynamic content or search capabilities are powered by Perl programs that handle requests from the webserver; turn these into queries for a database's server; collect, transform, and format the resulting data; and pass it back to the webserver. Because Perl makes it so easy to write programs that work between other programs, Perl is often referred to as a "glue" language. And because of its wide use sticking various things together throughout the Internet, Perl has also been called the "duct tape" of the Internet.

I mentioned that Perl was designed to grow and that it has a well defined module system. This means that many of the common tasks—and some uncommon ones—have already been encapsulated into *modules* that are freely available for anyone to use (see the discussion of CPAN later in this chapter). When you want to write a CGI program, write client software to do file transfer protocol (FTP), or interact with a database, you can use a well tested and *debugged* module that provides most of what you need, leaving you only to add the code to deal with your specific task.

Not only do modules make it easy to use Perl for common tasks, but some modules provide extensions that allow you to use Perl for problems for which Perl itself might be less well suited. I mentioned above that Perl may not be a good choice for numeric analysis. However, there are modules designed to extend Perl's handling of numeric data by providing arbitrarily large integers and floating point numbers. There is also the Perl Data Language (PDL) module package, which provides extensions for doing fast mathematical computations on large matrices of numeric data.

Some programming languages are *interpreted,* meaning that a program written in that language is read by an interpreter program that translates each statement into the appropriate machine code and executes it. In such languages, errors cannot be detected until the program is already running and the interpreter encounters a statement that generates an error. Other languages are *compiled,* meaning that a whole program is read by a compiler and translated into machine code before it can be run. In this case, many kinds of errors can be caught before the program is even run. (Some errors, called *run-time errors,* will still not be caught until the program is running.) Perl is both interpreted and compiled. When you run a Perl program, Perl reads the entire program and compiles it into an internal format (not machine code), then interprets this internal representation like a regular interpreter. Thus, in many places in this book, I will sometimes refer to the perl interpreter and sometimes to the perl compiler—but they both refer to perl itself. Perl, however, refers to the Perl language.

The advantage of such a compiled/interpreted system is that many kinds of errors can be detected during the compilation phase, before a program begins executing. Yet you do not need to separately compile and link your code into a binary executable each time you make a change, as you would for a strictly compiled language such as C. You can simply type in your program and run it. The perl compiler/interpreter takes care of the rest. The tradeoff is a little loss in speed. A program compiled into machine executable code runs somewhat faster than one whose statements are individually interpreted with each run through. That said, Perl programs usually run very fast, especially for text processing types of tasks.

Yet another benefit of Perl's interpreted nature is memory management. In many lower level compiled languages, like C, your program is required to deal specifically with allocating and releasing the necessary memory for storing data while your program is running. When you program in Perl, the perl interpreter takes care of allocating extra memory when needed and releasing that memory so it can be used again when it is no longer needed. This doesn't mean you can completely ignore memory issues. You still need to make choices such as whether to read a file completely into memory or read a file one line at a time. But you don't have to worry about actually allocating and releasing the memory yourself.

Later in this chapter, I will continue this discussion of Perl and why it is the greatest thing since peanut butter (sliced bread really wasn't such a big deal until peanut butter arrived on the scene). Right now, let's turn to the more practical matter of ensuring that you have a perl distribution up and running so that you can begin your Perl programming journey.

1.2.1 Getting started

If you are not using a system that has perl installed, you will have to obtain a perl distribution and install it yourself. The latest source distribution can be found on the Comprehensive Perl Archive Network (CPAN) at *http://www.perl.com/CPAN/ src*. Pointers to binary distributions for various platforms can also be found there in the */ports* directory. The distributions contain detailed installation information, and the process is usually painless.

Unix-like systems   On a Unix-like system, you will probably want to compile your own version of perl, assuming you have a C compiler installed. The process is simple, though it can be a little time consuming. The first thing you want to do, after downloading the latest distribution from the above mentioned CPAN site, is to unpack it, go into the resulting directory, and read the *README* file for your system and the *INSTALL* file. This should provide you with enough information to build your own version of perl. Essentially, the process is just

```
$ rm -f config.sh Policy.sh
$ sh Configure
$ make
$ make test
$ make install
```

The configure step will take awhile. You will have to answer a variety of questions about your system and where you want things installed. Picking the defaults is usually all that's needed in most cases.

Win/NT systems   On Win32 systems, your best bet is probably to obtain the ActiveState version of perl, which is available at *http://www.ActiveState.com/*

For Win95, you will probably need to get the DCOM package and install it before starting to install the perl distribution. You can find it at *http://www.microsoft.com/com/dcom/dcom1_2/download.asp*

Installing the ActiveState version of perl is a matter of double-clicking the archive. The install process will ask a few questions and you should accept the defaults unless you have good reason not to accept them. After this, you should be able to run perl from the command prompt and run the `perldoc` utility to access the documentation (see later in this chapter).

MacOS   You can get a compiled binary distribution of Perl for the MacOS in the ports section of CPAN: *http://www.perl.com/CPAN/ports/index.html#mac.* This link should automatically redirect you to a nearby mirror site.

Installing this version involves unpacking the archive, starting the program, and setting a few configuration details that are pointed out in the included *README* file. The major sections of the documentation should be accessible via the help menu.

1.2.2 Running Perl

Once you have perl installed, creating and running a Perl program is a simple process. The following is a simple, one line program that prints the string "Hello World":

```
print "Hello World\n";
```

Create a new text file (plain text) using any editor with which you are comfortable. This should be a text editor, not a word processing program—you can find a list of decent editors for various platforms by pointing your browser at *http://reference.perl.com/query.cgi?editors*

Now enter the above statement. Save the file as "first." You can then run the program from the command line as

```
perl first
```

On many Unix-like systems you can create your script to be run as if it is an executable program. This method means adding a special first line to your program and setting the executable bit on the file with the `chmod` Unix command. Here is the new program:

```
#!/usr/bin/perl
print "Hello World\n";
```

The first line, called the "pound-bang" or *shebang* line starts with the two characters # ! followed by the full path to where perl is located on your system— in other words, the absolute directory path to the perl program. If you save this as before and then type `chmod +x first` at the prompt, you can then invoke the program like:

```
first
```

If the current directory is not in your PATH (the environment variable listing search paths for executable programs), you may need to qualify the above call as

```
./first.
```

The ActiveState port comes with a `pl2bat` utility to turn your perl program into a batch file that can be placed in your PATH and called like any other program.

If you are using MacPerl then you should be able to simply choose `new` from the `file` menu, type in the script, and then choose `run script` from the `script` menu. The shebang line is not necessary on non-Unix systems, but it is always a good idea put one in, because perl will check it for command line switches such as -w (see chapter 2). With MacPerl, you can also save the script as a Mac-specific item called a "droplet," which is a version you can execute by double-clicking its icon.

1.2.3 Getting help

Perl is a relatively easy language to learn, but it is not a small language. This book does not attempt to be a reference for the Perl language. If you have perl installed, however, you already have the most up-to-date language reference available. The perl distribution includes a large amount of documentation that is installed as Unix manpages and/or HTML pages (or some other format, depending on installation configuration details). The raw documentation is in a plain text mark-up format called Plain Old Documentation (*POD*), and is also readable using the included `perldoc` utility (or `shuck` on the Mac). To view the initial perl pod-page you can enter `perldoc perl` at your command line prompt. This document provides a list of the remaining sections of the core documentation. Another useful starting page is `perldoc perltoc` which provides a more in-depth table of contents of the Perl documentation.

One extremely useful set of documents is the set of *perlfaq* documents. Very often one begins to tackle a problem by breaking it down into smaller problems and addressing those. However, when learning a new language, some of the smaller problems are often difficult because you do not yet know how to express the solution in the context of the language you are learning. This is when it is time to turn to the Frequently Asked Question (FAQs).

Do not assume that the FAQs only address simple or "little" questions and that your question will not be found there. Many FAQs do have simple answers, but they are no less valuable for that. On the other hand, there are also many real programming issues addressed in Perl's FAQs. No matter how easy or difficult your particular problem seems to be, you'll often have good luck finding something of use in the FAQs. In chapter 3, we will begin developing a tool to quickly search the FAQs for information we might need.

The FAQs are divided into nine sections, or files, named *perlfaq1* to *perlfaq9* and are viewable with the `perldoc` utility. The *perltoc* page describes each of these and lists all of the questions you will find answers to in each document.

Another source of help is the Usenet community. There are separate newsgroups for discussions on miscellaneous Perl topics (*comp.lang.perl.misc*), discussions on perl modules (*comp.lang.perl.modules*), and the Tk graphics toolkit (*comp.lang.perl.tk*). There is also a moderated group that you can read, but participation requires registration (*comp.lang.perl.moderated*). If you have never participated in Usenet newsgroups before, I recommend that you first take a look at *news.announce.newusers*.

Although all of the newsgroups are open to public participation, they are not forums for questions addressed in the perl documentation and FAQs. The people participating in these groups are knowledgeable and helpful, but you are expected to have tried to find answers to your questions in the documentation before turning to the newsgroup. These newsgroups are not free help desks. If you treat them as such, you will likely get ignored or worse.

On a related note, remember, programming is about problem solving. Beginners often approach a programming language as simply another application to learn. This can lead to asking questions like "How do I do "X" in Perl?" When learning a new word processor application, one might formulate a question such as "How do I create footnotes in my documents?" But a programming language is not simply an application. It provides ways to formulate solutions to problems. It does not provide single commands or functions for every conceivable problem.

Before you ask a "How do I…" question, search through the documentation on Perl's built-in functions (see `perldoc perlfunc`) to see if one meets your needs. Then search the FAQs to see if your question has already been answered. If these two approaches fail, ask yourself how you would go about solving the problem without a computer. For example, recently a question appeared on the *comp.lang.perl.misc* newsgroup asking (and not for the first time) how to tell if an integer is odd or even. There is no simple `even` or `odd` built-in Perl function that solves this problem for you directly. The obvious question to ask yourself is "How do *I* tell if an integer is even or odd?" Most people simply notice if the last digit is one of 0, 2, 4, 6, or 8. If so, the integer is even. Algorithms often arise from such simple beginnings.

You may not succeed in solving your particular problem, or your solution may not be the optimal solution, but this common sense approach is the first step in thinking like a programmer. One more avenue, before resorting to asking your question in the newsgroup, is to use one of the Usenet search engines (for example, *www.dejanews.com*) to search the Perl newsgroups for similar questions that may have been asked and answered in the past. Finally, if you have exhausted all avenues of inquiry without success, ask your question on the appropriate newsgroup. Be sure to include information on what you've tried so the helpful people there know you are not just looking for free handouts but are actually interested in learning.

Another place to begin exploring a wealth of Perl related information is the Perl home page at *www.perl.com*. From there you will find links to HTML versions of the Perl documentation and FAQs, plus pointers to the Comprehensive Perl Archive Network (CPAN). At CPAN, you can find and download not only the Perl source distribution, with its standard libraries and modules, but also a large number of contributed modules and scripts for various problem domains.

Jargon   If you are new to programming and/or Usenet in general, you may encounter quite a bit of jargon when using the above-mentioned resources. One very good, and quite extensive, resource you may want to look at is the *Jargon File*. This is a large dictionary or lexicon of common and not-so-common slang terms found in the hacker community. You can find this file at *http://www.tuxedo.org/~esr/jargon/*, or use your favorite search engine to locate a copy.

Just to get you started, I'll run through a few terms that you might happen upon as you begin to read the literature. For example, if you do ask a question on the newsgroup and it is answered in the FAQ, you're unlikely to get responses beyond the standard RTFM which means, "Read The F****** Manual."

Quite often, people will quote material from the "camel" or "llama" books. These are two standard Perl books by published by O'Reilly and Associates. The books feature pictures of the respective animals on their covers and are titled *Programming Perl* (camel) and *Learning Perl* (llama)—See appendix C. Both are very good books, by the way.

A couple of other frequently used terms are "grep," meaning to search, and "grok," meaning to understand. Grep derives from the standard Unix search utility of the same name. If you want to grok Year 2000 (Y2K) issues in Perl, you should grep the FAQs for the relevant entries.

Another common term is "parse." Specifically, parse means to break up a piece of data—such as a string (a sequence of characters or words)—according to a specified set of syntactic rules. More generally, parse is often used in the context of simply recognizing and/or extracting particular bits of data from a larger chunk of data.

You may also see reference to "p5p," which refers to the perl5-porters, a group of people responsible for maintaining and upgrading the actual Perl distribution across the many platforms on which it runs. Another group—set of groups really—is the Perl Mongers, a collection of user groups distributed around the world. (Visit *http://www.pm.org* to find your nearest group or to start one.) I happen to be a member of the Winnipeg Perl Mongers (Winnipeg.pm for short).

A variation of the Monger moniker seems to be Perl M(o|u)nger, which is regular expression talk (you'll learn about regular expressions in chapters 6 and 10) to refer to either Monger or Munger. Munger, then, is the noun form of the verb "to munge," which means essentially, in the context of data processing, to parse, process, slice, dice, julienne, massage, fold, bend, or otherwise mutilate (i.e., manipulate) data.

This little interlude barely scratches the surface of the jargon you will run into in your journey. If nothing else, at least I've warned you that you are entering not only a new area of study, but a new linguistic arena as well. Don't forget to check out the *Jargon File* mentioned above—it contains much more than mere definitions.

1.3 A bigger picture

The previous sections have dealt with basic information on programming and on Perl. Now we will take a brief step back and take in a larger view. My first choice for a title for this section was "Practical and Philosophical Remarks on Programming, Perl, and the Rest of this Book," but that was a tad long winded—even for me.

Several years ago, I worked as an inshore diver, doing a variety of underwater inspection, repair, and construction tasks, often in fast-moving water. Every job was different, and there was no such thing as a transportable stable work platform that could be used in every situation. Insted, we had the next best thing: a shop with a selection of tools, a wide variety of surplus construction steel (rings, bolts, rods, angle iron, and I-beams), and an arc-welder. This was a hacker workshop. We created reusable bracing and clamping components, and rigged up a variety of different scaffold systems that could be lowered from the barge, positioned, and anchored in various ways to bridge piers of different sizes and shapes, pilings, or dam gate systems. That arc-welder was the key to being able to quickly and solidly connect a variety of components into working solutions we could deploy in the field.

In the programming world, Perl reminds me very much of that workshop and, in particular, the arc-welder. Perl has been nicknamed the Swiss Army chainsaw of programming languages due to its multitude of built-in tools and overall brute force utility. I think a better analogy is that of a Swiss Army arc-welder, one quite capable of hacking out fast, sometimes crude, one-time solutions, as well as building and joining (virtually seamlessly) components for solving more complex or longer term problems.

Perl is not your average everyday programming language. In fact, it is an exceptional everyday programming language. There are currently more high level programming languages out there than you can shake a stick at. Of course, some computer scientists seem to get great pleasure from shaking a lot of sticks anyway, and Perl seems to have more than its fair share of detractors from computer science purists, who complain that Perl is too big, ugly, and redundant.

So what makes Perl so great? No single feature of Perl makes it outstanding, and any program you write using Perl could also be written using another language. Certainly, Perl makes some things easier to accomplish than they might be in other languages, but this can't be all there is to it. There are other languages that offer pretty much the same high level functionality as Perl, and do so in a way that seems to satisfy the above mentioned stick wavers. Yet Perl remains wildly popular. The language continues to evolve, and its user base is still growing unchecked. What appeal might Perl have beyond the sheer functionality that might first attract programmers from other languages, and why would experienced programmers fall in love with this language if other "better" programming languages exist?

I lay the blame squarely on the shoulders of Perl's creator, Larry Wall. (Well, more precisely, slightly above and between Larry's shoulders.) Besides being a computer programmer, Larry also has a background in linguistics. Consequently, the fact that Perl has the qualities of a natural language is no accident. You can read some of Larry's own musings on these qualities at *http://kiev.wall.org/~larry/natural.html*. Here I will touch upon only a couple of points in this regard.

Two of the things Perl receives criticism for are the richness and the redundancy in the language, which are by no means unrelated issues in Perl. By richness, I mean that Perl is a big language, incorporating and supporting a large number of powerful and specialized features directly in the language. In contrast, other languages tend to be minimal, providing standard libraries for specialized tasks. The list of Perl's specialized features includes regular expressions, pattern match operators, process management, file and directory manipulation, and socket programming tools, to highlight just a few. Another example of Perl's richness is its ability to provide more than one way of saying or accomplishing the same task. This is redundancy; it exists in natural languages and in Perl. Indeed, the Perl slogan is TMTOWTDI (pronounced "timtoady"), which stands for "There's More Than One Way To Do It."

Critics say that both richness and redundancy make the language harder to learn. But this is only true up to a point. Certainly, I may be able learn a complete minimalist programming language rapidly, but assuming there are libraries providing additional functionality, I would then still have to learn to use the various libraries to do the things I might want to do. Perl is not really more demanding in this respect. You do not have to learn the entire language before you start, merely the essential elements plus any extra built-in features you find necessary for your present task. Similarly Perl's redundancy doesn't require that you learn every possible way to say something before you begin. Redundancy merely expands your options. Indeed, the positive consequence of these natural language qualities is not that they make it easier to think in Perl; they make it easier to express your thoughts in Perl.

There is also a strong sense of community among many Perl programmers. More than just a large number of users sharing information on various forums, the Perl community shares a sort of Perl spirit. Perl's "naturalness" lends itself to playfulness—not merely clever programming tricks, but poetry, puns, and other games of the sort people play with natural languages. Of course, this community spirit is more than fun and games, but I think it is significant to note that programmers coming from other languages who have found their calling to be growing tedious have expressed gratitude that Perl has made programming fun again.

The Perl community also holds a strong concept of sharing. Help and advice are given freely on the newsgroups and many talented programmers cooperate on the development and evolution of Perl itself. Beyond that is CPAN—a vast collection of contributed modules from Perl programmers all over the world. Programming, unlike most creative acts, places a high premium on reuse rather than originality. The Perl community is no exception. Several hundred modules are available on CPAN, ranging from database interfaces to development tools to interfaces for several graphics libraries to Internet programming to date manipulation modules and much more. Whenever you find yourself facing a new programming challenge, check out CPAN. Chances are pretty good that someone has written a module that will make your task much easier.

By now you might be wondering when we will stop talking about Perl and start learning to program with it. The next two chapters concentrate on aspects of writing good code and the process of developing programs. In the latter chapter, we follow the development of two Perl programs from initial idea through to working programs. A good deal of Perl will be presented along the way.

C H A P T E R   2

Writing code

Writing code—that is, typing in the set of instructions in a programming language—is only one part of the programming process. In fact, as we will see in the next chapter, it is a relatively small part of the programming process. But, however small the act of writing code may be in the overall process, it is an important act. The decisions you make here can have a large effect on all other steps in the programming process. How well you write your code affects how easy it is to read, which in turn affects how easy it is to fix (if a problem arises), upgrade, and add additional features.

Perl is often derided as being a "write only" language—meaning that programs written in Perl are inherently hard to read and understand—but this is simply false. Mostly, these accusations arise from people unfamiliar with Perl. Some presumed difficulties arise as the result of all the funky symbols used in Perl (Perl uses every symbol on a standard keyboard for one purpose or another); some are due to the variety of shortcuts Perl offers the programmer; and some occur because people simply writing bad code (this happens in every language). Although at first glance, Perl appears to be a difficult language to read, it really isn't. Certainly, it is not terribly difficult to write hard-to-read code in Perl—but it is not terribly difficult to write easy-to-read code in Perl either. This chapter is about writing simple, clean code. Do not worry if you don't recognize or understand the Perl code in the following sections. They are only examples to illustrate style issues. You will have plenty of opportunity to learn Perl and apply these guidelines in the chapters that follow.

As we mentioned previously, high level languages exist for the benefit of the programmer, not the computer. The computer does not execute the instructions in a high level language. They must first be translated into the machine language of the particular computer system where the program will be run. As we saw in the last chapter, high level languages offer three advantages over low level machine code: They provide a level of portability across all the different machine types that have translators for that language; they make it easier for humans to write the instructions because certain operations that might take several lines of machine code can be written in a single simple statement in the high level language; and they make it easier for humans to read those instructions. This last benefit is the subject of this chapter.

It is up to the programmer to take full advantage of whatever facilities the high level language offers to produce easy-to-read programs. How easy a program is to read affects how easy it is to write, debug, and maintain. Let's begin with structure.

2.1 Structure

This book is organized into parts, chapters, sections, subsections, paragraphs, sentences, and words. Whitespace plays a large role in delimiting these elements. You wouldn'twanttoreadabookwithnowhitespaceinitnowwouldyou? Let's look at an example of bad code written in Perl:

```
$s=0;$i=1;while($i<=
10){$s=$s+$i;$i=$i+
1;}print"the sum of 1 through 10 is $s\n";
```

Virtually nothing about this fragment indicates the structure of the code to the reader. There is structure in this fragment, indicated to the Perl compiler by such things as semicolons, parentheses, and curly braces. These are enough for the Perl compiler to make sense of the above code, but human readers, even those familiar with Perl, have to decipher the structure before they can even try to decipher the code. Let's look at the same code written in a fashion that better mirrors its structure:

```
$s = 0;
$i = 1;
while ( $i <= 10 ) {
    $s = $s + $i;
    $i = $i + 1;
}
print "the sum of 1 through 10 is $s\n";
```

Both fragments accomplish the same task, as you can probably deduce from the print statement at the end of each fragment. However, the second example does not merely look nicer, its layout illustrates good use of whitespace to show the structure of the code. Each statement is now contained on its own line. (Note that a statement ends with a semicolon.) We have also used spaces between variables ($s, $i), operators (=, <=, +), and literal data (1, 10) in much the same way we use spaces to separate words in a sentence.

Finally, even though we have not introduced the while *loop,* if you guessed that the two indented statements somehow belong together and are probably related to the line immediately above them starting with the keyword while, you'd be right. It is important to realize, however, that the indentation does not group these statements together, the curly braces do that. Perl ignores the use of such whitespace and indentation, allowing the programmer to use such devices to write more human readable code.

Another common form of writing `while` loops and similar structures in Perl involves aligning the curly braces below the `while` *keyword* and indenting the *block* of statements as follows:

```
while ( $i <= 10 )
{
    $s = $s + $i;
    $i = $i + 1;
}
```

Another similar structure is the `if/else` structure. This is a decision structure rather than a looping structure (see chapter 3) and can be written in either of the styles we used for the `while` loop:

```
if ( CONDITION ) {
    statement;
    statement;
} else {
    statement;
    statement;
}
```

or,

```
if ( CONDITION )
{
    statement;
    statement;
}
else
{
    statement;
    statement;
}
```

Some variations exist of these two styles. Larry Wall, for example, favors something similar to the first style but with the `else` clause starting on a new line. The amount of indentation also varies. In this book, we will use the first style and an indentation equal to four spaces.

2.2 Naming

That first code example contained more problems than just a lack of structure. Let's take another look at the structured version:

```
$s = 0;
$i = 1;
while ( $i <= 10 ) {
```

```
    $s = $s + $i;
    $i = $i + 1;
}
print "the sum of 1 through 10 is $s\n";
```

This code is now nicely laid out in a way that highlights its structure, but without the print statement at the end, we still might have trouble discerning the purpose of this code fragment. A *variable* is a place in memory where we can store (and retrieve) data. What do the variables $s and $i represent here? We still have to examine the code closely to see how the variables are being used and what operations are being performed to even begin to understand the code. A much improved version of the same code might be

```
$sum     = 0;
$counter = 1;
while ( $counter <= 10 ) {
    $sum     = $sum + $counter;
    $counter = $counter + 1;
}
```

We have done two things in this new version. Most importantly, we have given names to our variables to indicate what the variables represent. We have also used spacing again to align related operations in related statements. Now, even before we look beyond the first line of code, we can guess that $sum is a variable that will be used to contain a sum of some kind. With the second line, we see a variable that will be used as a counter. It is now much easier to read and understand what the *loop* accomplishes, even without the print statement included in the fragment.

In Perl, variable names can be as long as you want them (as long as you don't want them to be longer than 255 characters). Variable names, other than built-in variables, must begin with a letter or an underscore and may be followed by upper or lowercase letters, underscores, or digits. Variable names are also always preceded by one of three symbols—$, @, or %—which represent the type of the variable. So far, we are only using *scalar* variables, which hold a single value and are preceded by the $ symbol. Let's look at another example:

```
$tot = $p + $st;
```

Using abbreviations is common, but these abbreviations are likely only obvious to myself, and we can be sure that if I had to come back and re-read this code next week it wouldn't be obvious to me either. In fact, with my memory, it is not likely they would be obvious two hours from now.

```
$total_price = $price + $sales_tax;
```

Now there is little chance that anyone who reads this code next week or next year (including myself) will have any problems figuring out what the variables represent right? Well, not entirely. We still have no indication of the units of the variables. Is the price in dollars or pennies? Often, in programs that deal with monetary values, the amounts may be input in dollar amounts such as 10.45 or 3.99, and, to avoid certain rounding problems, they may be converted to pennies (1045 and 399 respectively) for any internal calculations. We'll come back to this in section 2.3.

In the previous examples, I've used lowercase letters for variable names as well as the underscore character between distinct words in the same variable name. This is a common convention, but there are other styles. Some people prefer to avoid the underscore and instead use a single uppercase letter at the beginning of each new word:

```
$totalPrice = $price + $salesTax;
```

Both naming conventions are fairly common, but the former version using underscores to break up words is slightly easier to read. Try them both and use the one with which you are most comfortable.

So far we have only been using scalar variables, which hold a single value. Perl has two other variable types that represent collections of scalar data: the *array*, preceded by an @ symbol; and the *hash*, preceded by the % symbol. When using these variables to hold collections of similar data, it makes sense to give them names that reflect that plurality. At other times, the collection of data may be better viewed as a unit. For example, you might read a file into an array of lines and name it @file if you were working on it more as a unit, or you could name it @lines if the emphasis was on processing each line of the file.

Another naming technique is to use different cases for different kinds of variables. Variable names in Perl are case sensitive, so $Price, $PRICE, and $price are three different variables. (Note that I wouldn't recommend using the same name for different variables in a program.) Variables that are considered to be constants (i.e., not changing in value for the duration of the program) are conventionally named in all uppercase. Case is also sometimes used to distinguish *global* versus *lexical* variables. Lexical variables are those declared with the my keyword. (See part II.) Global variables begin with an uppercase letter while lexical variables remain all lowercase.

Like the previous section on structure and indenting and the next section on comments, the style you adopt or develop is a matter of choice. The important point is that you choose a style that works for you and use it consistently throughout your programs.

2.3 Comments

Programming languages usually allow some means of including text that is not actually part of the program itself, but is intended to explain some part of the program to human readers. These included bits of text are called *comments,* and serve as a means of documenting your program. So far, we have used whitespace and naming conventions to make our programs clearly readable. With comments, we can insert any explanatory text we wish.

There is some debate over the usefulness of comments. One camp insists on heavy use of comments to document everything, and the other camp firmly believing that, by adhering to good style guidelines like those above, a program should be self-documenting. The view of the second camp is that comments are not only a waste of time and space, but can make the program harder to read by cluttering up the code with unnecessary information. Neither camp is entirely right or entirely wrong.

In Perl, you can include comments in your programs by preceding them with the # symbol. When Perl sees the # symbol (and it is not part of something else such as string), it will ignore that symbol and everything that follows it until the end of the current line. Consider the program in listing 2.1 on pages 25–26.

This program uses comments liberally—far too liberally for some tastes. While definite problems exist with the commenting in the above program, the number of comments is not the issue, at least not directly. The main problem is that most of the comments are useless. They do not offer any information that isn't readily apparent in the code itself. Let's take a look at why these comments aren't very helpful in creating a readable program.

The large block comment at the beginning of the program does contain some useful information. In particular, it is a good idea to put a program description and copyright notice in the source of your programs. A usage statement is a good idea as well. However, the program description should be a simple statement or two of what the program accomplishes, not a detailed description of each step in the program. If you need to describe the individual steps of the program, describe them with comments next to the code itself.

Let's skip the warning notice for now and proceed to the variable declarations. It is a good idea to add comments to variable declarations to indicate useful information about the variables. In this program we have followed reasonable naming conventions for our variables. The additional comments are useless because they do not convey any additional information. It is no surprise that the variable $sales_tax will be used to represent sales tax.

```
#!/usr/bin/perl -w
#############################################################
# tax_calc: This is the tax_calc program, designed to make  #
#           it easy to figure out the sales tax on a given  #
#           price by accepting a price value in dollars and #
#           converting it to pennies and calculating the    #
#           sales tax using the built in rate of 7% and     #
#           adding that to the price, converting back to    #
#           dollars to output the total amount.             #
#-----------------------------------------------------------#
#    This program is copyright 1998 by Andrew L Johnson      #
#    and may be redistributed under the same terms as       #
#    Perl itself.                                            #
#-----------------------------------------------------------#
#                                                           #
#   Usage: perl tax_calc 12.15                              #
#                                                           #
#############################################################

    #################### !! WARNING !! #####################
    ## After converting to pennies, any fractional pennies ##
    ## are discarded, including any arising from internal  ##
    ## calculations.                                       ##
    #########################################################

use strict;

# This variable holds the tax rate
my $sales_tax_rate = 0.07;

# This variable will contain the initial price
my $price;

# This variable is to hold the sales tax
my $sales_tax;

# This variable will be used to hold the total price
my $total_price;

# call the get_price_input function to get a price from the
# user and assign it to $price
$price      = get_price_input();

# calculate sales tax by multiplying the tax rate by the
# price and use int() to remove any fractional portions
$sales_tax  = int( $sales_tax_rate * $price );

# add up price and tax and divide by 100 to get the total
# price in dollars
$total_price = ( $price + $sales_tax ) / 100;
# Print the total
print "Total price is $total_price\n";
```

```
#############################################
# SUB get_price_input()                     #
# This is just a dummy sub returning 1015   #
# at the moment and does not fetch any input#
# #########################################  #

sub get_price_input {
    return 1015;
}
```

Listing 2.1   Example program with bad commenting style

If a variable name already tells us what the variable will be used for, what else do we need to know? One thing we might want to know is how the data is represented. What are the units of a particular variable: pennies or dollars for monetary data? Inches or centimeters for length data? Other useful information might be the expected or allowable ranges of the data, or information on encoding schemes if a variable is to represent states of some kind. For example, (0 = off, 1 = on).

Now we get to the meat of the program, the three lines that do the main task of the program (not counting any statements in the subroutine). These are all heavily commented, but like the variable declaration comments, they do not convey any additional information about the code. A comment that merely restates the code in question is always useless. None of these comments will really help a programmer to understand the code here. The only marginally useful information here refers to $total_price being divided by 100 to obtain a price in dollars. This provides unit information. Of course, had the variables been commented on correctly, we'd already know what units were being used in each variable. We certainly do not need to be told that

```
$total_price = ( $price + $sales_tax ) / 100;
```

means that we are adding the price to the sales tax and dividing by 100. We can see that. A better comment might simply have been

```
# sum total and convert from pennies to dollars
$total_price = ( $price + $sales_tax ) / 100;
```

At least this comment focuses on the objective of the code, not the method.

Finally, let's look at the comments for the *subroutine*. Subroutines should be documented just like any other part of the code—no more, no less. A small header comment with a very short description of the routine may be appropriate. In this case, the header comment alerts us that this *function*—function is another word for subroutine—is just a dummy function. This would have been equally clear with a single comment following the return statement.

Aside from cluttering up the program with mostly useless information, the comments above have another drawback as well—formatting. One often sees comments boxed in one way or another like some of those above. You may think this looks nice, or helps highlight important information, but all we've done is made our comments harder to update if we make a change in the program. If I make even a small change to the text in one of the boxed comments, I also have to fiddle around reformatting the box to realign everything. Comments that are harder to update may get left unmodified "accidentally" and, therefore, be out of sync with the code. Comments that do not accurately reflect the code they comment are worse than no comments at all.

Thus far, I've been saying that the commenting above is nearly all useless. The program without comments is given in listing 2.2.

```perl
#!/usr/bin/perl -w

use strict;

my $sales_tax_rate = 0.07;

my $price;
my $sales_tax;
my $total_price;

$price       = get_price_input();
$sales_tax   = int( $sales_tax_rate * $price );
$total_price = ( $price + $sales_tax ) / 100;

print "Total price is $total_price\n";

sub get_price_input {
    return 1015;
}
```

Listing 2.2 Example program with no comments

Obviously, the comments may have helped a little, but even a novice programmer could probably figure out what is going on here with little effort—perhaps after wondering why the get_price_input() function merely returns 1015.

The version of the program in listing 2.3 on page 28, using the minimal commenting guidelines just presented, is not much longer than the uncommented version, yet more informative.

This program is shorter than the first version, more informative, less visually noisy, and easier to read and understand.

```
#!/usr/bin/perl -w
    # tax_calc - takes a dollar amount for input, computes
    #            the sales tax, and returns the total price.
    #
    #
    # note: converts to pennies for internal calculations
    #       and all fractional pennies are discarded.
    #
    # usage: tax_calc 12.15
    #
    # copyright 1998 Andrew Johnson, this software is
    # distributed under the same terms as Perl.

    use strict;

    my $sales_tax_rate = 0.07; # Manitoba rate: 7 percent

    my $price;       # in pennies
    my $sales_tax;   # in pennies
    my $total_price; # in dollars

    $price       = get_price_input();
    $sales_tax   = int( $sales_tax_rate * $price );
    $total_price = ( $price + $sales_tax ) / 100;

    print "Total price is $total_price\n";

    sub get_price_input {
        return 1015;       # dummy function for example only
    }
```

Listing 2.3   Example program with good commenting style

Other commenting techniques include creating headings and separators between sections of code. For example, you might prefer to include all your function definitions at the end of the program, separated by a heading comment line, and have similar functions grouped under subheadings with an organization similar to that shown in listing 2.4 on page 29.

This type of formatting attempts to give the program something of an outline structure and may make it easier to find sections of code when paging through a long program. Once you start looking at other people's code (always a good means of learning), you will find a variety of layout techniques, some good, some not so good, and many visually distracting and hard on the eyes. My only suggestion with regard to formatting here is that you try to find a balance between the visual noise of extra comment lines and the structural information they might convey.

```
######################################
########## MAIN PROGRAM ##########
######################################

    ...main code

########## Subroutines ##########

#-- initialization routines —

    ...some init routines

#-- input/output routines —--

    ...

#-- numeric routines ——

    ...
```

Listing 2.4   Comments as an organizational tool

2.4   Being strict

Programmers, like the rest of the human population, inevitably make mistakes. No programming language or environment can prevent design mistakes or mistakes in logic, but a programming language will catch errors in *syntax,* such as forgetting to put a semicolon on the end of a line.

Another simple mistake is using a variable only once in a program. This is generally caused by a typing error when you entered your code, resulting in the incorrectly spelled variable being used only once in the program. Other common errors include forgetting to set a variable before you use it, redeclaring variables in the same *scope* by accidentally giving a new variable the name of an existing variable, and redefining a function by accidentally using the name of a subroutine that already exists in your program or one imported from another program). A trickier error might be using a variable that contains a string in a numeric operation. Sometimes you might actually mean to do this. More often it is simply a mistake.

Perl offers the -w command line switch (seen above on the shebang line of the tax_calc program). The -w switch detects these and other simple mistakes and issues warnings about them. Using the -w switch helps you maintain a careful programming style. As mentioned above, Perl does not require you to declare your variables prior to using them:

```
#!/usr/bin/perl
$foo = $bar + 1;
print $foo;
```

This complete program will run and print out the number 1 without any hint of a warning. What's wrong with this program? The variable $bar is being used without having been set to any value. Perl creates this variable on-the-fly and gives it an undefined value. The undefined value is special in Perl: it is interpreted as zero in numeric context, as in the case above, and as an empty string if used in a string context). Perl then adds 1 to this value—the result of which is still 1—and assigns the result to $foo. This is most likely a simple mistake, a bad programming style, or an indication of a more serious problem in the code. Using the -w switch would have resulted in the following warnings in addition to the value of $foo being printed:

```
Name "main::bar" used only once: possible typo at try.pl line 2.
Use of uninitialized value at try.pl line 2.
1
```

Perl has detected that $bar was only used once in the program and has concluded that the error might be the result of a typo. It has also detected that a variable has been used in an expression before it was given a value. (Note that the warnings tell you the file name and the line number where Perl noticed a problem—in this case, line 2 in the file named *try.pl*.) One thing to note is that the variable $bar is referred to as "main::bar" in the warning because Perl created it as a package variable in the main package. We will discuss packages in more detail in later chapters (see chapter 16). You can find helpful information about any error or warning message in the *perldiag* (short for perl diagnostics) pod-page (see section 1.2.3). Checking this may help you understand the inevitable error messages and warnings that may pop up from time to time as a result of forgetting to *declare* variables, mistyping variable and function names, forgetting semicolons, or committing other common mistakes.

I am not inclined to issue blanket commandments regarding your programming style, but this is one exception: always use the -w switch in every one of your programs. If your program generates warnings, heed them, and fix your code. In the future, you may need to use a dubious construct that generates a warning. If you know that is what you really want to do, you can read about disabling warnings in the perlfaqs (specifically, *perlfaq7*).

Another way Perl can help you maintain a careful programming style is with the strict pragma. A pragma is just a directive to the compiler to enable or disable some specific behavior. The strict pragma is turned on with the statement use strict; as in the examples we've used in this chapter. Enabling this pragma tells the compiler to disallow certain constructs that are considered unsafe. The details of being strict must be left to later chapters. For now, being strict means you must always declare your variables using the my declaration. Other means of declaring variables will be covered in chapter 7). Consider the strict pragma as the second exception to my rule of not insisting on a particular programming style: always use strict;!

2.5 A quick style guide

Writing code is a fundamental part of the programming process. The style and manner in which you write code percolates through to the other stages in the process. The code you create should not be thought of as simply instructions for the computer to process. You could use machine language for that. Programming is a human endeavor, and your program should be written with human readers in mind. You'll be one of those human readers after all. Indeed, programming may be about problem solving, but when you have to fix or modify a program, reading and understanding the code itself should not be a significant part of the problem.

In this chapter we have seen a few examples of code and explored simple techniques to keep the code you write easy to read. None of these are rigid rules, and they do not cover all aspects of writing good code. The following is a summary of the stylistic guidelines presented in this chapter:

- Use whitespace to indicate the structure of your program.

- Choose variable and function names that are meaningful.

- Use comments sparingly to describe the objective or intent of your code, not the code itself.

- Add information, not visual noise, with comments to your programs.

- Always use the -w switch.

- Always use the strict pragma.

- Always declare your variables with my and comment the declarations if appropriate.

- Be consistent in your style.

- Break any one of these rules whenever you have a good reason.

The *perlstyle* pod-page makes a variety of points about coding style, some of which were covered above and some that are more particular to specific coding constructs that we haven't yet encountered. I recommend that you take the time to read it over once now, and then again after you've had a chance to learn about some constructs this source covers.

C H A P T E R   3

Writing programs

You can't learn to swim by reading about it in a book. The same holds true for programming. Of course, with programming, you can keep the book close by while you practice. So, now that we've seen what the pool looks like (see chapter 1) and learned a few basic safety rules (see chapter 2), it's time to plunge right in to the deep end.

The techniques presented in this chapter will provide you with a mental map of the programming process. This map will help you think about problem solving and designing good solutions as you learn the Perl language. If you find yourself too impatient to work through this chapter now, that's all right. You may skim through it now and return to it after chapter 5 or 6—but please do return and read this chapter before you sign your first programming contract.

The purpose of this chapter is not just to get your feet wet with a little Perl code, but to immerse you in the *process* of writing programs. Do not be concerned if some, or even a lot, of the details of the Perl code slip by you at this time. Focus on the concepts of the process of programming and the design issues in this chapter. In the chapters that follow we will begin teaching the fundamentals of the Perl language from the beginning. You will have plenty of time to put the knowledge you learn here to good use.

Programming is more than just writing code. Before you write any code you need to fine tune the initial idea or problem into a well-defined goal—the *specification*—and develop a solid plan for reaching that goal—the *design*. After you've finished the coding phase, you still need to test and debug the code before, finally, you enter the maintenance phase.

The latter two phases, testing/debugging and maintenance, can be seen as the major source for the ideas and problems that spark the process again. All of these phases overlap and feed back on each other, in what is referred to as a software development *cycle*.

Any programming assignment begins with an idea or problem to solve. This may originate from your boss, a request from a client, your own needs for a specialized tool, or an assignment in a programming course or book. Regardless of its origination, we will refer to the originator as the "client." Many assignments are not for complete programs, but rather individual components of larger programs. As a programmer with such an assignment you are still beginning at the specification stage. You need to make sure that your assigned component is well specified. In other words, you must have a clear goal or purpose. Then you design, code, test, and debug your component.

In this chapter, we will develop two small programs: one, an interactive math quiz, and the other, a tool to search the FAQ sections of the Perl documentation for a keyword or pattern. The first of these will be developed from idea through to a finished version in a great deal of detail. The second program is simpler in design and will take proportionately less time to develop. While program development is the key issue of this chapter, both programs will serve as introductions to many Perl language features as well. But don't worry if some of the Perl code whizzes by a little too fast. Concentrate on the development and the plain English version of the code, also known as the pseudo-code. The next several chapters are designed to introduce you to the elements of programming with the Perl language at a more reasonable pace.

3.1 A first program

Our first assignment comes to us from an imaginary client who wants a simple interactive program that his son can use to practice the basic multiplication and division tables. This program should repeatedly display random questions corresponding to the elementary multiplication table—multiplying two integers between 0 and 9—accept user responses each time, and check for correctness.

While the problem statement we have been given may seem reasonably clear, it is inadequate to serve as our programming goal. From this we need to develop a specification that defines *exactly* what the program will do and how it will operate from the user's perspective. This specification needs to be as detailed as possible so that a) you have a well-defined set of goals that your program design must meet, and b) you can check with the client to ensure that the program you are going to write is the program they actually want.

> *Rule 1:* Clients often don't know what they want until they see something, and then they want something different.

One of Perl's benefits is that it is easy to rapidly prototype something and show it to a client early in the process.

A preliminary query to our client has informed us that a simple, plain text interface is exactly what is desired. Having an imaginary client whose son does not live in the real world of video games and graphics overload makes our task so much easier. We can begin drafting our initial specification.

3.1.1 Specification

mathq is a program that repeatedly presents the user with a series of simple multiplication and division questions and checks the user's answers for correctness. The questions involve a single multiplication or division operation and correspond to the elementary multiplication table. All multiplication questions will involve two integers in the range 0-9 inclusive. All division questions will correspond to an inverse of a legal multiplication question. Example questions are

```
4 x 5 = ?
9 / 3 = ?
6 x 8 = ?
63 / 9 = ?
```

The program will be run from the command line. If you are a Mac user, the concept of the command line may be unfamiliar. A command line is just the spot in your program where you type in a command. The command-line prompt—in this case, >—is a symbol that tells you to enter your command. The program will display a welcome message on startup. Questions will be printed to the screen, and the program will wait for the user to type in an answer. A message will be displayed indicating if the answer was correct or incorrect. The correct answer will be displayed. A message will then appear, asking a new question.

Here's an example session:

```
> mathq
Welcome to the mathq program
  4 x 5 = ?
  20
Correct!
  21 / 7 = ?
  2
Incorrect: 21 / 7 = 3
  9 x 8 = ?
```

This specification is now reasonably complete so we show it to our client who, being imaginary, only asks us one question: "How does the user quit the program?" We also show it to another programmer who says: "What happens if the user inputs letters or other characters?" These are important, but often forgotten considerations that lead us to our other rule:

Rule 2:   Do not simply program for the expected cases. Plan to handle unexpected inputs.

We decide that if the user inputs a q, the program will terminate. Otherwise, any responses that are not simple integers will result in an error message, and the question will be redisplayed.

Now that we have a specification that defines the end product, we can begin laying out a plan to take us there.

3.1.2 Design
The first step in this design process is to list the major tasks that need to be accomplished. This is a top-down approach to design where we begin with the top level

description of the program tasks and continually break up each sub-task into a set of smaller tasks until each major task has been reduced to a simple set of instructions. Walking through our specification, we can identify the following list of tasks that need to be accomplished.

```
display startup message
generate a question and its solution
display question and get a valid response
test response and display right or wrong
display exit message
```

This is not yet an actual top level design because we have not indicated that the middle three tasks should be repeated until the user quits the program. A program normally executes its instructions in order from beginning to end. Often, we need to alter this flow of execution to either repeat some series of instructions or to select one or more sets of instructions to execute depending on a particular condition. Special constructs called flow-of-control constructs, or, more simply, *control statements,* allow us to alter the flow of execution through a program. The generic term for the repetition statement is a *loop.* With that in mind, we can roll out our first top level design of the program:

```
display startup message
LOOP until the user quits
    generate a question and its solution
    display question and get a valid response
    test response and display right or wrong
END LOOP
display exit message
```

Now we have a top level design of the program in what we call pseudo-code, that simple set of English instructions will later be converted to real code. Some of these instructions have simple translations already, notably, the first and last display statements. We already know how to display information to the screen with the print() function, so these statements need no further refining. However, each of the statements inside the loop is more complex and needs to be broken down into sets of simpler statements until a direct translation into code is possible.

I will use a particular notation for pseudo-coding (and for many of the example programs later on in the book) borrowed from a method of programming known as *Literate Programming* (LP). (See section 9.2.) In this method, we use each complex statement as a placeholder for the refined pseudo-code that belongs there. We mark each complex statement by surrounding it with double angle brackets (<< >>). Each of these represents a spot where the more refined code will be inserted. We use the suitably technical term *chunk* to refer to the chunk of code to be inserted, and chunk names for the representative statement acting as a place-holder. To make it easier to identify what is code, or pseudo-code, and what is not, all chunk names will be typeset in italics.

Our design process is then one of designing each of these chunks. This allows us to focus on one particular goal at a time. Some of these chunks will consist of a few simple statements, and others will contain further chunks to be defined. Our uppermost chunk, the "root" chunk, is simply the program itself. Let's encapsulate this top level design as a definition of the program:

```
<<mathq>>=
display start up message
LOOP: until user quits
    <<generate a question and its solution>>
    <<display question and get a valid response>>
    <<test response and display right or wrong>>
END LOOP
display exit message
```

You can see that we begin a chunk definition with the name of the chunk in angle brackets, followed by an equals sign (=). We then lay out the code design that defines the chunk. Now we repeat the entire process for each chunk, refining the chunks into a series of simple statements that perform the task described by the chunk name. Outer chunks read more like an outline or table of contents of the program. Inner chunks, or nested chunks, contain more detail about a particular task or step being performed.

Our first inner chunk needs to generate a simple multiplication or division question and calculate its solution. To create a question that corresponds to the basic multiplication table, we need to pick two random integers from the range 0 to 9 inclusive. We also need to randomly pick either multiplication or division as the mathematical operator for the question.

Perl has a function we can use to generate random integers, but how might we pick between multiplication and division? We can simply generate another random integer between 0 and 1. If it is 1, we will do multiplication. If it is 0, we will do division. Let's map this out into a pseudo-code definition of the chunk:

```
<<generate a question and its solution>>=
set first_number to random integer from 0 to 9
set second_number to random integer from 0 to 9
set operator to random integer from 0 to 1
IF operator is 1 THEN
    <<create multiplication question and solution>>
ELSE
    <<create division question and solution>>
END IF
```

The first primary control structure we used in this program was the loop. Here we introduce the other primary control structure, the if/else selection or decision structure. This structure allows us to execute one set of statements if a condition is true, or another set of statements if the condition is false. So, in the example above, IF the operator value is equal to 1, the program executes the block of statements immediately following and skips the statements in the ELSE block.

The multiplication chunk is fairly simple to derive:

```
<<create multiplication question and solution>>=
set solution to first_number times second_number
set question to "first_number x second_number = ?"
```

However, the division chunk requires a little more thought. We cannot simply calculate the result of the first number divided by the second number as that might not correspond to a question from the multiplication table. We need to first calculate the result of multiplying two numbers, then switch the result with the first number. For example, if the first number was 4 and the second number was 6, the solution would be calculated as 24 giving us: 4 x 6 = 24 for the three values. To turn this into a division question, we merely need to swap the 4 and the 24 and change the operation sign from multiplication to division, giving us 24 / 6 = 4.

```
<<create division question and solution>>=
set solution to first_number times second_number
swap values of solution and first_number
set question to "first_number / second_number = ?"
```

We have now fully reduced our <<generate a question and solution>> chunk down to simple statements. We can work our way back up to the top, replacing each chunk name with its corresponding definition as we go:

```
<<mathq>>=
display start up message
LOOP: until user quits
    set first_number to random integer from 0 to 9
    set second_number to random integer from 0 to 9
    set operator to random integer from 0 to 1
    IF operator is 1 THEN
        set solution to first_number times second_number
        set question to "first_number x second_number = ?"
    ELSE
        set solution to first_number times second_number
        swap values of solution and first_number
        set question to "first_number / second_number = ?"
    END IF
    <<display question and get a valid response>>
    <<test response and display right or wrong>>
END LOOP
display exit message
```

This demonstrates how we replace each chunk name with its corresponding definition to fill in the program. We continue this process, creating definitions for each chunk name until we have a completed program. To get a valid user input, we need to set up a loop to repeatedly ask the user for input until a valid input is received:

```
<<display question and get a valid response>>=
set is_valid to 0
LOOP: until is_valid is 1
    display question
    accept user response
    <<test if input is valid>>
END LOOP
```

In order to test if the response is valid we need to determine whether it contains only digits or only the letter "q."

```
<<test if input is valid>>=
IF input is all digits or the letter q THEN set is_valid to 1
END IF
```

Finally, we need to test the response and display an appropriate message depending on whether the response is correct or not. Since we've already validated the input, we know the response may be either the letter q or a number. We will use a new form of the selection structure to test for these cases:

```
<<test response and display right or wrong>>=
IF response is q THEN
    set loop control variable to indicate the user has quit
ELSE IF response equals solution THEN
    display correct message
ELSE
    display incorrect message
END IF
```

Now we see how the if/else control statement can be extended to select among more than two sets of instructions. In the above chunk, the response is tested to see if it is equal to q. If it is, we set the quit variable to 1. The quit variable controls the loop, in that the loop will repeatedly execute until the quit variable is 1. If the response is not q, we test to see if it equals the solution. If so, we display the message indicating a correct answer. Finally, if the response was neither q nor equal to the solution, it must have been an incorrect answer. In that case, we display the appropriate message in the final else block.

Our entire pseudo-code program now appears as

```
display start up message
LOOP: until user quits
    set first_number to random integer from 0 to 9
    set second_number to random integer from 0 to 9
    set operator to random integer from 0 to 1
    IF operator is 1 THEN
        set solution to first_number times second_number
        set question to "first_number x second_number = ?"
    ELSE
        set solution to first_number times second_number
        swap values of solution and first_number
        set question to "first_number / second_number = ?"
    END IF
    set is_valid to 0
    LOOP: until is_valid is 1
        display question
        accept user response
        IF input is all digits or the letter q THEN
            set is_valid to 1
        END IF
    END LOOP
    IF response is q THEN
        cause outer LOOP to terminate
    ELSE IF response equals solution THEN
        display correct message
    ELSE
        display incorrect message
    END IF
END LOOP
display exit message
```

3.1.3 Coding

In this phase, you translate the pseudo-code statements into their equivalent statements of your target programming language. Here I will illustrate the translation of each code chunk of the program in the same manner as we developed the pseudo-code, beginning with the root chunk of the program. As before, actual code is in plain text and the chunk syntax is shown in italics. I will warn you now that the actual code that follows contains a couple of minor bugs that we will work out in the debugging and maintenance phases of the cycle.

We are now writing code, so we begin our root chunk by turning on warnings on the initial line, followed by the strict pragma as recommended in the previous chapter.

```
<<mathq>>=
#!/usr/bin/perl -w
use strict;
print "Welcome to the mathq program\n";
my $quit = 0;
until ($quit) {
    <<generate a question and its solution>>
    <<display question and get a valid response>>
    <<test response and display right or wrong>>
}
print "exiting the mathq program\n";
```

Here we have simply used the print() function to display our startup and exit messages. We have also set up our main loop for the program. Perl has two forms of indefinite looping constructs, the while and until loops. Each one tests the condition within the parentheses every time it starts the loop. The only difference between the two is that the while will execute the loop as long as the condition is true, and the until will execute it until the condition is true. In Perl, a condition is false if it *evaluates* to zero, the empty string, or an undefined value. All other values are considered true.

We have declared the variable $quit and set its value to zero. Hence, it is false when evaluated in a conditional. A variable is simply a name that is associated with a memory location. Once we declare a variable, we may assign values to it or read values from it using only its name. This is a scalar variable, meaning it can only hold a single value. In Perl, all scalars begin with a $ symbol. The until loop will evaluate this variable each time it starts the loop. The loop will terminate when this variable evaluates to any true value—in other words, anything besides one of the possible false values just mentioned. We will consider control structures and truth and falsity in detail in chapter 5.

In our next chunk, we need to pick random integers to use as the numbers in our question. Perl has a rand() function, which returns a random number from 0 up to, but not including, the number given to the function or from 0 to 1 if no number is given. The number returned is fractional, so to get an integer we use the int() function, which returns the integer part of any number given to it by cutting off any decimal portion. So, to get a random integer from 0 to 9 inclusive, we need to get a random integer between 0 and 10 and take the integer value of that number:

```
<<generate a question and its solution>>=
my $first_number  = int(rand(10)); # range 0 to 9 inclusive
my $second_number = int(rand(10)); # range 0 to 9 inclusive

# choose random operator code: 0 or 1
# operator codes: 0 is division
#                 1 is multiplication
my $operator      = int(rand(2));
```

```
my $solution
my $question;
if ($operator == 1) {
    <<create multiplication question and solution>>
} else {
    <<create division question and solution>>
}
```

Here we also see Perl's `if/else` selection structure. The syntax is very similar to the `until` loop we saw earlier. We use the `if` keyword followed by a condition inside of parentheses. If the condition is true, then the block immediately following is executed. If it is not true, the block following the `else` keyword is executed.

The inner two chunks that create either the multiplication or division version of the question are straightforward.

```
<<create multiplication question and solution>>=
$solution = $first_number * $second_number;
$question = "$first_number x $second_number = ?";

<<create division question and solution>>=
$solution = $first_number * $second_number;
($solution, $first_number) = ($first_number, $solution);
$question = "$first_number / $second_number = ?";
```

The only tricky part above is the swap. In Perl, you may assign a list of values to a list of variables. In this case we create a list of values on the right side consisting of the values of the first number and the solution. These are then assigned back to the same variables in reversed order, achieving a swapping of the variables' values.

The other thing to note in the preceding code is that we can place variables within double-quoted strings. This string first *interpolates* the values of the variables before the assignment takes place. So, if our first number was 4 and our second number was 5, the variable `$question` above would receive the string 4 x 5 = ?.

The only new thing in the next chunk is obtaining the user input. For this we use the input operator `<STDIN>` to read a line of input from the keyboard.

```
<<display question and get a valid response>>=
my $response;
my $is_valid = 0;
until ($is_valid) {
    print "$question\n";
    $response = <STDIN>;
    chomp($response);
    <<test if input is valid>>
}
```

The `until` loop here will continue to execute until the variable `$is_valid` contains a true value. The `chomp()` function removes any end-of-line character from the variable given. We need to do this because, when we read a line of input from the keyboard, that input retains the end of line character, caused by pressing the <enter> key. Neglecting the chomp() function is a common mistake.

To test whether the input is valid we need to determine that the response is either equal to q, or contains only digits. To test string equality, we use the eq operator. We could set our valid indicator to a true value if the response equals q in the following fashion:

```
if ($response eq 'q') {
    $is_valid = 1;
}
```

To test if the input contains only digits we use a regular expression inside the match operator m//, which returns a Boolean (true/false) value. In a regular expression, the pattern \d will match any single digit, and the pattern \d+ will match a sequence of one or more digits. Two other key patterns are the ^ character which, when used at the beginning of a pattern, means "match the beginning of the string," and the $ character which means "match the end of the string." So, the pattern ^\d+$ means "match the beginning of the string, then match one or more digit characters, then match the end of the string." This pattern can only match if the string contains only digit characters from beginning to end.

To have the match operator attempt to match against the contents of a variable, you need to use the binding operator, =~, between the variable and the match operator. So, to test if our response variable contains only digits we apply the match operator as

```
$response =~ m/^\d+$/
```

We can combine our two tests into a single condition using the logical or operator:

```
<<test if input is valid>>=
if ($response eq 'q' or $response =~ m/^\d+$) {
    $is_valid = 1;
} else {
    print "Invalid Input: enter an integer or 'q' to quit\n";
}
```

The conditional reads like this: if the response equals q, or the response contains only digits, then set the valid indicator to 1.

Finally, we translate the last chunk, which tests whether we should end the loop, or whether the response was right or wrong.

```
<<test response and display right or wrong>>=
if ($response eq 'q') {
    $quit = 1;
} elsif ($response = $solution) {
    print "Correct\n";
} else {
    print "Incorrect: $question $solution\n";
}
```

Once again, performing our chunk substitution from the low level back up to the top level, we have our completed program:

```
<<mathq>>=
#!/usr/bin/perl -w
use strict;
print "Welcome to the mathq program\n";
my $quit = 0;
until ($quit) {
    my $first_number  = int(rand(10)); # range: 0 to 9 inclusive
    my $second_number = int(rand(10)); # range: 0 to 9 inclusive

    # choose random operator code: 0 or 1
    # operator codes: 0 is division
    #                 1 is multiplication
    my $operator      = int(rand(2));

    my $solution
    my $question;
    if ($operator == 1) {
        $solution = $first_number * $second_number;
        $question = "$first_number x $second_number = ?";
    } else {
        $solution = $first_number * $second_number;
        ($solution, $first_number) = ($first_number, $solution);
        $question = "$first_number / $second_number = ?";
    }

    # get valid user response
    my $response;
    my $is_valid = 0;
    until ($is_valid) {
        print "$question\n";
        $response = <STDIN>;
        chomp($response);
        # valid input is 'q' or  only digits
        if ($response eq 'q' or $response =~ m/^\d+$/) {
            $is_valid = 1;
        } else {
            print "Invalid Input: enter an integer or 'q' to quit\n";
        }
    }
```

```
    # test response
    if ($response eq 'q') {
        $quit = 1;
    } elsif ($response = $solution) {
        print "Correct\n";
    } else {
        print "Incorrect: $question $solution\n";
    }
}
print "exiting the mathq program\n";
```

We have inserted a few small comments for each main section of the code. In the interests of space, I have not included an opening comment block describing the program. You should add one to your version. We can now begin the next phase of programming.

3.1.4 Testing and debugging

If we have been careful during the previous stages, we should not encounter many difficulties in this phase of the cycle. However, no matter how careful one is, mistakes can and will creep into the program. Testing our program is not simply a matter of running it and seeing if it appears to work, we need to formulate a plan to try test all of the possible conditions that may occur.

The first test in any plan is to make sure the program compiles correctly. We can do this using the -c option when starting Perl. This option causes Perl to read in the program and compile, but not run it.

We then test our program under various inputs. We need to verify that correct and incorrect responses both produce the appropriate messages on the screen. We need to test that an input of q causes the program to terminate. And, finally, we need to make sure that invalid input is handled correctly. Our test plan is:

1 Run the program under the -c option.

2 Provide correct responses to several questions.

3 Provide incorrect responses to several question.

4 Test invalid input: abc, 12.4, 1a.

5 Test that an input of q exits the program.

If you copied the above program exactly, running our first test results in a bunch of errors being output to the screen. We always consider only one error at a time. The first error, in this case, is

```
syntax error at mathq line 15, near "$solution
    my "
```

An important note to keep in mind when examining error messages such as this is that the line number indicates where Perl ran into trouble parsing the code, not necessarily where the actual error is located. In this case, we do not see anything wrong with line 15, so we look at the line right before that line. We notice that this line lacks a semicolon after the variable declaration. Without the semicolon, Perl has tried to continue reading the next line as part of the same statement, resulting in a syntax error being generated for that line. We fix this by adding the semicolon and try the test again.

This time, Perl reports mathq syntax OK. We proceed to the second test, running the program and entering correct responses. This run looks like

```
Welcome to the mathq program
35 / 5 = ?
7
Correct
6 x 6 = ?
36
Correct
7 x 3 = ?
21
Correct
```

The program appears to be correctly determining correct responses for both multiplication and division questions, so we continue the testing by responding with incorrect answers:

```
7 x 6 = ?
12
Correct
12 / 3 = ?
0
Correct
```

Immediately, we see that we have a real problem. For some reason our program is not identifying incorrect responses. We look at the code where we test for correct responses which begins at line 40:

```
# test response if ($response eq 'q') {
    $quit = 1;
} elsif ($response = $solution) {
    print "Correct\n";
} else {
    print "Incorrect: $question $solution\n";
}
```

The problem lies in the `elsif` condition. We have made the common error of using = instead of == to test for equality. The = operator does not compare the two variables, it does an assignment. We quickly change this line to read

```
} elsif ($response == $solution) {
```

Now we begin our tests from the beginning. We have a successful compile. Correct responses are still identified as being correct and now incorrect responses are also correctly identified. We now test invalid inputs, and we try to quit the program:

```
9 x 8 = ?
abc
Invalid Input: enter an integer or 'q' to quit
9 x 8 = ?
1a
Invalid Input: enter an integer or 'q' to quit
9 x 8 = ?
12.4
Invalid Input: enter an integer or 'q' to quit
9 x 8 = ?
72
Correct
4 x 1 = ?
q
exiting the mathq program
```

The program passes all tests. We slap a version number on it (version 0.01), and release it to the client. We are now entering the maintenance phase of this program.

3.1.5 Maintenance

There are several reasons we may need to revisit this program. The client may wish small modifications to the interface, or may wish a new graphical interface (i.e., buttons, icons, and scroll bars). The client might also request that the program be extended to handle negative integers or that the program be generalized to include addition and subtraction questions as well.

In this case, however, we need to return to the program due to a bug report. The client informs us that the program sometimes asks a question involving division by zero. In fact, these division by zero questions are always zero divided by zero, and the program often insists that the answer is a non-zero integer.

Our first thought is to simply not allow division by zero questions to ever occur because division by zero is an undefined mathematical operation, at least for the purposes of this program. We first need to check the question generation routine to ensure that simply disallowing division by zero will, in fact, solve the problem and not create new problems. So we look to the code that creates the division question:

```
} else {
    $solution = $first_number * $second_number;
    ($solution, $first_number) = ($first_number, $solution);
    $question = "$first_number / $second_number = ?";
}
```

In order to diagnose the problem, we need to see what values are being used when the program enters this section of code. A common debugging technique is to insert some print() statements before and after the problem area to print the current values. So we place one print statement right after the line where the solution is calculated and another right after the swap is performed. We also know that the problem involves division by zero, which will only occur when the second number is zero. So, rather than running the program and waiting until such a situation occurs, we will set the second number to zero right at the beginning of this block of code:

```
} else {
    $second_number = 0;                                       #DB
    $solution = $first_number * $second_number;
    print "* $first_number:$second_number:$solution *\n"; #DB
    ($solution, $first_number) = ($first_number, $solution);
    $question = "$first_number / $second_number = ?";
    print "* $first_number:$second_number:$solution *\n"; #DB
}
```

We have added debugging comments, #DB, to make the debugging statements easy to locate and remove. We now run the program:

```
Welcome to the mathq program
* 8:0:0 *
* 0:0:8 *
0 / 0 = ? 0
Incorrect: 0 / 0 = 8
9 x 0 = ?
q
exiting the mathq program
```

This explains both why the only division by zero questions appear as zero divided by zero and why the solution is not zero. Anytime the second number is zero, the solution will be calculated as zero, then swapped with the first number. The fix of preventing the second number from being zero will solve the problem. We can do this by adjusting the statement where we originally choose a random number for the second number. Remember to delete the debugging statements from your code.

The statement where we generate a random integer for the second number is located near the beginning of the main loop:

```
my $second_number = int(rand(10)); # range: 0 to 9 inclusive
```

We need to change the range of possible numbers to 1 to 9 inclusive rather than 0 to 9. We can easily accomplish this by simply changing the statement to create a random integer between 0 and 8 and then adding 1 to it.

```
my $second_number = int(rand(9)) + 1; # range: 1 to 9 inclusive
```

The program will no longer generate division by zero questions. We run the full sequence of tests on the program to ensure we did not make a simple syntax error or create any new problems. All tests pass. We slap a new version number on it (version 0.02) and release the new version back to the client.

3.2 faqgrep

Our next program project will allow us to perform searches on the nine separate files in the standard Perl documentation that contain frequently asked questions (FAQs) and their answers. These files are located in the */pod* directory in the main source directory (refer to section section 1.2.3). They are also installed somewhere on your system, depending on how you configured Perl during the installation process.

The nine files are named *perlfaq1.pod* to *perlfaq9.pod* and they are written in standard plain old documentation (POD) format. POD is a simple mark-up language that allows you to write documents in plain text and include simple formatting directives. You can run these files through one of several formatting utilities to produce output in different formats such as as PostScript, HTML, or native manpage formats. We will discuss POD in more detail in chapter 9.

The perlfaq files themselves contain a large number of questions relating to programming with Perl that have arisen over the years, along with standard answers to these questions. These documents are extremely useful, and you should consult them whenever you find yourself wondering how you might go about doing something in Perl.

The program we will develop here has the following specification: faqgrep is a program that performs searches on the perlfaqs. The user invokes the program on the command line along with a keyword or pattern. The program searches each perlfaq file for any questions containing the specified pattern. If a matching question is located, the name of the particular perlfaq file will be printed along with the matching question. For example, if users wanted to know if any questions involved sorting arrays, they could run the program searching for all questions containing sort:

```
> faqgrep sort
perlfaq4.pod:
 How do I sort an array by (anything)?
perlfaq4.pod:
 How do I sort a hash (optionally by value instead of key)?
perlfaq4.pod:
 How can I always keep my hash sorted?
```

Users would then know that the information they seek is located in section 4 of the perlfaq documents, which can be read using the command perldoc perlfaq4.

Before we begin designing the program, we need to know a little bit about the format of the perlfaq pod files. The format of these files is relatively simple. Any question is contained on a single line and starts with a pod directive that looks like =head2. So we know that, when we read through each file, we only need to search for our pattern on a line that begins with that sequence of characters.

You will also need to know where the perlfaq files were installed on your system. On my system, they were installed into a directory named

```
/usr/local/lib/perl5/5.00502/pod
```

To find the pod installation on your system you can type perl -V, which will result in a lot of output regarding the configuration of Perl on your system. Near the end of this output is a list of the directories contained in the special @INC array. You should find a /pod subdirectory under one of these listed directories. Once you have located the perlfaq files on your system, we can begin designing our program. In the previous example, we did not begin with a complete pseudo-coded design of the program. This program is much simpler, so we can begin from a completely pseudo-coded design:

```
set faq directory
set list of filenames
get search pattern
LOOP: foreach file in list of filenames
    LOOP: until end of file
        read a line from the file
        IF line starts with =head2 and line has pattern THEN
            print filename and line
        END IF
    END LOOP
END LOOP
```

To transform this into Perl code, we may still break this into a few large chunks that we will refine as before:

```
<<faqgrep>>=
#!/usr/bin/perl -w
use strict;
<<set directory and filename list>>
<<set search pattern>>
<<search all files for pattern and print matches>>
```

In the previous example we only used scalar variables, that is, variables that hold one value. Now we want a variable that can hold a list of values. Perl's list variable is called an array. Array variable names are prefixed with an @ symbol. We can assign to an array by providing a list of values on the right hand side of an assignment operator—that is, after the = operator. Our first two lines of pseudo-code translate as:

```
<<set directory and filename list>>=
my $faq_directory = '/usr/local/lib/perl5/5.00502/pod';
my @faq_files = ('perlfaq1.pod', 'perlfaq2.pod', 'perlfaq3.pod',
                 'perlfaq4.pod', 'perlfaq5.pod', 'perlfaq6.pod',
                 'perlfaq7.pod', 'perlfaq8.pod', 'perlfaq9.pod'
                );
```

Remember, Perl doesn't care about most whitespace, so we can make our list assignment span multiple lines. We can also indent subsequent lines to keep the list organized and make it clear where the list assignment ends. The next thing we need to do is get the keyword from the command line. When you invoke a Perl program on the command line with additional *arguments,* Perl automatically places those arguments into a special array named @ARGV. For example, one might invoke the faqgrep program like:

```
> faqgrep sort
```

In this case, the argument sort is available to the program as the first element in the @ARGV array. You can refer to a single element of an array using a *subscript* denoting the position of the element in the list. Arrays begin counting positions at zero, so the first element in the @ARGV array can be referred to as $ARGV[0]. We use a $ now because we are not talking about the whole array, just one scalar value in the array. In our program, the pattern we want to search for will be given as an argument to the program, so we may set our search pattern variable like:

```
<<set search pattern>>=
my $pattern = $ARGV[0] or die "no pattern given: $!";
```

We will explain the or die syntax shortly. In this case, it simply means that if $ARGV[0] is empty or contains a false value, then the program will exit with the given error message.

We have seen the while and until loop structures in the previous example. Perl has another looping construct that is designed specifically to loop over lists of values. This structure is called the foreach loop. The syntax of the loop is

```
foreach variable (list of values) {
    statements;
}
```

In this structure, the loop executes once for every value in the list. During each execution, the loop variable is assigned the next value in the list. You may declare your loop variable prior to the loop or directly in the foreach line. To iterate over each file in our array of filenames, we may use

```
<<search all files for pattern and print matches>>=
foreach my $filename (@faq_files) {
    <<read files and print matching lines>>
}
```

Before you can read a file, you need to open it and associate it with a file handle. A file handle is a Perl data-type that is associated with an input or output channel. Recall our method for reading input from the keyboard using <STDIN>. Perl automatically opened the file handle STDIN for reading. STDIN reads from what is called the *standard input,* usually the keyboard by default, unless you've explicitly redirected it to be read from elsewhere. Once we open a file and associate it with a file handle, we may read lines from the file using the same syntax: <FILE>.

The syntax of the open() function is: open(filehandle, $filename). Opening a file is a system operation that may fail for reasons such as the file does not exist, or the user does not have permission to read that file. We want to know if such a failure occurs, so we always check the *return value* of the open() function. We may do this using an if conditional, but it is more commonly done using a logical or operator like so:

```
open(filehandle, $filename) or die("can't open '$filename': $!");
```

You will often see this written using the || operator instead of the or operator. The former is just a higher precedence version of the same operator. (See chapter 4 for a discussion of precedence.) When Perl encounters such a statement, it first tries to evaluate the expression on the left, the open() function in this case. If that expression evaluates to true Perl ignores the right hand expression. If the left expression fails, Perl then evaluates the right hand expression. In this case, the right hand expression is a call to the `die()` function, which causes the program to exit and prints its argument to the screen. The special Perl variable `$!` holds the value of the current system error, so we include it in the string we pass to the `die()` function to provide a better diagnostic message about what went wrong. We may define our next code chunk as

```
<<read files and print matching lines>>=
open(FILE, $filename) or die("can't open '$filename': $!");
while (<FILE>) {
    <<print line if matches pattern>>
}
close FILE;
```

It is important to remember that the `<>` is the input operator and `FILE` is the file handle being read. You do not `close()` an input operator, just a file handle: `close FILE;`

Perl does some extra magic when we use the input operator as the only thing within a `while` conditional. It automatically converts the conditional to read

```
while ( defined($_ = <FILE>) ) {
```

When you read from a file using `<FILE>`, the input operator (`<>`) returns an undefined value at the end of the file. So, in this conditional, a line is read from the file and assigned to a special Perl variable, `$_`. This value is then checked to see if it is defined. In this way, the loop will be executed once for every line in the file, setting `$_` to each line in turn. The loop will exit when the end of the file is reached.

We use regular expressions again to test for matches against our pattern. This time we introduce the substitution operator, `s/pattern/replacement/`. This works the same as the match operator with regard to matching the pattern, but, instead of just matching, Perl replaces the found pattern with whatever is in the second half of the `s///` operator. The replacement part of the substitution operator is just a string, not a regular expression. We will use this to find lines beginning with `=head2` and to strip off those characters without replacing them so we don't see them if we print out that line from the file.

```
<<print line if matches pattern>>=
if (s/^=head2// and m/$pattern/) {
    print "$filename:\n$_";
}
```

Notice that we did not use the `=~` binding operator with either the substitution or the match operators. This is because when either operator occurs without being bound to a particular variable, it is automatically bound to the special `$_`

variable, which, remember, is the variable that contains each line in our file due to the magic while condition mentioned above.

That completes the whole program. All that remains is to insert the code chunks into their relative places to create the whole program listing:

```
<<faqgrep>>=
#!/usr/bin/perl -w
use strict;
my $faq_directory = '/usr/local/lib/perl5/5.00502/pod';
my @faq_files = ('perlfaq1.pod', 'perlfaq2.pod', 'perlfaq3.pod',
                 'perlfaq4.pod', 'perlfaq5.pod', 'perlfaq6.pod',
                 'perlfaq7.pod', 'perlfaq8.pod', 'perlfaq9.pod'
                );
my $pattern = $ARGV[0] || die "no pattern given: $!";
foreach my $filename (@faq_files) {
    open(FILE, $filename) or die "can't open '$filename': $!";
    while (<FILE>) {
        if (s/^=head2// and m/$pattern/) {
            print "$filename:\n$_";
        }
    }
    close FILE;
}
```

This compiles fine with perl -c but running it to search for a pattern of sort produced an immediate error about not being able to open a file. This illustrates the kind of extra information that the $! variable can provide.

We check our open() call and realize that we are trying to open the files without giving the full pathname. We knew we needed the FAQ directory location, and this is where it was needed. We have to change the open() function to use the full path and filename when trying to open the file:

```
open(FILE, "$faq_directory/$filename") or die "can't open file: $!";
```

Now running perl faqgrep sort produces the output we showed in our intitial specification. We will not proceed further with this script at this time, but we will return to it and modify it to optionally print out the full answers to matching questions rather than just the filename locations.

We have covered a lot of ground in this chapter. We have taken two programming projects from initial ideas through to working programs. We have also been exposed to quite a bit of Perl code in the process.

If you had no previous experience with the Perl language prior to this chapter, don't worry if some of it seemed a little over your head. The main purpose of this chapter was not to teach Perl, but to introduce you to the process involved in creating programs. Too often, it is tempting to jump right into writing code when given a problem, especially if it seems like a simple problem. But simple problems often have a way of requiring more complex solutions than we first imagine.

When you sit down to write an essay, you need to first have a clear idea of the topic and purpose or goal of the essay. Then you need to do the necessary research and develop an outline of your arguments. Finally, you can write the essay, then edit and revise it. Programming has a similar development cycle. The more attention you give to the early specification and design stages, the less time you'll have to spend debugging or redesigning and rewriting your program. There is no single right way to design a program, or to decompose a problem into subproblems. Still, the prevailing wisdom is that you should *design* your program first before diving in and writing code.

3.3 Exercises

1 Modify the `mathq` program to keep a running score of right and wrong answers.

2 Design and pseudo-code a program that simulates the rolling of two standard six-sided die and prints out the total of the roll. Then consider how it might be modified to display the faces of each dice rolled, for example: a roll of 3 and 5 might be displayed as

```
######  ######
# #   #  # # # #
#  #  #  #  #  #
#   # #  # # # #
######  ######
```

PART II

Essential elements

CHAPTER 4

Data: types and variables

At a basic level, a program operates on data. Not surprisingly, a source of fundamental variation among programming languages is in how they carve up the world of data into meaningful or interesting types of discrete data.

Some languages are splitters, drawing fine-grained distinctions between various kinds of data. For example, in some languages, what we normally think of as simply numeric data (numbers) might be divided into integer numbers and floating point numbers. These may be further divided based on their size (i.e., how much storage space they require in memory). Other languages are lumpers and might differentiate only between numeric data and character data.

These type distinctions are applied in two ways: first, in terms of the operations defined on a given type of data, and second, as restrictions on the types of data a variable may contain. A variable, as we mentioned in the previous chapter, can be thought of as simply a named memory location where a value of a particular type can be stored. In a splitter language, you may have several different types of variables: an integer type that can hold only integers (again, perhaps further divided into short and long integer types based on the size of the integer), a float type for holding floating point numbers, a char type for holding a character, and perhaps other types as well.

Variables may also be classified as primitive (scalar) or structured. Primitive or scalar variables hold a single piece of data; structured variables hold a collection of data. In a splitter language, you may have an array type of variable that is defined to hold a list of integers, and another array variable defined to hold a list of floating point numbers.

Perl is very much a lumper language. It draws a primary distinction between singular or scalar values and plural or list values. Perl has only one variable type for holding single pieces of data—the *scalar* variable. A scalar variable may hold a number (such as 42 or 3.14159) or a character string (such as h or hello or this string has 29 characters). It may also hold a reference to another variable or memory location (see section 4.5).

Similarly, Perl has a list type of variable called an array that can hold an ordered list of scalar values. The scalars need not all be the same type, for example, such a list might be: (42, 'hello', 3.14159). Perl also has another plural variable type called the *hash* or *associative array* (see section 4.3.2).

4.1 Scalar data

The simplest way to use data within a program is as literal data—that is, explicitly represented directly within the program. We have already seen this with our hello world program in chapter 1 where the program printed out the literal string

`Hello World` followed by a newline (represented by \n). Here are a few literal representations of numbers with comments:

```
print 42;        # an integer
print 3.14159;   # a floating point number
print -2;         # a negative integer
```

Perl also allows for a few other literal representations of numeric data such as scientific notation:

```
2.31e4   is 2.31 times 10 to the 4th power, or 23100
2.31e-4  is 2.31 times 10 to the -4th power, or 0.000231
```

Additionally, in literal representation only, a number preceded by a zero is taken to be a number in octal (base 8) notation, and a number preceded by an 0x is taken as a number in hexidecimal (base 16) notation. (If you are unfamiliar with binary, octal, and hexidecimal numbers, please refer to appendix D.)

```
0213    is 139 in decimal (base ten) notation
0x1fa   is 506 in decimal (base ten) notation
```

Finally, Perl allows one further notational convenience for representing numbers. We can use underscores with numbers to enhance readability, just as we use commas when writing out large numbers:

```
1_369_253         is 1369253
7_214_300.312_413 is 7214300.312413
```

It is important to realize that these integers and floating point numbers (and character data for that matter) are not internally represented and stored as the sequence of digits you see on your screen (or in this book). They are stored in binary format. Not all floating point decimal numbers have a precise binary representation. The number 0.2, for example, if printed out to 20 decimal places turns out to be a representation of 0.20000000000000001110. This leads to occasions when the results of some mathematical operations are not exactly what one might expect. This is not a Perl problem but a fact of binary representation (see `perldoc perlfaq4` for further discussions of such data issues).

String or character data comes in two basic forms in Perl: single-quoted strings and double-quoted strings. Single-quoted strings, delimited with single quotation marks or apostrophes, are the more literal of the two forms. We will look at double-quoted strings first. Recall our Hello World program from chapter 1:

```
print( "Hello World\n" );
```

This prints out the string of characters `Hello World` followed by a newline. The `\n` is a special sequence denoting a newline in a double-quoted string. This is referred to as backslash interpretation. There are several backslash interpretations available within double-quoted strings, as shown in table 4.1:

Table 4.1   Backslash interpretation in double-quoted strings

\a	alarm	\cX	control X
\b	backspace	\0nnn	octal byte
\e	escape	\xnn	hexadecimal byte
\f	formfeed	\l	lowercase next letter
\n	newline	\L	lowercase until next \E
\r	carriage return	\u	uppercase next letter
\t	tab	\U	uppercase until next \E
\\	backslash	\Q	backslash non-alphanumerics
\"	double quote	\E	end \L,\U,or \Q

For any other character, the backslash means interpret the next character literally (losing any special meaning it may have had). This is usually referred to as *escaping* a character. So, to include a double-quote character or a backslash character within a double-quoted string, you *escape* them with a backslash:

```
print "This \\ is a backslash";    # prints: This \ is a backslash
print "Here \" is a double quote"; # prints: Here " is a double quote
```

Aside from backslash interpretation, double-quoted strings also allow variable interpolation. This means that a variable in a double-quoted string will be replaced by its present value:

```
$variable = 'Hello';
print "$variable World"; # prints: Hello World
```

Array variables may also be interpolated, but hash variables are not subject to interpolation in this manner. All scalar variables begin with a `$` symbol and all array variables begin with a `@` symbol, so a consequence of this interpolation is that if you want to have to one of those symbols in your string you must precede it with a backslash so that it is interpreted literally:

```
$variable = 'Hello';
print "\$variable World"; # prints: $variable World
```

Single-quoted strings cannot interpolate variables. Single-quoted strings only allow for two special cases of backslash interpretation: a backslash may be used to escape a single quote (i.e., to allow a single-quoted string to contain a single quotation mark), or to escape a backslash as in a double-quoted string.

It is often helpful in terms of maintenance to adopt a style of coding where you only use double-quoted strings when you require a double-quotish interpolation or interpretation not offered by single-quoted strings. Use single quotation marks for all simple strings.

Of course, specifying data literally every time we want to use it in a program would be tedious and error-prone at best. If we could name an item of data, then just use the name to refer to it, we would be much better off. Well, we don't do exactly that, but we can create named containers (i.e., variables) to hold bits of data. Then we can access the data through the name of the container.

4.1.1 Scalar variables

A variable is a container or slot of memory, associated with a name, where you can store data values. Perl's scalar variable type can hold any scalar value: a number, a string, or a reference. We discussed variable naming in chapter 2, but let's quickly review the particular naming rules for variables in Perl here.

A variable name in Perl, apart from its type symbol, must begin with a letter or an underscore character and may be followed by any number of letters, digits, or underscore characters (well, any number less than 255 characters anyway). Perl has a large number of special built-in variables that do not follow these rules. Consequently, you seldom have to worry about giving your variables names that conflict or clash with built-in variable names. The following list provides examples of legal and illegal variable names you may use with your own variables:

```
$amount                         legal
$total_amount                   legal
$_private                       legal
$field_3                        legal
$abc123                         legal
$This_is_a_LONG_variable_name   legal

$!var      illegal (must start with letter or underscore)
$13_var    illegal (starts with digits)
```

While Perl does not force you to declare your variables before you use them, the strict pragma discussed in chapter 2 does force you to declare your variables or use fully qualified variable names (discussed in chapters 7 and 16). The simplest way to declare your variables is with the my declaration:

```
my $variable;
my $name;
my ($foo, $bar);
```

As you can see, you can declare a list of variables by using parentheses around a comma-separated list of variables.

Once you've declared a variable, you'll need to know how to assign a value to it. The equals sign (=) is the assignment operator:

```
$foo = 42;
$bar = 'Hello';
$greeting = "$bar World\n";
print $greeting;
```

Figure 4.1 shows the relationship between a variable name and its value in memory during declaration and assignment statements.

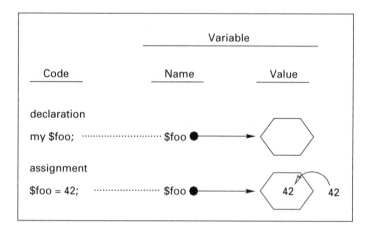

Figure 4.1 Scalar variable declaration and assignment

Assignment may also be combined with declaration either singly or in list form:

```
my $greeting = 'Howdy';
print "$greeting World\n";

my ($first, $second) = ('Hello', 'World');
print "$first $second\n";
```

It is important to note that assignment writes a value into the variable (i.e., into the memory location), but using a variable, as in the print statements above, does not remove the value from memory, but only accesses the value from the variable.

If programs were confined to the literal data contained within them, they would be of limited use. We need to obtain data from outside the program from, for instance, a user typing at a keyboard or by reading data from a file stored on disk. We will examine this more in depth in chapter 6 when we discuss input and output. For now, we consider only the simple case of obtaining scalar values from a user at the keyboard. We can do this using the input operator and the standard input file handle STDIN as follows:

```
my $input;
print "Enter a value: ";
$input = <STDIN>;
print "You entered $input";
```

In a scalar context, such as assignment to a scalar variable, the <STDIN> operator reads in one line of input from the standard input, which is usually the keyboard unless you've otherwise redirected it. So, in the snippet above, the first print statement prompts the user to enter a value. The assignment statement takes everything the user types at the keyboard up to and including the newline (generated by hitting the enter key) and assign that input to the variable $input.

4.2 Expressions

An *expression* is something that evaluates to a value. It may be a literal value, a variable, a function that returns a value, or the result of an operation on one or more values or expressions. Perl supports the basic mathematical operations you are familiar with, addition, subtraction, multiplication, and division, represented by the *operators* +, -, *, and / respectively. For example:

```
$foo = 3 + 5;
$bar = ($foo + 7) / 5;
```

The addition operator returns the value of the sum of its two operands, which in this case are the two simple expressions represented by the literals 3 and 5. In the second line, the division operator also has two operands: the literal value 5 on the right and the result of the expression ($foo + 7) on the left.

Operators also have a relative precedence level associated with them, as demonstrated in the above example. Of the four basic arithmetic operators, multiplication and division have a higher precedence than addition and subtraction, meaning that multiplication and division operations are evaluated before any addition and subtraction. In the example above, we used parentheses to override the standard precedence, causing the addition to take place before the division because parentheses have the highest precedence. Had we not used parentheses, then the value of $foo would have been added to the result of 7 / 5.

Perl has two additional numeric operators: exponentiation and modulus. The exponentiation operator is **. Like the four simple arithmetic operators above (and the modulus operator), it is a binary operator. In other words, it takes two operands. It returns the result of its left operand raised to the power of its right operand:

```
$foo = 4 ** 2;    # $foo is 4 raised to the power of 2, or 16
$bar = $foo ** 3; # $bar is 16 raised to the power of 3, or 4096
```

The modulus operator (%) may be less familiar. It returns the remainder after dividing the left operand by the right operand. Both operands are taken to be integers (or converted to integers if necessary by removing any fractional portions). The result of 10 % 3 is 1 because 10 divided by 3 is 3 with 1 left over. 1 is the remainder and is the value returned by this expression. If you recall the question of testing an integer to see if it is even or odd, you might realize that this operator can provide a ready means of making such a test. The result of any integer N, modulo 2 will only have a non-zero remainder if N is an odd integer.

Perl also has two binary string operators: *concatenation,* represented by a dot (.), and repetition, represented by an x. There is also one built-in function that will be handy to know right away, the chomp() function, which removes a trailing newline from a string. This is useful to remove the newline from an input value obtained using the <STDIN> operator described above.

```
$foo = 'hello ';
$bar = $foo . 'world'; # concatenation: $bar is now 'hello world'

$foo = 'bo' x 3; # $foo is now 'bobobo'

print "Enter a value: ";
$input = <STDIN>;
chomp($input);      # removes newline from $input
```

Perl also offers several shorthand assignment operators that combine a scalar operator with the assignment operator, the complete list of these is available in the *perlop* pod-page (perldoc perlop), here are a couple examples to illustrate the concept:

```
$a = 42;
$a += 5;   # same as: $a = $a + 5

$b = 'hello ';
$b .= 'world';   # same as: $b = $b . 'world'
```

You might now wonder what happens if a scalar variable contains a string and you attempt to use a numeric operator such as addition to add it to a number. This is the second application of type distinction I mentioned in the opening section. Numeric operations are only defined for numeric values, and string operations are only defined for string operations. In a strongly typed language where each variable can only hold a particular type of value such as an integer or a character string, the compiler can detect an attempt to add two mismatched variables and

```
```

cause an error before the program is actually run. In Perl, with only one scalar data type for both strings and numbers, such information is not available to the compiler. An attempt to add a string and a number cannot be detected until the program is running and the variables are evaluated for their values.

Perl solves this problem in a very relaxed manner. If a number is used where a string is expected, the number is converted to a string. (For example, the number 3.14 becomes the string of characters 3.14.) Similarly, if a string is used where a number is expected, it is converted to a number according to the following rule: Any leading spaces in the string are ignored. If the first non-space characters are something reasonably interpreted as a number (or a plus or minus sign followed by a number), they are taken as the number. Any trailing non-numeric characters are ignored. If the string does not have an obvious numeric interpretation, a value of 0 is used.

```
'3.14'      converts to 3.14
'  3.14'    converts to 3.14
' 3.14abc'  converts to 3.14
'abc123'    converts to 0
'number'    converts to 0
```

This conversion is a useful device that allows you to read a number from the keyboard, which is read as a string, and use it as a number. Similarly, after you have done some calculations and wish to print out the results, a number is converted back to a string for output. Run the following example program a few times using different values for input. Try using: 42, 42abc, and hello.

```
#!/usr/bin/perl -w
use strict;
print "Enter a value: ";
my $input = <STDIN>;
my $result = $input + 5;
print "result is $result\n";
```

If you are using the -w switch for warnings, which I highly recommend, the program will issue warnings when a string value does not have an obvious numeric interpretation. Try running the preceding script again with the same inputs but without the -w switch.

4.3 List data

A list is simply an ordered collection of scalar values. It is represented literally as a comma-separated list of scalar values or expressions enclosed within parentheses:

```
(1,2,3,4)           list of four values
('a', 42, "red")    list of three values
(4 + 5, $foo, 1)    list of three values
```

A nested list, where a list is inserted within a list, is simply evaluated to a single flat list:

```
(1, 2, (3, 4), 5)  is the same as (1, 2, 3, 4, 5)
```

We've already seen an example of using a list in the previous discussion of variable declaration using the my declaration. The print() function also takes a list as its argument, though we've only used it so far with a single element in the list:

```
print("the value of \$a is $a\n");
print('the value of $a is ', $a, "\n"); #same output as above
```

In the second version we've used a list of three scalar values to produce the same output as the first version. The first element is the single-quoted string. (Hence, we did not have to use a backslash to get a $ symbol in the string.) The second is the value of the variable $a. And the third element is simply a double-quoted string producing a newline. The practical utility of variable interpolation in double-quoted strings is demonstrated here by the simplicity of the first version.

Perl has a convenient list-making function for producing lists of quoted strings—the quote function. Consider the following list:

```
('one' , 'two', 'three', 'four')
```

Creating this type of list in your code can make it difficult to read for long lists, and is prone to the error of forgetting a quote. The qw() function takes a sequence of whitespace-separated "words" and produces a list of quoted "words":

```
('one' , 'two', 'three', 'four')
is the same as:
qw(one two    three four)
```

I used quotes in the above paragraph to describe "words" because they don't have to be words in the ordinary sense—just sequences of non-whitespace characters separated by any amount of whitespace. The qw() function does not have to use parentheses to delimit its argument. One can use any non-alphanumeric character. Common choices are slashes or vertical bars:

```
qw/one two three/
qw|one two three|
```

4.3.1 Array variables

A list value may be stored in an array variable (see figure 4.2). An array variable is prefixed with an @ symbol (think of it as a stylized "a" for array), but otherwise follows the same naming rules as those for scalar variables mentioned earlier. Assignment to an array variable is the same as for scalar variables. Simply use the assignment operator to assign a list value to an array variable:

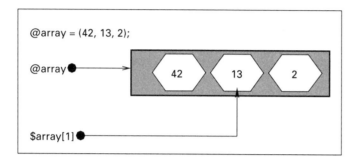

Figure 4.2   An array variable is a list of scalars.

```
@foo = (1, 2, 'three');
@bar = ($a, $b, 3 + 4);
@copy = @foo;
```

Whenever you picture an array, you should keep the list representation in mind. That way you won't find it surprising that you cannot store an array as an element of a list:

```
@foo = (1, 2, 'three');
@bar = ('four', 5, 6);
@new = (0, @foo, @bar, 7);
    is the same as:
@new = (0, (1, 2, 'three'),('four', 5, 6), 7);
    which resolves to:
@new = (0, 1, 2, 'three', 'four', 5, 6, 7);
```

Lists and arrays are ordered. We can access individual elements of them using a subscript notation to refer to the position, or index, of a value in the list:

```
@array = (9, 10, 11, 12);
$second = $array[1]; # assigns 10 to $second
```

You might find two things odd at this point: why the second position is numbered 1, and why the access into the array is prefixed with a $ instead of an @ symbol. First things first. Perl, like many programming languages, starts counting from zero. This means that the four element list stored in the array has positions or indices numbered from 0 to 3.

On the second point, recall that an array holds a list of scalars, so the type of any given element in the array is always a scalar type denoted by a $ symbol. When we say

```
@foo = (42, 12, 2);
```

this performs the equivalent assignment of

```
($foo[0], $foo[1], $foo[2]) = (42, 12, 2)
```

Well, it's not quite the same thing. In the first case, the entire array is set to equal that three element list, while in the latter case, only the first three elements are set to those values. If the array previously held ten items, the last seven remain unchanged.

Each element of the array is a scalar in its own right. All the array variable does is allow us to refer to the whole collection as one named list and to perform certain operations on the list itself such as adding or removing elements to the beginning, the middle, or the end of the list.

Before we proceed to discuss some of these array operations, we should realize that the above assignment from a list of scalar values to a list of scalar variables does not just apply to array elements. You can assign a list of scalar values to any list of scalar variables just as we saw earlier when declaring and assigning multiple scalar variables:

```
($foo, $bar) = (42, 12);      # $foo gets 42, $bar gets 12
($foo, $bar) = ($bar, $foo); # swaps $foo and $bar
```

That last line is possible because the list on the right is evaluated first. The values of the two variables create the list on the right, which is then assigned to the list of variables on the left. I point this out so that you don't mistakenly assume that list assignments happen sequentially—$bar assigned to $foo, then $foo assigned to $bar—which would leave both variables with the same value.

Aside from accessing individual elements, we may access what is referred to as a *slice* of an array or list—that is, a sublist corresponding to a list of indices into the array:

```
@foo = (10, 12, 14, 16);
@bar = @foo[1,2];            # @bar gets the list (12, 14)
```

When we are accessing a slice (sublist), we use the @ symbol in combination with a subscript list. A slice of an array is still a list or array type value. Also, these slices need not be in a consecutive order:

```
@foo = (10, 12, 14, 16);
@bar = @foo[3,0,1];        # @bar gets the list (16, 10, 12)
```

There are two pairs of built-in functions for adding and removing elements from the beginning or end of an array. For adding to or removing from the beginning of an array, we use unshift and shift respectively:

```
@foo = (11, 12, 13);

unshift(@foo, 10);    # @foo is now (10, 11, 12, 13)
unshift(@foo, (8, 9));# @foo is now (8, 9, 10, 11, 12, 13)

$bar = shift(@foo);   # $bar gets 8; @foo is now (9, 10, 11, 12, 13)
```

For working at the end of an array, we use the push and pop functions for adding and removing respectively:

```
@foo = (1, 2, 3);

push(@foo, 4);        # @foo is now (1, 2, 3, 4)
push(@foo, (5, 6));   # @foo is now (1, 2, 3, 4, 5, 6)

$bar = pop(@foo);     # $bar gets 6; @foo is now (1, 2, 3, 4, 5)
```

One last point to make about array variables concerns how they are interpolated within double-quoted strings. If you print an array using print @array, no space or comma separates the values printed. Perl will just treat the array as a comma-separated list of values to be printed. However, if you print an array in a double-quoted string like print "@array", the array will be printed with a space between each value. Both behaviors are good defaults, but can be changed by altering the values of the special variables: $, the output field separator, and $" the list separator.

4.3.2 Hash variables

Perl has one other variable type that holds collections of scalar values—the hash variable (formerly known as an associative array). A hash variable is prefixed with a % symbol. A hash does not have a convenient literal representation in the way an array can be represented as a list, because the elements of a hash are stored in an order completely independent of the order in which they were assigned.

A hash is like an array that is not ordered, where each value is associated with a name, called a *key* (which must be a string), rather than a positional index. These keys are used as subscripts to access individual elements just as indices are used as subscripts into arrays. But while array subscripts are contained inside square brackets, hash subscripts are contained in curly braces.

Even though a hash is not a list, a list can be used to assign values to a hash. In such a case, the list is taken to be a list of key/value pairs:

```
%hash = ('first', 42, 'second', 12);
```

The hash above has two elements, one corresponding to the key first and one corresponding to the key second:

```
%hash = ('first', 42, 'second', 12);
print "$hash{second}\n"; # prints: 12
```

Perl has an alternative to the comma operator that is useful when using lists to assign to hash variables, the => operator. This works the same as the comma except that it also automatically causes the value on the left to be quoted:

```
%hash = (first => 42, second => 12);
print "$hash{second}\n"; # prints: 12
```

The list in the first statement still has four elements, but now it looks more like two pairs of elements separated by a comma, and it is easier to read because the quotes are no longer necessary. Just remember that a hash is not a list, but a list may be interpreted as a hash (see figure 4.3 on page 72).

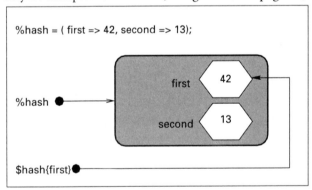

Figure 4.3 A hash variable associating keys with scalar values

Because a hash is not a list, no functions exist to add or remove elements from the beginning or end of a hash: there is no beginning or end of a hash. You can always add a new element by simply assigning a value to a new key in the hash:

```
%hash = (first => 42, second => 12);
$hash{third} = 7;
```

And you can delete a key (and its value) using the `delete` function:

```
delete $hash{first}; # removes the key 'first' and its value
```

You can get a list of the keys or the values in a hash using the appropriately named `keys()` and `values()` functions. However, do not expect these to return the list of keys or values in any particular order. Remember, a hash is not an ordered list. The `keys()` function merely returns a list of keys depending on the order in which Perl internally stored those keys.

```
%hash = (first => 42, second => 12);
$hash{third} = 7;
@keys = keys(%hash);
print "@keys\n";  # printed: first third second
```

Perl also allows hash slices, similar to array slices, with which you may access a list of values by providing a list of keys as a subscript to the hash. You use an `@` symbol, rather than the normal `%` symbol, for hash slices:

```
%hash = (third => 7, first => 42, second => 12);
@h_slice = @hash{'third','second'}; # @h_slice gets (7, 12)
```

Here, `@h_slice` is an ordinary array and `@hash{'third','second'}` is the hash slice.

The `each()` function iterates through key/value pairs in a hash. This is generally done with one of the looping constructs shown in the next chapter.

Hashes are powerful tools for organizing sets of data. We will make heavy use of them in examples in later chapters.

4.4 Context

Perl draws a primary distinction between scalar values and list values. This distinction extends farther than just what type of value may be assigned to a particular type of variable. It also affects how certain expressions are evaluated. Expressions are evaluated within a context that may be either scalar or list (or void, but we won't consider that here). Consider the following:

```
@foo = (11, 12, 13);
$bar = @foo;
```

In the first statement, we have a list on the right being assigned to an array. An array expects a list so the list is evaluated in a list context. In the second statement, an array on the right is being assigned to a scalar variable. In a strongly typed language, this would be a type mismatch. How can you assign an array to a scalar? The assignment is expecting a scalar value; it is providing scalar context for the array. Perl has a rule for evaluating an array in scalar context: return the number of elements contained in the array. So, in the above example, $bar would be assigned a value of 3.

Similarly, you might assign a scalar to an array in one of two ways:

```
@foo = (12);
@foo = 12;
```

The first statement assigns a list with one element to the array @foo. The second statement tries to assign just the scalar value 12 to the array. In this case, the scalar value is evaluated in list context, and Perl produces a single element list, (12), which is assigned to the array.

We saw an example of context in the earlier examples of array assignment:

```
@foo = (2, 3, 4);
@bar = (0, 1, @foo); # @bar gets (0, 1, 2, 3, 4)
```

A list provides a list context to any element within, which is why the array @foo is evaluated as a list in the second statement rather than as a scalar. Many of Perl's built-in functions return different values depending upon the context in which they are called. If a function has different return value behavior, depending on context, the *perlfunc* pod-page entry for that function will clarify that different behavior.

4.5 *References to variables*

Earlier we mentioned that a scalar value can be a number, a string, or a *reference,* but we never said what a reference is or how to make one. If you think of a variable as a storage bin with a name and an address, then you can think of a reference as a forwarding address. When you store a reference to another variable in a scalar variable, you are not storing that variable's value, but the address where its value is stored.

Internally, Perl maintains its own lists of variable names and their associated addresses. Whenever you access a variable, Perl looks up the address for that variable name and follows it to the correct storage bin. If you examine the variable diagrams given earlier in this chapter, you'll see that each variable name is immediately followed by a black circle pointing to a storage bin—that circle represents the address associated with the variable name.

Whenever Perl encounters something like $foo, it expects the $ symbol to be immediately followed by something that evaluates to an address where a scalar value is stored. Perl checks its internal scalar name lists for the name foo. If it finds it, then foo is replaced by its address, and the scalar value in that bin is retrieved (or set if we are assigning something to $foo).

Perl allows you to assign the address of one variable's storage bin, rather than its value, to another variable using the backslash operator. This is called assigning a reference to a variable:

```
$foo = 42;
$bar = \$foo;  # $bar gets address of $foo's bin
```

It is important to realize that $bar is a scalar variable with its own storage bin. In this case, however, the value stored in that location is the address of another bin. Hence, if you print out the value of $bar you will not see 42 but a representation of the address that looks like: SCALAR(0x8050fe4). This printed representation consists of the type of reference—a reference to a scalar—and a representation of the address. To actually use the reference to access the contents of that storage bin, you need to *dereference* it. Remember that Perl expects to find something that resolves to an address immediately following the $ symbol, so if we place another $ symbol before our reference variable, it will be followed by something that resolves to an address:

```
$foo = 42;
$bar = \$foo;
print "$bar\n";  # prints the reference: SCALAR(0x8050fe4)
print "$$bar\n"; # prints: 42
```

In the first print statement, Perl sees $bar as a $ followed by a scalar variable name that immediately resolves to an address. Perl looks up the address in its internal tables and prints the value stored there (another address). In the second print statement, Perl discovers a dollar sign followed by another dollar sign. It first evaluates the second dollar sign, which is followed by a valid variable name, and retrieves the value, which is an address as we have already seen. Now the first dollar sign is followed by an address, so Perl follows that address, retrieves the scalar value stored there (42), and prints it out.

Figure 4.4 shows a graphic depiction of a scalar variable containing a value, and another scalar variable containing a reference to that variable. As in the earlier diagrams, an address is denoted by a black circle pointing to a storage bin.

A reference value is always a scalar value, although it may refer to the address of an array value or a hash value:

```
@array = (11, 12, 13);
$aref  = \@array;
print "@$aref\n";
```

In this case, Perl expects the @ symbol to be followed by either a valid array name, which corresponds to an address, or an address pointing to an array value.

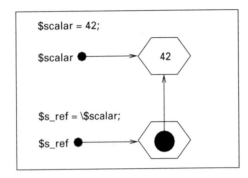

Figure 4.4 A reference to a scalar variable

As in the previous example, $aref evaluates to an address. So, in the print statement above, the @ symbol is followed by an address that Perl uses to retrieve the stored array value. Figure 4.5 depicts an array variable and a scalar variable containing a reference to that variable.

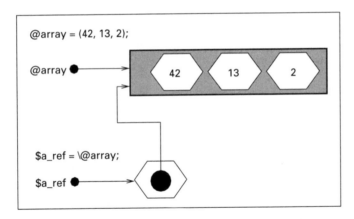

Figure 4.5 A reference to an array variable

At this point, it is only important that you understand the basic concepts of references. Their usefulness won't come into play until later chapters when we deal with passing *parameters* to functions and creating data structures. We will cover references more fully in those chapters.

4.6 Putting it together

In this chapter, you've been presented with all Perl's basic data and variable types as well as many simple operators and functions for reading in data, manipulating data, and displaying the results. You may not realize it, but already you can write a

CHAPTER 4   DATA: TYPES AND VARIABLES

variety of simple but complete programs using only what has been covered so far. For example, consider a program that asks for a measurement in inches and displays the equivalent measure in centimeters. Here is a version of such a program with excessive comments to remind you of various operations. We convert inches to centimeters using the approximation that 1 inch equals 2.54 centimeters:

```
#!/usr/bin/perl -w
use strict;

my ($inches, $centimeters);  # declare variables

print "Enter a measurement in inches: "; # display a prompt

$inches = <STDIN>;    # read input value from user
chomp($inches);       # remove newline from input value

$centimeters = $inches * 2.54; # calculate converted value

print "$inches inches is approximately $centimeters centimeters\n";
```

You could write more complex programs as well, taking many more values from the standard input and calculating complex mathematical formulas using these values. Such programs may become long because they must repeatedly prompt for a value and read a line of input. The next chapter addresses ways of repeatedly executing the same piece of code to simplify such problems.

I mentioned earlier and repeat here that you will learn far more by writing and running Perl programs than by reading about them. I encourage you to do the exercises that follow. Quite a few more functions and operators exist in addition to those we have presented here. We will cover many of them in the following chapters. Remember, the *perlfunc* and *perlop* pod-pages are always available to you. Use them either to get a second viewpoint on things we've already covered or to take a first look at some functions we haven't yet explored.

4.7 Exercises

1 Write a program that asks for a weight in pounds and displays the equivalent weight in kilograms (1 kilogram equals 2.2 pounds).

2 Write a program that calculates the gross pay of an employee. The program should ask for the hourly rate of the employee, how many regular hours, and how many overtime hours the employee worked. Pay for overtime hours should be calculated at time and a half (1.5 times the regular hourly rate).

C H A P T E R   5

Control structures

A program is a series of *statements* that are, by default, executed in sequence from beginning to end. This sequence of execution is referred to as the flow of control of the program. Not all problems are amenable to being solved by executing a series of instructions in a strictly linear fashion. Some problems require a choice among two or more courses of action, depending on particular criteria or condition. Other problems require a series of steps to be repeated a certain number of times or until some condition is met.

In the previous chapter, we discussed simple expressions but we did not explicitly address the concept of statements. In short, a statement is an expression (or combination of expressions) followed by a semicolon. For example

```
12;
```

This is a statement, but it doesn't do anything. It is just a literal value in a void context. Such a statement will generate a warning when using the -w switch (and we are assuming that the -w switch is being used throughout this book). More realistic examples of statements are

```
foo = 12;
print "$foo\n";
```

Statements are usually written on a single line, but this is not a requirement of the language. Occasionally, statements are too long to fit reasonably on a single line. Consider the following statement, which might have been used in the solution to the final exercise in the previous chapter:

```
$gross_pay = $regular_hours * $hourly_rate + $overtime_hours *
$hourly_rate * 1.5;
```

This is a perfectly valid statement, though it is not particularly readable when written in this fashion. This statement might be better written as

```
$gross_pay = $regular_hours  * $hourly_rate +
             $overtime_hours * $hourly_rate * 1.5;
```

Using whitespace in this manner helps the reader understand that this is a single statement. An even better way to rewrite this statement is to use three statements:

```
$regular_pay  = $regular_hours  * $hourly_rate;
$overtime_pay = $overtime_hours * $hourly_rate * 1.5;
$gross_pay    = $regular_pay + $overtime_pay;
```

Multiple statements may be grouped into compound statements called *blocks* by enclosing them within a pair of curly braces. A block also introduces a *scope* on variables declared within it, which simply means that a variable declared in a my declaration within a block only exists within that block. In other words, the variable in question is visible only within that block:

```
my $foo = 42;
{
    my $bar = 13;              # both $foo and $bar exist
    print "$foo and $bar\n"; # within this block
}
print "$foo and $bar\n"; # warning, $bar does not exist here
```

Scope is an issue we will address more closely in chapter 7, for now we are declaring all of our variables with the my declaration and all such variables are private to the block in which they are declared. Blocks can be nested. Your entire program is considered a block—think of Perl automatically putting curly braces at the beginning and end of your source code file. Aside from introducing scope, a block serves to group statements into a compound statement that can be selected or repeated with the use of control statements.

5.1   Selection statements

The basic selection statement in Perl (and many other languages) is the if statement. This statement has the following general syntax:

```
if ( Condition ) { Block }
```

There is no semicolon after the closing brace on a block. Often, the block contains multiple statements and the structure is written as follows (according the principles laid out in chapter 2):

```
if ( Condition ) {
    statement;
    statement;
}
```

When Perl encounters an if statement it evaluates the condition. If true, then the block of statements is executed. Otherwise, execution skips the block and continues with the next statement following the block (see figure 5.1).

But what is a condition and what is true and false? The condition is simply any expression. This expression is evaluated in a scalar context to produce a scalar value. Remember, Perl interprets variables and expressions slightly differently, depending upon context (i.e., scalar or list context). When something is evaluated in a scalar context, the result of the evaluation is the scalar value. A value is false if

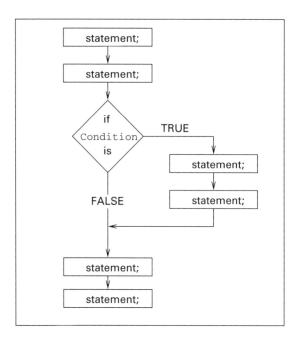

Figure 5.1 Flow diagram of an `if` statement

it is undefined (a variable that has no value stored in it), a zero, an empty string, or a string containing only a zero. Every other value is considered true.

```
my $foo = 1;
if ( $foo ) {
    print "$foo is a true value\n";
}
```

If you run the snippet above as a Perl program, it will execute the print statement inside the `if` block. If you change the initial assignment to `$foo` to be one of: 0 (or anything that evaluates to zero; 0.0 or 0e12 for example), `' '`, or `'0'` then the `if` block will be skipped.

Often we do not want to merely test a variable's value. We want to evaluate that value in terms of another value. In other words, is the variable's value less than, greater than, or equal to another specific value? There are operators, called *relational operators,* for each of these tests. These operators come in two forms: one tests numeric relations and one tests string relations (see table 5.1 on page 82). It is a common mistake to use the wrong type of relational test, especially to mistakenly use a numeric test for string data. Perl will issue a warning about this if -w is being used. (You are using -w, aren't you?).

Table 5.1 Relational operators

Numeric	String	Result
$a < $b	$a lt $b	True if $a is less than $b
$a <= $b	$a le $b	True if $a is less than or equal to $b
$a > $b	$a gt $b	True if $a is greater than $b
$a >= $b	$a ge $b	True if $a is greater than or equal to $b
$a == $b	$a eq $b	True if $a is equal to $b
$a != $b	$a ne $b	True if $a is not equal to $b

You can use the `if` statement to choose set up choices. Perl can do one thing if the condition is true or something else if it is false. This form has the general syntax

```
if ( Condition ) { Block } else { Block }
```

Again, this is better written as an indented structure according to principles outlined in chapter 2. Figure 5.2 shows the flow of control in such a structure.

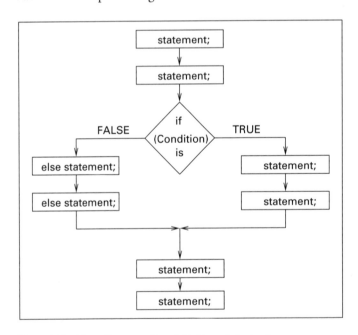

Figure 5.2 Flow diagram of an `if/else` statement

The following example displays one thing if $foo is greater than $bar, or something else if the relation is false:

```
if ( $foo > $bar ) {
    print "$foo is greater than $bar\n";
} else {
    print "$foo is not greater than $bar\n";
}
```

Additionally, you may select one of several blocks to execute by using multiple selection criteria in elsif clauses (note, there is no "e" before the "i" in the elsif keyword), which can be inserted between an if block and an else block (see figure 5.3).

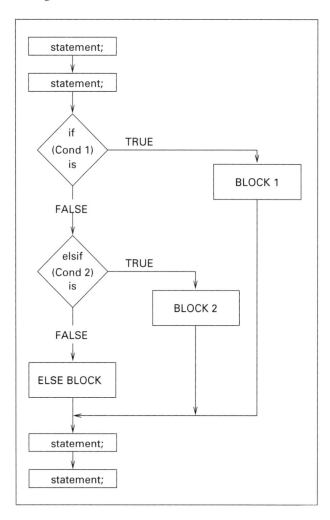

Figure 5.3   Flow diagram of an if/elsif/else statement

In this manner, we can determine if a value is greater than, equal to, or less than another value:

```perl
if ( $foo < $bar ) {
    print "$foo is less than $bar\n";
} elsif ( $foo > $bar ) {
    print "$foo is greater than $bar\n";
}
else {
    print "$foo must be equal to $bar\n";
}
```

5.2 Repetition: loops

The other primary flow of control structure is the *loop*. A loop allows you to specify a block of code that is to be repeatedly executed a specific number of times (determinate loop) or until some condition is met (indeterminate loop). Consider a program to calculate the average of ten values input by a user. You could write out ten pairs of statements that prompt for and accept user input. Or you could write the code once and loop over it 10 times.

What if you do not know in advance how many values will be averaged? In this case, you must use a loop to repeat the input statements until a special value, called a *sentinel value,* is entered.

The basic indeterminate loop, which you'll find in many other languages, is the while loop:

```perl
while ( Condition ) { Block }
```

Here the condition is tested and, if it is true, the statements in the block are executed. Once the block is finished, control returns to the top of the loop and the condition is tested again. The block will be repeatedly executed as long as the condition evaluates to a true value. Once the condition returns a false value, execution will continue with the next statement following the block. Whenever you write an indeterminate loop, you should always double-check the statements in your loop-block to ensure that the conditional will eventually fail. Otherwise, you will have an infinite loop that won't stop running until you kill the program.

Here is an example that calculates the average of an undetermined number of grades:

```perl
#!/usr/bin/perl -w
use strict;
my ($average, $total, $count) = (0, 0, 0);
my $grade = '';
```

```perl
while ($grade ne 'q') {
    print "Enter a grade or 'q' to quit: ";
    $grade = <STDIN>;
    chomp $grade;
    if ($grade ne 'q'){
        $count = $count + 1;
        $total = $total + $grade;
    }
}
$count ||= 1;   # avoid division by zero if nothing entered
$average = $total / $count;
print "The average is $average\n";
```

In the example above, we first declare our variables for the average, the total, and the count of how many values will be eventually entered. These variables are initialized with values of zero, using the list assignment we saw in the previous chapter. We also declare a variable to hold each grade as it is input and initialize it with the empty string. We then enter the loop statement. If the value of the grade is not equal, (ne), to the string q, the block is executed. Inside the block, we prompt the user for a grade, or the sentinel value q, and read this into the grade variable. We chomp() off the newline and use an if statement to determine if the sentinel was entered. If the sentinel was not entered, we add one to our count and add the grade to the total. This entire loop will be repeatedly executed until the user enters a single q, at which point the loop is finished, and the program goes on to calculate the average and display the result.

A while loop may also have an optional continue block immediately following the main loop block.

```perl
while ( Condition ) { Block } continue { Block }
```

The continue block is executed each time the while loop continues to be executed by default (see figure 5.4 on page 86). The continue block is not used much in practice. When it is, it is usually in conjunction with additional loop control statements we will discuss later in this chapter. However, we can use the while statement, complete with its continue block, to help define the next kind of loop, the for loop:

```perl
for (initialization; condition; iteration) { Block }
```

In this statement, the first time the loop is encountered, it evaluates the initialization expression and tests the conditional expression. If the condition is true, the loop body is executed. When the loop body is finished executing, the iteration

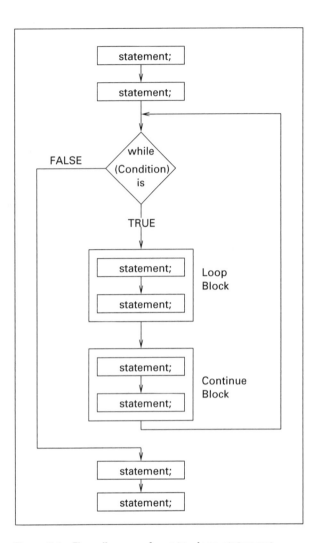

Figure 5.4   Flow diagram of a `while` loop statement

expression is evaluated, and the condition is tested again. An example will help show what happens:

```
for (my $count = 0; $count < 10; $count++) {
    print "$count\n";
}
```

The first time this loop is entered, the variable $count is declared and set to zero. The condition is tested, and it is true. Zero is less than 10. The block is executed. When the block is finished, the iteration expression is evaluated, $count++, which increments the variable by one. This is a short way of saying $count =

$count + 1. The condition is then evaluated once again. This sequence of condition, block, iteration continues until the condition is false. In other words, the above loop will execute ten times, printing the values from 0 to 9 inclusive. This is equivalent to the following while loop:

```
my $count = 0;
while ( $count < 10 ) {
    print "$count\n";
} continue {
    $count++;
}
```

The for loop is a determinate loop because you can specify how many times the loop will execute. Obviously, you can do the same thing with a while loop, making it a determinate loop in a sense. The converse is also true, a for loop without any of the three expressions (i.e., with empty parentheses) considers the condition to be true. Consequently, the following two loops are both infinite loops and will never stop running:

```
for (;;) {
    print "still running\n";
}
while ( 1 ) {
    print "still running\n";
}
```

Infinite loops have no value in programming unless you can somehow force the loop to exit with some other statement. Perl provides a last statement to do just this sort of thing.

```
while ( 1 ) {
    print "Enter a value: ";
    my $input = <STDIN>;
    chomp $input;
    if ( $input eq 'q' ) {
        print "You are exiting the loop\n";
        last;
    }
    print "You entered $input, here we go again\n";
}
```

The last statement will force an exit of the immediate enclosing loop.

Perl provides two other loop control statements in addition to the last statement, the next and redo statements. Briefly, the next statement causes the rest of the loop block to be skipped and the continue block to be executed. Control then returns to the condition of the loop. In the case of the for loop, the loop body is skipped, and the iteration expression is evaluated again before returning to the conditional expression. A simple example might be to count the number of non-empty lines in a file:

```
#!/usr/bin/perl -w
use strict;
my $count = 0;
while( <> ) {
    next if length($_) < 2; # next if line contains only \n
    $count++;
}
print "There are $count non-blank lines in the file\n";
```

Note, there is some magic going in this example that will be made clear when we introduce reading files in the following chapter.

The `redo` statement causes control to return to the beginning of the loop block without executing the `continue` block or re-testing the condition.

The third kind of looping statement is the `foreach` statement. This statement does not evaluate a condition, but instead evaluates a list value and executes the loop block once for each scalar value in the list. Each value in the list is assigned to a loop variable for each execution of the loop block.

```
foreach my $loop_variable ( LIST ) { Block }
```

The list may be a literal list, a list of scalars, an array, a function that returns a value, or any combination of these.

```
my @array = (12, 13, 14);
foreach my $item ( @array ) {
    print "the current item is $item\n";
}
```

If you do not provide a loop variable, then the special $_ variable will be used as the loop variable. This special default variable is often used in Perl programs and is the default target of many operations. I'll point out the operators and functions that make use of this variable as they are introduced.

One important point is that, if a value in the list is a variable, then the loop variable is an *alias* for that variable. Changing the value of the loop variable will change the value of the corresponding value in the list:

```
my @array = (1, 2, 3);
foreach my $item ( @array ) {
    $item = $item * 2;
}
print "@array\n";  # prints '2 4 6'
```

In this example, each element of the array has been assigned, in turn, to the loop variable, $item. Because this variable is an alias to the real variable, changing its value has changed each value in the array.

In review, the loop constructs can be divided into three loose categories of functionality:

```
To execute a loop while/until a given condition is true:
    while ( condition ) { Block }
    until ( condition ) { Block }

To execute a loop for each item in a LIST:
    foreach my $loop_variable ( LIST ) { Block }

To execute a loop a certain number of times:
    for ( initialization; condition; iteration ) { Block }
```

5.3 *Logical operators*

The conditional expressions we have used thus far have all been easily understood expressions, such as tests for true/false values, or simple relational tests such as ($foo < $bar). Expressions may be combined into more complex expressions through the use of logical operators. There are three logical operators, two of which may be used to combine two expressions. These operators come in two forms: a low precedence, easy to read form (and, or, and not), and a higher precedence symbolic form (&&, ||, and !), respectively. These behave just as you might expect them to. For example:

```
if ( $foo < $bar  and  $foo != 0 ) {
    print "$foo is less than $bar and is not zero\n";
}
```

Here we have combined two relational expressions with the logical and operator. The if block will only be executed if both relations are true. Similarly, we can use the or operator to combine two simple expressions:

```
if ( $foo < 15  or  $foo > 20 ) {
    print "$foo is less than 15 or greater than 20\n";
}
```

The not operator can be used to negate the truth/false value of an expression:

```
if ( not $foo ) {
    print "$foo is false\n";
}
```

This is usually not necessary, however, as Perl provides negated versions of the both the `if` and `while` constructs: the `unless` and `until` statements:

```
if ( not $foo ) {block}
# does the same as:
unless ( $foo ) {block}

while ( not $foo ) {block}
# does the same as:
until ( $foo ) {block}
```

A list of each logical operator and how it evaluates is given in table 5.2. To simplify matters, this table uses the capitalized word for each operator, and is meant to stand for either its low or high precedence form.

Table 5.2 Truth tables for logical AND and OR

Operand 1	AND	Operand 2	Result
TRUE	AND	TRUE	TRUE
TRUE	AND	FALSE	FALSE
FALSE	AND	TRUE	FALSE
FALSE	AND	FALSE	FALSE

Operand 1	OR	Operand 2	Result
TRUE	OR	TRUE	TRUE
TRUE	OR	FALSE	TRUE
FALSE	OR	TRUE	TRUE
FALSE	OR	FALSE	FALSE

	NOT	Operand	Result
	NOT	TRUE	FALSE
	NOT	FALSE	TRUE

The logical AND and OR operators are lazy evaluators. They do only the minimum amount of evaluation to determine their result. Consider the AND operator. It can return a true value only if both of its operands are true. Hence, if the first expression is false, the whole combined expression must be false. Therefore, the second expression is never even evaluated. Similarly for the OR operator—if

CHAPTER 5 CONTROL STRUCTURES

the first expression is true, the whole combined expression will be true regardless of the result of the second expression. So the second expression is not evaluated if the first results in a true value. We saw an example of this back in chapter 3 when we used the die() function if the open() call to open a file failed.

Now, it should be pointed out that the AND and OR operators do not return TRUE or FALSE or 1 or 0, but instead return the value of the last expression evaluated, which itself will evaluate as either true or false depending on the expression. This is convenient because logical operators are not confined to conditional tests in loops and selection statements. They can also be used in other forms of statements, like assignment statements, to provide a default value:

```
$foo = $bar || 42;
```

Here, $foo will get the value of $bar if it is a true value. Otherwise, it will be assigned 42. We have used the higher precedence form of OR in this example because it has a higher precedence than the assignment. This means that the || is evaluated first providing a value for the assignment. Had we used the lower precedence or operator, we would have needed parentheses to obtain the proper evaluation:

```
$foo = ( $bar or 42 );
```

Otherwise, the assignment would have been evaluated first, assigning the value of $bar to $foo and then evaluating the logical OR value of the assignment's result with the value of 42. Logical AND operators can also be used in a manner similar to simple if statements:

```
$foo && print "$foo is a true value\n";
```

Here the first operand of the AND operator, $foo, is evaluated. If it is true, the second expression is evaluated causing the print statement to be executed. Due to lazy evaluation, if $foo has a false value, then the combined expression is known to be false so the second expression is never executed. This is the same as:

```
if ( $foo ) {
    print "$foo is a true value\n";
}
```

5.4 Statement modifiers

All of the control statements above can also be used as statement modifiers—that is, rather than setting up a block containing a single statement, you can append the control structure to a single simple statement:

```
if ( $foo ) {
    print "$foo is true\n";
}
# same as:
print "$foo is true\n" if $foo;
```

This type of conditional statement can improve the readability of your code. Consider a simple case such as looping through an array and printing only those elements that are greater than five:

```
@list = (1,6,3,9,2,7);
foreach my $var (@list){
    if ($var <= 5) {
        next;
    }
    print "$var\n";
}

# compare to:
@list = (1,6,3,9,2,7);
foreach my $var (@list){
    next if $var <= 5;
    print "$var\n";
}

# or even this
@list = (1,6,3,9,2,7);
foreach my $var (@list){
    print "$var\n" if $var > 5;
}
```

The simplifying effect can be even more apparent in more complicated loops, but this illustrates the point. Sometimes it is more natural to say "next if condition" rather than "if condition then next."

5.5 Putting it together

At this point, you have tools to create programs to solve problems of practically any complexity level. Indeed, research in the mid 1960s showed that any program could be written in terms of just three control structures: sequence, selection, and repetition.

Consider a program that asks for a number to serve as an upper limit, then finds and displays all of the prime numbers less than or equal to that number. A prime number is defined as a positive integer greater than 1 that has only 1 and itself as integer divisors. It cannot be evenly divided by any other integer other than 1 and itself. We are going to use a method called the "sieve of Eratosthenes" to find prime numbers that are less than or equal to a given number N. In this method, we first create a list of all the integers from 2 to N. Rather than finding primes directly, we will rule out numbers that are not prime from the list. To begin with, we consider all the numbers to be good prime candidates. Our method of ruling out non-primes is simple, we start at the beginning of the list (with the number 2) and apply the following rule: if the number has not been crossed out it is prime and left on the list. All multiples of that number are then crossed out on the list. We proceed to the next number that is not crossed out and repeat the process.

Programming is a matter of practice. Now is a good time to sit down with a pencil and paper and design and code a program that asks for a number, then prints out all the primes less than or equal to that number (don't forget chapter 3). When you've finished, or made a good attempt, come back and continue reading for an example of one way to create such a program.

In this example, we will use the notation from chapter 3 to break the program into smaller more manageable chunks. The first thing we have to do is define our overall program in terms of a set of smaller chunks. We will need to declare some variables, obtain a number from the user, set up a list of integers, cancel out the non-primes of this list, and finally, display the primes that remain. Our top level design for this program, which we will call `primes.pl`, is:

```
<<primes.pl>>=
#!/usr/bin/perl -w
use strict;
<<declare variables>>
<<get upper limit from user>>
<<initialize array of prime candidates>>
<<find primes and cancel non-primes>>
<<display the primes>>
```

We can see from the top level design that we will need two main variables: a scalar to hold the upper limit and an array to hold the array of prime candidates (i.e., list of integers).

```
<<declare variables>>=
my $limit;
my @primes;
```

Obtaining a value from a user is a simple matter of prompting and accepting the input. Normally, we simply accept the input and then use chomp() to remove the newline, but it is common practice to do both at the same time as in the following chunk:

```
<<get upper limit from user>>=
print "Enter an integer as an upper limit: ";
chomp( $limit = <STDIN> );
```

Now we need to initialize our array of prime candidates. Before we do, we need to decide what we will put in this array. An obvious choice is to simply store the list of integers from 0 up to the $limit in the array. However, there is an alternative: we could simply store a list of 1s, one for each position in the array from the 0'th position up to the $limit'th position. Then we could use the positions as the list of integers. Later we could set to zero any position that is to be crossed out. This would amount to using the array as a list of *Boolean* values (i.e., true and false values) with 1s representing true and 0s representing false. Since any non-zero number is considered true in Perl, we will use a list of the actual integers, but still set crossed-out values to zero so we can later simply print out all the true values in the list.

The most obvious way we know of thus far to initialize our array is with a for loop like so:

```
for ( my $index = 0; $index <= $limit; $index++ ) {
    $primes[$index] = $index;
}
```

While that is a perfectly good way to initialize our array with a list of integers from 0 to $limit, we may as well take this opportunity to introduce another operator—the 'range' operator, which consists of two dots (..). This is a binary operator which, in list context, produces a list of values counting by ones from the value on the left side to the value on the right side.

```
@foo = (3, 4, 5, 6, 7, 8);
@foo = (3 .. 8);   # same as above
```

This will make it easy to initialize our array. However, we do not need to simply initialize our array to the list (0 .. $limit) as we already know that the first two numbers of this list should be crossed out (set to zero) because 2 is the first prime integer:

```
<<initialize array of prime candidates>>=
@primes = (0, 0, 2 .. $limit);
```

All of our chunks have been fairly simple up to this point, but the problem of how to cancel out non-primes is a little more complex. Each number in the array from 2 up to the $limit corresponds directly with its position in the array. For example, if the $limit is 20, then $primes[9] is 9 and $primes[20] is 20. We can use a for loop to count through positions in the array, starting at position 2, and check if the number stored there has been crossed out (is zero). If the number's value is not zero, that number must be a prime number. Consequently, we will need to cancel out all later multiples of that number.

One last, but important, consideration here is when to end the for loop. Obviously, we should not count any higher than the value of $limit, but do we need to count that high? The answer is no. In fact, we only have to count through values of the list that are less than or equal to the square root of the $limit. Why this is so is a mathematical exercise for the reader. Perl has a built-in function to calculate the square root of a number: sqrt(). Let's use this in the conditional expression of the for loop:

```
<<find primes and cancel non-primes>>=
for (my $index = 2; $index <= sqrt($limit); $index++) {
    if ( $primes[$index] ) {
        <<cancel multiples of this prime>>
    }
}
```

Notice our if condition above. Because any non-zero value is considered true, we did not have to test for a zero value at that position, if ($primes[$index] != 0). We simply used the value itself for its truth value.

If we are in the if block, it means that the number at the current index has not been canceled and is therefore a prime number. We now need to go through the rest of the list and set the value of any position that is a multiple of this number to zero (i.e., cancel it out). We can do this with another for loop, but just for a little variety, we will use a while loop to do it in this case. We need to declare a new variable to use as a positional index. We initialize that variable to a value twice that of the current index:

```
<<cancel multiples of this prime>>=
my $cross_out = $index * 2;
while ( $cross_out <= $limit ) {
    $primes[$cross_out] = 0;
    $cross_out += $index;
}
```

Consider the first index value, 2, in the above code. The value at index 2 has not been crossed out, so 2 is a prime number. We then set a new index variable called `$cross_out` to twice the value of the current index. The cross out index is now 4, which is the first multiple of 2 in the list. We set the value at that position in the array to zero. In other words, we cross it out. The next multiple of 2 is obtained by adding 2 (the `$index` value) to the cross out index and repeating the loop, canceling out the value at position 6. This continues until we have canceled out all multiples of 2 from the list and this `while` loop ends. The whole process continues again in the outer loop as the index is incremented to 3, which is not canceled, so all of its multiples are canceled. The third time through the loop the index is 4, which has already been canceled as a multiple of 2. So the value at position 4 is zero and if the `if` block is skipped. (Any multiple of 4 is also a multiple of 2 and has already been canceled out.)

When the canceling out process is completed, every number in the array `@primes` is either zero or a prime number. To display the primes, we can use a `foreach` loop to loop through the array and print out each value that is not zero.

```
<<display the primes>>=
foreach my $prime_number ( @primes ) {
    if ( $prime_number ) {
        print "$prime_number is prime\n";
    }
}
```

And that completes the program. The whole thing, when each chunk name is replaced with its corresponding code is:

```
#!/usr/bin/perl -w
use strict;
my $limit;
my @primes;
print "Enter an integer as an upper limit: ";
chomp( $limit = <STDIN> );
@primes = (0, 0, 2 .. $limit);
for (my $index = 2; $index <= sqrt($limit); $index++) {
    if ( $primes[$index] ) {
        my $cross_out = $index * 2;
        while ( $cross_out <= $limit ) {
            $primes[$cross_out] = 0;
            $cross_out += $index;
        }
    }
}
foreach my $prime_number ( @primes ) {
    if ( $prime_number ) {
        print "$prime_number is prime\n";
    }
}
```

5.6 Exercises

1 Write a program that prompts for and accepts up to twenty numbers (i.e., provide a way for a user to enter less than twenty values) and prints out these values in reverse order.

2 Modify the above program to remove any duplicate values from the list, while still telling how many times a given value was entered.

3 Write a program that will either convert a length in inches to a length in centimeters or convert a length in centimeters to a length in inches.

CHAPTER 6

Simple I/O and text processing

Until now, we've limited ourselves, and our programs, to a simple means of input and output (I/O). We have used <STDIN> to read single lines of input from the keyboard, and we've used the print() function to produce output to the screen. Though simple, we are already using the two basic components for most input and output operations on files: the angle operator (input operator) (<>) and file handles such as STDIN.

6.1   File handles

A file handle is both another kind of Perl identifier and another data type. If you think of a variable as associating a name with a region of memory, then you can think of a file handle as associating a name with what we may simply call an I/O channel—or, even more simply, a stream of bytes. This bytestream doesn't even have to be associated with a file stored on disk. It may be associated with input from the keyboard as with STDIN (see below) or with the input or output of another program altogether (see chapter 13).

A file handle is simply a line of communication between your program and some other device such as your keyboard, a console, or a file on a disk. You may read from or write to a file handle and, in either case, your program will read data from or write data to whatever is on the other end of file handle.

When your Perl program starts it automatically has three predefined file handles opened that it inherits from the shell: STDIN (standard input), STDOUT (standard output), and STDERR (standard error). Unless you provided some input/output redirection when you started the program, STDIN is generally attached to the keyboard device. STDOUT and STDERR are attached to the console. You've already used the STDOUT file handle implicitly with all of the print() statements used in earlier chapters. The print() function may optionally be told to print to a file handle opened for writing. If a file handle is not given, STDOUT is used:

```
print "Hello World\n";        # prints to STDOUT
print STDOUT "Hello World\n"; # same as above
```

To create a new file handle and attach a file to it we use the open() function:

```
open(FILEHANDLE, 'filename');
```

This opens the file named *filename* and attaches the file handle identifier FILEHANDLE to it. By default, any file opened as above is opened for reading only. The symbols < and > may be used in front of the file name to specify reading or writing respectively. The double >> can be used to open a file for appending (i.e., writing to the end of the file):

```
open(HANDLE, 'filename');   # opens 'filename' for reading only
open(HANDLE, '<filename');  # same as above
open(HANDLE, '>filename');  # opens 'filename' for writing only
open(HANDLE, '>>filename'); # opens 'filename' for appending only
```

Opening a file for writing by using the > symbol will truncate the file if it already exists. You may also open a file for both reading and writing using the + symbol in conjunction with either the < or >. However, you usually want to use +< to open a file for reading and writing because using +> will first wipe out the contents of the file.

Before we try to use one of the file handles we've just opened, we need to think about what will happen if the named file could not be opened for some reason—for example, incorrect permissions or the nonexistence of the file. You should always test a call to the open() function before trying to use the file handle. The standard way to do this is by using the die() function:

```
open(FILE, 'filename') || die "can't open the file: $!";
```

The open() function returns 1 on success and undef (a false value) on failure. This means we can use the logical OR operator (either || or or) and rely on its short circuit behavior as mentioned in the last chapter. If the open() call succeeds, it returns 1 (a true value) and the right hand expression is not evaluated. However, if the open() call fails, the right hand expression is executed, which calls the die() function with the given string. The die() function prints the string to STDERR and exits the program. The $! variable is a special Perl variable and is set to the last error message returned by a system call such as the open() function.

Now that we can open a file, let's read something from a file:

```
open(FILE, 'data.txt') || die "can't open file: $!";
my $line = <FILE>;
close FILE;
```

This snippet opens the file *data.txt* for reading, or dies with an error message. It reads in one line from the file into the variable $line and then closes the file.

Often we want to do more than read in the first line of file. We usually want to read through an entire file or at least read until we find a particular item. The input operator is context sensitive. If we use it in a scalar context (i.e., assigning to a scalar variable), one line will be read from the file handle. However, if we use it in a list context, such as assigning to an array, the entire file will be read as a list of lines:

```
@lines = <FILE>; # @lines contains whole file
```

This is one way to read an entire file, but it is not efficient for large files that might occupy too much memory if read all at once. Another way to work on a file is to process it line by line:

```
open(FILE, 'filename') || die "can't open file: $!";
while ( <FILE> ) {
    print $_;
}
close FILE;
```

There is a lot going on in that little loop statement. When the input operator is used as the only thing in the conditional part of a `while` or `for(;;)` loop, Perl does some extra magic for you. Each time through the loop, a single line is read from the file and assigned to the special `$_` variable. This is also checked to see that it is defined even if the value of the line is false (as in instances where the line contains only the string `0`). The loop will continue reading lines until the end of the file is reached. This loop is the same as the following:

```
open(FILE, 'filename') || die "can't open file: $!";
while ( defined( $_ = <FILE>) ) {
    print $_;
}
close FILE;
```

The `defined()` function returns true if the expression has a defined value, including zero, the empty string, or `'0'`. Because the input operator returns `undef` at the end of a file, the condition remains true for any value read in from the file until the end of the file is reached. We should also note here that, if the `print()` function is not given any expression to print, it will assume you wanted to print the `$_` variable. Hence, inside the loop above, we could have just used `print;` rather than `print $_;`.

You should know about a few special and convenient Perl variables associated with input and output, beginning with the `$.` variable. The `$.` variable contains the current line number of the file being read.

In many cases, when we store data in a file, we organize it terms of records and fields. A record is a unit of data made up of one or more fields. For example, to store employee data in a file we might want to store an employee ID number, last name, first name, and department name as fields for one employee record:

```
1201:Jones:William:Sales
1202:Smith:Jane:Operations
```

In the example above, each record is one line of data (the record separator is a new-line) and consists of four fields separated by colons. This is referred to as a colon-separated file. Other common formats use comma-separated fields and pipe (|) separated fields.

The $/ variable is the input record separator variable. Normally, this is set to the string \n (a newline), which is why we often refer to reading a file in terms of lines. But you may not always want to read a file this way. You may set this variable to the empty string to read in "paragraph" mode. This is a special case where the file will be read in chunks separated by one or more blank lines.

```
ID: 1201
Last Name: Jones
First Name: William
Department: Sales

ID: 1202
Last Name: Smith
First Name: Jane
Department: Operations
```

In this example, each record is a paragraph, and each line contains the field name and the field data. You may also set this variable to the undefined value, $/ = undef();. The entire file will then be read in as one single scalar value (one long string), but, again, this could cause memory problems if the file is large or your system doesn't have a lot of memory. It is often a good idea to localize changes to Perl's special variables—we will discuss local() in chapter 7.

There are also two output special variables. $, is the output field separator and determines what is printed between arguments to the print() function. Normally, a statement such as print "one", "two", "three"; will produce 'onetwo-three' because $, is an empty string by default. Setting this variable to a space, $, = ' ' will cause the statement above to produce 'one two three'. The $\ special variable is the output record separator. This is an empty string by default, meaning nothing is printed following a print() statement's arguments. This could be set to a newline so that each print() statement wrote a newline after its arguments. Appendix B lists several more of the special built-in variables, and the *perlvar* pod-page lists the complete set of such special variables.

You have seen how to open a file for reading or writing (or both) and how to get data to and from a file. But Perl has more magic to offer. When you invoke a Perl program, any arguments you give it on the command line are available in the special array called @ARGV Quite often, you give filenames as arguments to a program and the program operates on those files. Perl makes it easy to process files given on the command line by using the empty input operator <>.

```
#!/usr/bin/perl -w
use strict;
while ( <> ) {
    print;
}
```

The above is a complete program. You may invoke it with one or more file names that will be placed in the @ARGV array. Each element of this array will be automatically treated as a filename and opened for reading in the while loop. Inside the loop, the name of the current file is available through the special $ARGV variable. The file is opened as the special file handle ARGV. If no arguments are given to the program, then <> is treated as <STDIN>. This also means that, if you have list of literal file names in your program that you wish to open and read, you do not have to manually open, read, and close each one. You can simply assign this list to the @ARGV array, then use a while loop on the empty input operator:

```
#!/usr/bin/perl -w
use strict;
@ARGV = ('file1', 'file2', 'file3');
while ( <> ) {
    print;
}
```

Most often, however, we want to do much more than just read lines from files and print them out. We want to examine the data and do different things depending on what we find.

6.2   Pattern matching

Probably the single most used method of examining data in a Perl program involves the match operator or its partner, the substitution operator. The match and substitution operators can be used to test whether a string matches a given pattern (or part of the string matches a given pattern), to extract portions of a string that match a pattern, and to replace portions of a string that match a pattern with new string data. Both operators use regular expressions to express patterns. Regular expressions are very much a programming language in their own right. We will discuss Perl 's regular expression (regex) language in depth in chapter 10. For now, we will only present a simple subset of Perl 's regex capabilities.

The match operator m// has a syntax of

```
m/PATTERN/
```

Other *delimiters* may be used (such as: m|PATTERN|, or m!PATTERN!, or even paired delimiters like: m(PATTERN) or m<PATTERN>. However, when the slashes are used, the m may be omitted and the operator written simply as: /PATTERN/. The match operator is applied to a target string by means of the binding operator =~.

```
TARGET =~ m/PATTERN/
```

The target may be a string, a variable containing a string, or any other expression that evaluates to a string. If the binding operator and target are not given, then the match is performed against the contents of the special $_ variable. A negated form of the binding operator, !~, reverses the sense of the match operator. In that case, the whole expression will be true only if no part of the target string matches the given pattern.

But what exactly is a pattern? A pattern is a description, expressed as a regular expression (regex, or regexen for plural), of some sequence of textual data. There is a great deal to know about regular expressions. In this chapter, we cover the basics of creating and using regular expressions. Later, in chapter 10, we will also present a way of thinking about how a pattern match is applied to a target string.

The simplest kind of pattern is one that literally describes a sequence of characters. In a regex, any literal alphanumeric character stands for itself. The pattern foo will match against any string containing the sequence of characters foo. A program that prints out any line containing foo can be written as:

```
#!/usr/bin/perl -w
use strict;
while( <> ) {
    if ( m/foo/ ) {
        print;
    }
}
```

This program uses a lot of default behavior. The while(<>) automatically opens each file specified on the command line and loops through the file, assigning each line in turn to the special $_ variable. The match operator, not being bound to a particular target string, is automatically applied to $_. And, finally, the print() function also prints out the $_ variable when used with no arguments. You will likely see a lot of code that takes advantage of Perl's default behavior, and you will probably want to do so yourself. The alternative would be to code the above in a fully explicit fashion:

```
#!/usr/bin/perl -w
use strict;
my $line;
```

```
foreach my $file ( @ARGV ) {
    open(FILE, $file) || die "can't open file: $!";
    while( defined( $line = <FILE> ) ) {
        if ( $line =~ m/foo/ ) {
            print $line;
        }
    }
    close FILE;
}
```

You can see that once you get used to Perl's default behaviors, writing and reading code can be greatly simplified.

Patterns, like `foo` in the above example, are case sensitive. That is, strings like FOO or Foo would not be matched by a match operation such as m/foo/. However, the match operator has several modifiers that can be placed immediately following the final slash, one of which is the case "insensitive" modifier /i. If the program above used m/foo/i then it would print out any line containing any sequence of f, followed by o, followed by o, regardless of case: FOO, fOo, and fOObar would all be matched by such a pattern.

6.2.1 Matching constructs

Inside a match operator (except when single quotation marks are used as the delimiter as in m'pattern'), the backslash escapes used in double quoted strings are also available (see chapter 4, table 4.1). The notable exception is the \b sequence, which we will discuss shortly. The backslash can also be used to interpret any special regex character literally (we will also see what these are shortly), or to escape a delimiter such as a forward slash when using slashes as the match operator's delimiters. (Of course, the whole point of being able to choose your delimiters is to avoid having to escape literal occurrences of a given delimiter in a pattern.)

Regular expressions don't just specify every character literally. You can specify a set of characters, called a character class, to match at a given point in the pattern. This is done by enclosing the set of characters within square brackets. For example, the pattern foo[bc]ar will match a string that contains the sequence foobar or the sequence foocar but not foobcar. When you use a character class in a pattern such as a[bc]d it can be read as: match an a followed by one of the things in the character class (in this case a b or a c), followed by a d. A complement to a character can also be specified using the ^ (caret) symbol as the first thing inside the character class, making it a negative character class. The pattern a[^bc]d reads: match an a followed by any character not in the set (b or c) followed by a d. When the caret appears anywhere else inside a character class other than the first position, it has no special meaning and merely matches itself.

Ranges can be expressed inside of a character class by using a dash between two characters. Thus the character class [abcdefg] could also be written as [a-g]. There are several special backslash sequences that stand for particular character classes. For example, \d stands for any digit and is equivalent to the characterclass [0-9]. Its converse, \D, is equivalent to the class [^0-9] (i.e., any character that is not a digit).

Two other common classes exist with shorthand sequences. The "word" character class \w which corresponds to the class [a-zA-Z0-9_]. You might recognize this class as being all the legal characters that can be used in a variable name. The other is the "space" or whitespace class \s, which means [\n\r\f\t] or any whitespace character (space, newline, carriage return, formfeed, and tab, respectively). Each of these special classes also has a complement: \W and \S (any non-word character and any non-space character, respectively).

```
m/abc[def] \w\s\d[^a-z]/
```

The above pattern can be read as: match the sequence abc followed a single character that is either d, e, or f, followed by a space then any word character, then any whitespace character, then any digit, and, finally, any character that is not a lowercase letter. This pattern would match against a string such as blabcf D7Kook because it contains a sequence of characters, abcf D 7K, that conforms to the pattern.

One last shorthand character class is represented by a dot (.). This stands for anything that is not a newline. (The /s modifier can be used to include a newline in the class represented by the dot.) Thus, the dot is a sort of wildcard character that will match anything but a newline when used in a regular expression.

There are also special regex characters that match positions rather than characters. These are often called *anchor* characters as they anchor patterns or subpatterns to particular positions within a string. The caret (^) is used to match the start of a string or the start of a logical line when the /m modifier is used. (See chapters 10 and 11.) For example, the pattern m/^abc/ will only match against strings that start with abc.

Similarly, the $ character will match the end of a string when it is used in a place that can sensibly match the end of a string, like the end of a pattern. For example, the pattern m/xyz$/ will only match against strings that end in xyz.

A useful consequence of this is that the pattern m/^foo$/ can only match a string that contains foo and only foo since the string contains only the three-character sequence foo from start to finish).

Another positional matching construct is the \b sequence. This matches a position between a word (\w) character and a non-word (\W) character (called a word boundary position) or between a \w character and the beginning or end of a string. For example, m/\babc\b/ can only match when a string contains the sequence abc and it is not immediately preceded or followed by a \w character. The strings abc, foo abc bar, and foo!abc would match, but xabcy and foo_abc3 would not since, as you should recall, the underscore and digits are word characters.

The basic constructs for matching covered so far are presented in table 6.1. We will take up some additional anchoring constructs in chapter 10.

Table 6.1 Special constructs for matching in regular expressions

Special Construct	Special Meaning
[...]	character class
[^...]	negative character class
\w	word character, from the class [a-zA-Z0-9_]
\W	non-word character, from the class [^a-zA-Z0-9_]
\d	digit, from the class [0-9]
\D	non-digit, from the class [^0-9]
\s	whitespace, from the class [\n\r\f\t]
\S	non-whitespace, from the class [^ \n\r\f\t]
.	wildcard, from the class [^\n]
^	beginning of string
$	end of string
\b	word-boundary: matches between \w and \W
\B	non-word-boundary

6.2.2 Regex language constructs

I mentioned earlier that regular expressions are very much a programming language in their own right, but the constructs given so far are not enough to justify this position. Regular expressions also have constructs that work like operators, allowing you to say "match this OR that" (alternation) and "match this some number of times" (repetition). You can also group subpatterns within a larger pattern using parentheses, and you can capture parts of a match into special variables for use later in the pattern (i.e., backreferencing) or for use outside of the match operation.

Alternation   The | character is the alternation operator, which allows you to specify a series of alternatives to match. A pattern such as m/foo|bar/ will match a string that contains either foo or bar. Parentheses can be used to group a set of alternatives and to limit the scope of the alternation. For example, the pattern m/ab|cd/ is very different from the pattern m/a(b|c)d. The former says to match either ab or cd while the latter says to match an a followed by either a b or c followed by a d. In other words, m/a(b|c)d/ matches the same things that m/a[bc]d/ matches, but while a character class is limited to matching one character within its class, the alternation and parentheses can provide choices of arbitrary subpatterns.

Consider the following pattern:

```
m/^Date: (\d\d|[A-Z][a-z][a-z]):\d\d:\d\d/
```

This pattern might be expected to match a line that begins with Date: and is followed by a date representation of either 09:29:63 or one that uses a month abbreviation, such as Sep:29:63. The alternation group allows either two digits to match or an uppercase letter followed by two lowercase letters.

Repetition   Several special constructs exist that represent repetition with a regex. These are termed *quantifiers*. Normally, any character or sequence that matches something in the target string matches just once. Any character, character class, or subpattern delimited by parentheses may be followed by a quantifier that tells it how many times in a row it is allowed to match the given sequence. The first such quantifier is the ? character, which says that the previous character (or subexpression) may be matched zero or one times—that is, it makes the previous character or subexpression optional). A pattern such as m/ab?c/ will match if the string contains either abc or ac.

Two less restrictive indeterminate quantifiers are the * and + quantifiers, which mean "zero or more" and "one or more," respectively. A pattern of m/ab*c/ will match ac, abc, abbbc, or, generally, an a followed by any number of b characters in a row (including none), followed by a c. Similarly, the pattern m/ab+c/ will match abc, abbbc or, generally, an a followed by one or more b characters in a row followed by a c.

In the previous chapter, we gave an example of counting the non-empty lines in a file. That example counted any non-empty line, even one containing only spaces. One thing programmers often want to do is count the lines of code a program contains. In this case you might want to avoid counting those lines containing only whitespace or beginning with a comment character:

```
#!/usr/bin/perl -w
use strict;
my $count = 0;
```

```
while ( <> ) {
    next if m/^(#|\s*$)/;
    $count++;
}
print "File contains roughly $count lines of code\n";
```

Quantifiers can apply to special sequences and subpatterns as well. The pattern m/abc\d+/ will match if the string contains the letters abc followed by one or more digits. And the pattern m/a(foo|bar)*d/ will match a string containing an a followed by any number of repetitions of either foo or bar (including zero repetitions), followed by a d. Thus, that pattern would match against strings containing any of the following sequences of characters:

```
ad
afood
abard
afoofood
abarbard
afoobarfoofoobard
```

The * and + are indeterminate and can be thought of as similar to a while loop of sorts in that each will continue to match as many times as the previous character or subpattern occurs in the string.

There is also a determinate form of quantifier that has the general form of {n,m} (where n and m are integers), which means to match the previous pattern thing at least n times and no more than m times. Omitting the comma and the m as in m/a{3}/ means to match an a exactly three times. Leaving the comma but omitting the m, as in m/a{3,}/, means match an a three or more times.

Capturing subpatterns   Parentheses do not just group subpatterns; they also cause the text matched by that subpattern to be captured and remembered for use later inside, or even outside, of the regex. Each parenthesized subpattern is implicitly numbered starting at 1 in the order of their appearance in the regex. You may *backreference*—that is, refer back to a particular subpattern—by using a backslash and an integer representing the particular subpattern you want to reference.

The pattern m/foo(\w)bar\1/ will match foo followed by a \w character followed by bar followed by the same character that was matched inside the first parenthesized subpattern. This would match strings like fooTbarT and foosbars but not foodbars. In other words, a backreference does not refer to the subpattern itself but to whatever literal sequence was matched by that subpattern.

Outside of the regular expression itself, a captured subpattern is available in a special variable consisting of a dollar sign followed by an integer representing the particular subpattern. For example

```
$string = 'xyzfooTbarTabc';
$string =~ m/foo(\w)bar\1/;  # \1 refers to the subpattern here
print "$1\n";                # $1 refers to the same subpattern here
```

Note, $1 will obviously only refer to that subpattern if the regular expression successfully matched against the string. Otherwise, it will retain whatever value it had (if any) prior to the match operation. A safer approach would be to print the value only if the pattern matched:

```
$string = 'xyzfooTbarTabc';
if ($string =~ m/foo(\w)bar\1/) { # \1 refers to the subpattern
    print "$1\n";                  # $1 refers to the same subpattern
}
```

This provides a standard way of using regular expressions to extract particular pieces of data from a string or line. Let's say that you have a file in which each line is an entry of a number of hours worked for a particular person on a particular project formatted as follows:

```
Mathew    17
Smith      3
Jones      5
Jones      2
Smith      4
Mathew     3
Mathew     2
```

Each filename represents the project. For example, the file above might be named *proj_X.txt*. There might also be files named *proj_Y.txt* and *proj_Z.txt* and so on. These data files have been created by some other process. Your job is to create a program that reads through all the project files given on the command line and summarizes each person's hours on each project:

```
#!/usr/bin/perl -w
use strict;
my %project_hours;
while ( <> ) {
    m/^(\w+)\s+(\d+)$/;
    my ($employee, $hours) = ($1, $2);
    $project_hours{$employee} += $hours;
    if ( eof(ARGV) ) {
        $ARGV =~ m/^(\S+)\.txt/;
        print "$1\n";
```

```
        foreach my $name (keys %project_hours){
            print "\t$name:$project_hours{$name}\n";
        }
        %project_hours = ();
    }
}
```

You should create two or three data files similar to the one above and run the program above in a file called *proj_hours*. You can then try out this program by running it from the command line as

```
perl proj_hours proj_X.txt proj_Y.txt proj_Z.txt
```

Depending on the hours you entered for each person in each file, you should get output similar to this:

```
proj_X
        Smith:7
        Mathew:22
        Jones:7
proj_Y
        Smith:18
        Mathew:11
        Jones:13
proj_Z
        Smith:12
        Mathew:2
        Jones:11
```

The program above used only one thing we have not discussed yet, the eof() function. This function returns true when the file handle given returns undef on the next attempt to read a line. Recall that the special while(<>) loop automatically opens each file in the @ARGV under the file handle ARGV and sets the special variable $ARGV to the name of the current file. Let's go through this program in more detail. You are already familiar with the first two lines. The fourth line declares a hash that will use each person's name as a key and store the total hours worked on a given project for each name. The magic while(<>) reads through each file in turn and sets each line to the default $_ variable. On the next line, we use the match operator with no target, thereby defaulting to the $_ variable as the target. The regular expression matches lines that start with one or more word characters, followed by one or more spaces, followed by one or more digits, followed by the end of the string.

Two subpatterns, enclosed in parentheses, are meant to capture the employee names and hours from each line: (\w+) and (\d+), which are then available in the variables $1 and $2 respectively. We assign these to more meaningfully named variables on the next line. Next we use the $employee variable as a key in the hash and add the hours to the value associated with that key.

The if block tests if we are at the end of the current project file. If so, we create our output for that project. The first thing we do is to use a regex with capturing parentheses to extract just the first part of the file name. We use \S+ to grab all the leading non-whitespace characters before the .txt into the $1 variable. We have to backslash escape the dot; otherwise, it would have its special meaning of matching anything. We don't bother saving this value to a more meaningfully named variable because we only use it once on the next line to provide a heading for the following project hours output.

We use a foreach loop to iterate through the list of keys in the hash (provided by the keys() function mentioned in chapter 4), assigning each key in turn to the new variable $name. We then simply print out a tab, \t, to indent our output below the project heading, the employee name, and the total hours worked for that employee.

When we are finished with the output loop, we need clear out the hash so we can start from scratch when we process the next data file in the while loop. Otherwise, we would be adding hours from another project to the hours we've already calculated and printed for the current file.

That pretty much covers the basic elements of Perl 's regular expressions. Should you wish to learn more about regular expressions, you may look ahead to chapter 10. You can also check out the documentation in the *perlre* pod-page. For now, we will turn back to the matching and substitution operators and consider a few other useful string processing functions.

6.2.3 Matching and substitution operators

You have seen the matching operator used in several examples and snippets above, but we have not yet considered the substitution operator. The substitution operator has the following general syntax:

```
s/PATTERN/REPLACEMENT/
```

Unlike the matching operator, you cannot omit the s, but you can use different delimiters just as with the match operator: s!pattern!replacement!, s<pattern><replacement> among others. The first half of the substitution operator, the pattern part, operates in the same way as the match operator so the entire discussion above regarding patterns applies equally here. The difference with the substitution operator is that the part of the target string matched by the pattern is replaced by whatever is in the replacement half of the operator. (The target string is modified *in situ*.) The replacement portion is interpreted as a double-quoted string—the special regular expression characters are not special on this side of the operator.

```
my $string = 'abcdefghij';
$string =~ s/def.*/...xyz/;
print "$string\n"; # prints: abc...xyz
```

You can use variables on the replacement side just as you can inside double-quoted strings, including captured subpattern variables such as $1, $2, and so on.

```
$_ = 'The truth is out there';
$repl = 'somew';
s/out t(here)/$repl$1/;
print "$_\n";        # prints: The truth is somewhere
```

Both the match and substitution operators can take optional modifiers like the /i modifier mentioned earlier. Another common modifier is the /g modifier which means to operate repeatedly or globally. When the /g modifier is used with a substitution, the first substring that matches the pattern is found and replaced. The pattern is then tried again from that point in the string.

```
$_ = 'abracadabra';
s/ab/ud/g;
print; # prints: udracadudra
```

We will delay further discussion of the match and substitution operators and their remaining modifiers, as well as regular expressions, until chapters 10 and 11. At this point, we will consider two additional functions useful in text processing and give a few examples to wrap up what we've covered in this chapter.

6.3 Split and join

The split() function provides another way to use regular expressions to extract data from a string. This function takes a regular expression as its first argument and a string as its second argument. It returns a list created by splitting the string at every place the pattern matches. The part that matches is discarded unless all or some of it is parenthesized. Often, the pattern is simply a single character that has been used as a field delimiter in the data:

```
$string = 'name:age:favorite_beer';
@fields = split( /:/, $string); # split on colons
print "@fields\n"; # prints: name age favorite_beer

$string = 'andrew,35,ale';
@fields = split( /,/, $string); # split on commas
print "@fields\n"; # prints: andrew 35 ale
```

Longer patterns can also be used. You may have a data file delimited by colons, but with varying amounts of space. You can use a pattern that includes whitespace surrounding the delimiter. Note the difference in the following two examples:

```
$string = 'foo    :bar:car   :   last';
@fields = split( /:/, $string );
print "<$fields[2]>\n";  # prints: <car   >

@fields = split( /\s*:\s*/, $string );
print "<$fields[2]>\n";  # prints: <car>
```

If you do not specify a string to be split, Perl uses the $_ variable. As a special case, you may provide a string containing a single space, instead of a regex. Perl will split the target string on any amount of whitespace, ignoring any leading or trailing whitespace. If you do not provide a pattern at all, this special case behavior is assumed.

The join() function does the opposite of split(), joining together elements of a list into a single string, using a string argument to supply the delimiter:

```
@list = ('one', 'two', 'three');
$string = join( ':', @list);  # $string is now: one:two:three
print "$string\n";

$string = join( '|', @list); # $string is now: "one|two|three"
print "$string\n";
```

6.4 The DATA file handle

You can use another special file handle within your Perl programs—the DATA file handle. Normally, you do not need to do anything special to end a Perl program. It simply exits when it reaches the last line of executable code. However, you may explicitly place one of two special tokens to mark the end of the executable portion of your code: the __END__ token or the __DATA__ token. Any text following these tokens is ignored, but can be read using the DATA file handle.

```
#!/usr/bin/perl -w
use strict;
while( <DATA> ) {
    print;
}
__END__
foo
bar
blah
```

This can be helpful for including data that your program needs within the same file as the program itself. I have always found this feature useful for experimenting with and trying out new ideas or features. For example, let's say you have just learned about simple patterns and the split() function, and now you find yourself needing to process a data file of addresses where each line contains several fields separated by the | character. You can open your editor, create a simple loop over the DATA file handle, and put some example data at the __END__ of your script. Then you can try various techniques to turn each line of data into an array of fields. Your first attempt might look like

```perl
#!/usr/bin/perl -w
use strict;
while( <DATA> ) {
    chomp;
    my @fields = split /|/;
    print join(':', @fields), "\n";
}
__END__
Bill Jones|19 Some Street|Some City|Some State|Some Postal Code
Anne Smith|219 Greenway Bay|Springfield|North Dakota|90201
```

Now we can run the program and see the results. By the way, many editors can be set up to run the contents of (or a selection of) the current buffer straight through Perl to display the output. This can be convenient for testing little snippets or scripts like this one. The output of the previous script, truncated to fit the line here, appears as:

```
B:i:l:l: :J:o:n:e:s:|:1:9: :S:o:m:e: :S:t:r:e:e:t:|:S:o:m:e:
```

Apparently, you have split each line at every character rather than at the | characters. This is a common mistake. Remember, the | is special. In a regular expression pattern, it is the alternation operator. So a pattern of /|/ matches nothing OR nothing and succeeds between every character in the line. You need to escape the | symbol with a backslash using a pattern of /\|/ in the split() function:

```perl
#!/usr/bin/perl -w
use strict;
while( <DATA> ) {
    chomp;
    my @fields = split /\|/;
    print join(':', @fields), "\n";
}
__END__
Bill Jones|19 Some Street|Some City|Some State|Some Postal Code
Anne Smith|219 Greenway Bay|Springfield|North Dakota|90201
```

This produces the following output

```
Bill Jones:19 Some Street:Some City:Some State:Some Postal Code
Anne Smith:219 Greenway Bay:Springfield:North Dakota:90201
```

Using `split()` and `join()` with different delimiters shows that you've properly split the data into the fields you wanted. You can go on with designing the program to do what you want with those fields.

6.5   *Putting it together*

Let's consider putting together a simple word frequency analysis program. This program should count all the words in a file over a certain size and provide the following simple statistics: the total number of words, the number of unique words, and the average word length.

Before we even begin, you'll need to know about the `length()` function, which simply returns the length (number of characters) of the string given as an argument.

```
$string = 'this is a string';
print length($string);  # prints: 16
```

One of the first things we need to decide is what will constitute a word. Should a word be any sequence of non-whitespace characters, any sequence of `\w` characters, or only sequences of alphabetical characters? For now, let's say we want to count only things that might be considered words in the English language, so we don't want to count such things as `ab345.x` or `$#*%` as words.

When we read through a file, we can break up a line of text into possible words using the `split()` function with no arguments—giving us a list of non-whitespace sequences. We can then iterate through this list, testing each element to see if it conforms to our definition of a word:

```
while ( <> ) {
    my @words = split;
    # now test and count real words in @words
}
```

A first attempt at counting only words in the `@words` array might be to test them against the pattern `m/^[a-zA-Z]+$/`, which matches only when the string contains lowercase or uppercase letters from beginning to end:

```
my $count = 0;
while ( <> ) {
    my @words = split;
    foreach my $word ( @words ) {
```

```
        $count++ if $word =~ m/^[a-zA-Z]+$/;
    }
}
print "$count words\n";
```

However, this does not allow contractions like "isn't" or "you're," nor does it allow for hyphenated words like "built-in,". A somewhat better pattern is

```
m/^[a-zA-Z]+([-'][a-zA-Z]+)*$/
```

This now matches a sequence of one or more letters of any case at the start of a string, followed optionally (zero or more times) by a hyphen or apostrophe and another sequence of letters, followed by the end of the string. This is not perfect because we know that a contraction will not have more than two letters following the apostrophe, but we let it stand as it is. The reader is invited to work out a more precise regex. So our simple word counting loop becomes:

```
my $count = 0;
while ( <> ) {
    my @words = split;
    foreach my $word ( @words ) {
        $count++ if $word =~ m/^[a-zA-Z]+([-'][a-zA-Z]+)*$/;
    }
}
print "$count words\n";
```

Now we need to consider the actual specifications mentioned at the beginning of this section: We need to be able to set a size and count only words of that size or larger; we need to know the number of unique words; and, we need to be able to calculate the average word length. Obviously, using a single variable to count all the words will not be adequate for our needs.

Whenever you find yourself thinking about data in terms of sets of unique values, you should immediately think about using a hash. In this case, if we use each word we find as a key in hash, we can maintain separate counts for each unique word we find:

```
my %count;
my $size = 4; # minimum length of words to count
while ( <> ) {
    my @words = split;
    foreach my $word ( @words ) {
        next if length($word) < $size;
        $count{$word}++ if $word =~ m/^[a-zA-Z]+([-'][a-zA-Z]+)*$/;
    }
}
```

The next statement only applies to its immediately enclosing loop. So if the current word is less than $size characters long, this statement skips ahead to the next word in the foreach loop.

With a hash of unique words as keys, and the counts of each word as the corresponding values, we can proceed to calculate our statistics:

```
my $uniq_words   = keys %count;
my $total_count  = 0;
my $total_length = 0;
foreach my $word ( keys %count ) {
    $total_count  += $count{$word};
    $total_length += length($word);
}
my $avg_length = $total_length/$total_count;
```

We covered the keys() function back in chapter 4, but here we use it not only to iterate though the list of keys in the foreach loop, but to assign a value to a scalar variable. The keys() function in a scalar context returns the number of keys present in the hash. (This is similar to the way that assigning an array to a scalar results in the assignment of the number of elements in the array.)

One other thing we need to watch for here is division by zero. It is always a possibility that no words exist in the file on which we run this program. The file might be empty, it may contain no sequences that match our word pattern, or all the words in the file may be less than $size. We will take care of the problem when we string our complete program together. (You may want to think about how you would handle these contingencies before reading further.)

The last thing we need to do is display our word count statistics. We can simply use multiple print statements to achieve this:

```
print "Stats for words of length $size or greater\n":
print "----------------------------------------\n";
print "total words         = $total_count\n";
print "unique words        = $uniq_words\n";
print "average word length = $avg_length\n";
```

A useful method for quoting multi-line literal strings involves the *here-document* (here-doc) syntax. A here-doc is simply a way of quoting a block of text and has the following syntax:

```
print <<MARKER;
line of text
another line
etc...
MARKER
```

The marker or delimiter is just a string you supply. The final marker, marking the end of the block of text, must begin at the left margin and be the only thing on that line (no trailing spaces). The convention is to use all caps for these delimiters. This kind of here-doc is treated as a double-quoted string that allows variable interpolation. If you wanted a single-quoted here-doc, you would use:

```
print <<'SINGLE';
stuff here
SINGLE
```

We can now rewrite our output code as

```
print <<STATS;
Stats for words of length $size or greater
------------------------------------------
total words          = $total_count
unique words         = $uniq_words
average word length  = $avg_length
STATS
```

We can pull all this together to get our final program:

```
#!/usr/bin/perl -w
use strict;
my %count;
my $size = 4; # minimum length of words to count
while ( <> ) {
    my @words = split;
    foreach my $word ( @words ) {
        next if length($word) < $size;
        $count{$word}++ if $word =~ m/^[a-zA-Z]+([-'][a-zA-Z]+)*$/;
    }
}
my $uniq_words   = keys %count;
unless ($uniq_words) {
    print "No words in file\n";
    exit;
}
my $total_count  = 0;
my $total_length = 0;
foreach my $word ( keys %count ) {
    $total_count  += $count{$word};
    $total_length += length($word);
}
my $avg_length = $total_length/$total_count;
print <<STATS;
Stats for words of length $size or greater
------------------------------------------
total words          = $total_count
unique words         = $uniq_words
average word length  = $avg_length
STATS
```

We have taken care of the possible division by zero problem by exiting the program if no words were found. If there are no keys in the hash %count, then no words were found. In this case, we don't even have to bother trying to calculate the rest of the statistics. This introduces the exit() function, which simply causes the program to quit and returns an exit status to the shell. The exit status is zero by default.

At this point you have covered all of the programming constructs used in the example programs presented in chapter 3. This would be a good time to turn back to those programs and review them in light of everything we've covered so far.

6.6 Exercises

1 Consider a data file consisting of lines that contain user names and time online in minutes, separated by colons like so:

```
bjones:27
asmith:102
asmith:12
jdoe:311
bjones:45
```

Write a program that reads this file and calculates the total time spent online for each user. The final program should create a report that appears like:

```
User: bjones
Total time online: 72 minutes

User: asmith
Total time online: 114 minutes ...
```

Hint: Use a hash with user names as keys and add each time period to that user's hash value.

2 The word count program only counted words of length 4 or greater. Modify this program to take a command line option for the minimum word size. So a user could invoke the program as

```
wordcount -s5 filename
```

to count words of length 5 or greater. If no size option is given, the program should default to a size of 4.

Hint: The command line arguments are in @ARGV, so you can test if the first element of this array matches m/-s\d+/ and act accordingly.

Second hint: Acting accordingly also means removing -s5 from the argument array before using the input operator.

C H A P T E R   7

Functions

Back in chapter 4, after discussing various ways to specify literal data, we found that we could use named variables to hold this data and then access or operate on it through the variable name. A function is a similar concept applied to bits of code rather than bits of data.

A *function* or *subroutine*—we will use the terms function and subroutine interchangeably—is simply a name given to a piece of code defined somewhere in the program, in a module, or built-in to Perl itself. We can call (invoke) this code by name and execute it from anywhere in a program. (Anonymous subroutines that have no name also exist. We will cover those in chapter 8.) We have used several built-in functions in the previous chapters, notably: `print()`, `open()`, `sqrt()`, and `chomp()`. Defining your own function is as simple as

```
sub SUBNAME {block}
```

The `sub` keyword declares this as a subroutine definition and associates the name SUBNAME with the block of code that follows. The block of code is only executed when the subroutine is called within the program, so you may place your subroutine definitions anywhere in your program. Typically, such definitions are placed at the end of the file, below the main code of the program. However, some people place all their function definitions at the beginning of the file. As with many things in Perl, it is up to you to choose your style.

A simple function might be

```
sub greetings {
    print "Greetings Earthling, we come in peace.\n";
}
```

And a trivial program that defines and uses such a function is simply

```
#!/usr/bin/perl -w
use strict;
greetings();  # calls the greetings() subroutine

sub greetings {
    print "Greetings Earthling, we come in peace.\n";
}
```

You can call the function in the example above in one of two ways: by using the function name with parentheses for its arguments, or by prepending the & symbol to the function name. In the first case, the parentheses will contain an empty list if there are no arguments; in the second case the parentheses can be dropped if there is no argument.

```
greetings();
&greetings();
```

These two methods of calling a function have slightly different semantics (i.e., meanings), which we will consider shortly. If you define your subroutine before it is used, you can also call it just using the bare subroutine name by itself (but you'll have to read the *perlsub* pod-page for more details on that style of usage).

Arguments can be passed to a user-defined function just as they can to a built-in function such as print() or sqrt(). In the function itself these arguments are available in the special @_ array. This is the default argument list—not to be confused with the default scalar variable $_. The elements of the default argument list are accessed as $_[0], $_[1], and so on:

```
#!/usr/bin/perl -w
use strict;
print "Enter your name: ";
chomp( my $name = <STDIN> );
greetings($name);

sub greetings {
    print "Greetings $_[0], take me to your leader.\n";
}
```

Now, while @_ is a convenient container for the list of arguments to your function, using the individual elements like $_[0] goes against the principle of using meaningful names for your variables. Usually, we immediately assign this list of arguments to more appropriately named variables:

```
sub greetings {
    my $name = $_[0];
    print "Greetings $name, take me to your leader.\n";
}
```

Didn't we already have a variable named $name in the program itself? Yes, but if you recall in chapter 5 we mentioned that a my() declaration creates a new variable that exists only within the block in which it was declared, and a function defines a new block. That said, now is a good time to take a closer look at variable scope. This is not the easiest concept to understand, but we will proceed slowly.

7.1 Scope

The scope of a variable reflects both its time of existence and its visibility within a program. Scope can be a tricky concept if you only think of a program as a single linear series of statements executed in turn. Blocks, and the scopes they introduce, impose a hierarchical structure upon the code. Before we look at this structure in a general way, we will first look at two kinds of variable scoping and the effect each has.

When you declare a variable using my(), you are creating a new variable that exists only from its point of declaration to the end of the block in which it was declared. These are called *lexical variables*. A lexical variable is simply one that is private to a block—or a file, because, as we mentioned previously, a file is a block. Perl sets up a little scratchpad for each block on which it maintains a list of the lexical variables defined in that block. Whenever you use a variable in a statement, such as in print "$foo";, Perl looks at the current block's scratchpad to find a variable with that name. If Perl finds a matching name, it uses that variable's value. If Perl fails to find the variable there, it looks "outward" to the next outer or enclosing block to see if it exists on that block's scratchpad. This continues until Perl finds a variable of that name. It is important to note that Perl will only look outwards from a block; it will never look inside another block to find a variable. An example will demonstrate this point better than words:

```
my $foo = 'Outermost foo';              # outermost scope/block
my $bar = 'Outermost bar';              # outermost scope/block

{
    my $foo = 'inner foo';              # inner scope/block
    print "1: $foo : $bar\n";           # inner scope/block
    {
        my $bar = 'inner inner bar';    # inner-inner scope/block
        print "2: $foo : $bar\n";       # inner-inner scope/block
    }
    print "3: $foo : $bar\n";           # inner scope/block
}
```

In the first print statement above, Perl finds $foo in the scratchpad of the current (inner) block and, so, uses the value of that lexical $foo. However, it does not find $bar in the scratchpad, so it looks outward to the next enclosing block — the file scope or block that is outermost in this case—to find $bar.

The second print statement operates in a similar manner. We are now in a block within a block, all inside the file block. Here, a new lexical variable $bar has been created and installed on the inner-inner block's scratchpad. This $bar is the one that gets used in the print statement. The variable $foo is not found here, so Perl proceeds outward where it finds $foo on the enclosing block's (inner) scratchpad.

The last statement is the same as the first. The important point here is that when Perl looks at this block's scratchpad, it can't see into the inner-inner block. It can only look at its own pad or outward. The variable $bar that was created in the inner-inner block no longer exists. When a block is finished, its scratchpad is discarded, and its private lexical variables are no longer available. The one exception is in the case of closures. (See section 8.3.1.)

All of the variables we've been creating so far in this book are lexical variables created with the `my()` declaration. We've also been using variables such as `$_`, `@ARGV`, and other special Perl variables that we haven't declared. These are *global variables*. They are not listed on scratchpads at all, but in the main program's *symbol table*. A symbol table is just a fancy name for a scratchpad of identifiers—such as variables, file handles, and function names—used in the program.

You cannot create a lexical version of one of these special global variables, but you can localize its value for the duration of a block (scope). This is done with the `local()` declaration, which saves the original value of the global variable and restores it when the current block is exited:

```
$_ = 'I am global';
{
    local($_) = 'I am a localized global';
    print "$_\n";
}
print "$_\n";
```

One very important point to remember here is that no new `$_` variable is created in the inner block. Nothing is added to the inner block's scratchpad, and no new variable is added to the main program's symbol table either. After it localizes `$_`, Perl takes the value stored in `$_` and stores it in the one and only global variable. Once the block is finished, it restores the previous (pre-localized) value of `$_`. You can achieve something similar to the same overall effect by creating your own extra variable to hold the old value and restore it at the end of the block:

```
$_ = 'I am global';
{
    my $old_underscore = $_;
    $_ = 'I am temporarily changed';
    print "$_\n";
    $_ = $old_underscore;
}
print "$_\n";
```

But doing this risks forgetting to restore the original value at the end of the block.

The above examples of `my()` and `local()` and their interaction with scope is not the whole story. Functions add a slight twist that often confuses beginners. Consider the following example:

```
my $foo = 'Outer';
$_      = 'Global';
{
    local($_) = 'localized';
    my $foo   = 'inner';
    show_me();
}
```

```
sub show_me {
    print "$_  : $foo\n";
}
```

Now, what values of $_ and $foo do you expect to be printed by the call to the show_me() function in the inner block? (C'mon, don't simply enter the program and run it to find out.)

When you run a program, each statement has both a time of execution and a location of execution relative to the other statements, and the block structure of the program. Scope involves both properties—time and location. Figure 7.1 shows these two aspects of scope in relation to the code example above.

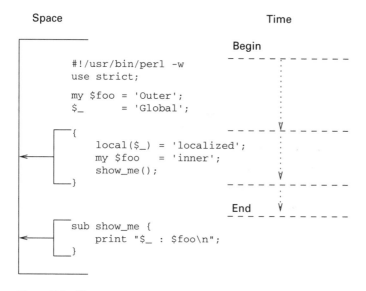

Figure 7.1 Time, space, and scope of execution

This means that the call to the show_me() function is executed while the program is in the inner block. Hence, the local() declaration of that block is in scope (i.e., is in effect). But, and this is the tricky bit, the show_me() function itself always runs where it is defined in the file. So, when show_me() runs, it can only access variables within its own block or an outer enclosing block (the file block). The result is that the program will print

```
localized : Outer
```

We should note here that a function like show_me() above is not a good model for a function because it depends on variables defined outside of its own scope. Sometimes this is necessary, but you should try to keep functions as independent of the rest of the program as possible. Parameters can pass a function the values you want it to use at the time it is called. Using parameters, you can avoid much potential confusion that may arise about scoping rules, such as that in the program example above.

7.2 Global variables

A global variable is a variable that is visible throughout the program (including within other packages, which we will discuss in part IV). Under the strict pragma, you may use global variables only if you fully qualify their name. That means that means you must supply the package name for the variable like so:

```
#!/usr/bin/perl -w
use strict;
{
    my $lexical   = 'file scoped lexical';
    $main::global = 'fully qualified global';
}
print "$main::global\n";
```

The main:: prefix to the variable $global is just the package name. (All the programs we are writing at this time are in the main package. We will create new packages in part IV.) Notice that we did not use any sort of declaration for the global variable. They only need to be qualified. You can also use the vars pragma to inform Perl of your intent to use one or more globals. In that case, you don't need to provide the fully qualified name:

```
#!/usr/bin/perl -w
use strict;
use vars qw/$s_global @a_global/;
$s_global = 'declared global scalar';
@a_global = (1, 2, 3);
print "@a_global\n";
```

The use vars LIST syntax lets Perl know about globals that you want to use without package name qualification. Globals can be useful on occasion, but it is generally considered bad practice to use globals without good reason. Using globals is convenient when you are coding extremely short scripts or running Perl as a command line tool. (See appendix A.) We won't use or discuss user-created global variables again until we get into packages and modules in the advanced section.

7.3 Parameters

You have already seen that you can pass arguments to a Perl program and those arguments will be available within the special @ARGV array inside the program. A function is like a little program within a program. In fact, some languages refer to them as subprograms rather than subroutines. It can receive arguments much like a full fledged program.

The arguments you pass to a function when you invoke it are called parameters. In Perl, the parameter list is passed to the routine in the special @_ array. Like any list, when you include another list or list variable inside the parameter list, it is flattened out into a single list. Consider the following function call:

```perl
my @array = (1, 2, 3);
my $foo   = 42;
something($foo, @array);
```

The something() function will not receive a list of two parameters. Its @_ array will receive a list containing the value of the variable $foo, followed by the values of the elements of the array variable @array. In other words, the parameter list will be (42, 1, 2, 3). But even this is not the whole truth about the parameter list contained in @_.

Whenever you pass a variable to a function, the resulting element of the @_ parameter array is an alias for the rea variable. Changing this value directly will change the value of the variable. This is best shown by example:

```perl
my @array = (1, 2, 3);
my $foo   = 42;
something($foo, @array); # prints: 13 1 4 3
print "$foo @array\n";    # prints: 13 1 4 3

sub something {
    $_[0] = 13;
    $_[2] = 4;
    print "@_\n";
}
```

You've seen a similar aliasing effect in the foreach loop back in chapter 5. Here, each element of the @_ array is an alias for the variable (or array element) that was passed into the function.

Sometimes we want to use this aliasing effect for a function that is supposed to change the value of the arguments passed to it. Consider the built-in chomp() function, for example, which removes any trailing newline from its arguments. For most functions you create, you will want instead to assign the parameter list to lexical variables immediately within the function and use those variables to avoid any accidental or unintended changes to the original arguments.

```perl
my @array = (1, 2, 3);
my $foo   = 42;
```

```
something($foo, @array);  # prints: 13 1 4 3
print "$foo @array\n";    # prints: 42 1 2 3

sub something {
    my @parameters = @_;
    $parameters[0] = 13;
    $parameters[2] = 4;
    print "@parameters\n";
}
```

Now we have left the original variable arguments intact and made changes to only a private copy of the parameters. This is a much safer way to handle parameters.

Previously, I mentioned two methods of calling function: use the function name followed by an argument list in parentheses or prepend the & symbol to the function name. Remember that, in the first method, the argument can be empty but the parentheses are required. The latter method can be used both with parentheses to pass an argument list, or without parentheses, in which case the current contents of the @_ array (if any) are passed to the function.

```
my_func(1, 2, 3);   # calls my_func with @_ set to (1, 2, 3)
my_func():          # calls my_func with @_ set to ()
&my_func(1, 2, 3);  # calls my_func with @_ set to (1, 2, 3)
&my_func;           # calls my_func with current value of @_
```

The &my_func or &my_func() syntax also disables "prototype" checking on functions defined with prototypes. We won't be covering prototypes in this book, but if you're interested, see *perldoc perlsub* for more information.

7.4 Return values

So far, the sample functions we've been using have been used for what they do rather than what they return. All functions or subroutines in Perl have return values, a result returned from the function. Think of a return value as the "answer" that a function gives back. For example, when you call the square root function with an argument of 25 (sqrt(25)), you are asking: "What is the square root of 25?" The square root function returns the answer so you can use it or store it:

```
my $number = 25;
my $s_root = sqrt($number);
print "$s_root\n";# prints: 5
```

In Perl, you can explicitly denote the return value of a function by using the return statement. Otherwise, the return value will be the result of the last statement executed in the function.

```
sub sum {
    my @list = @_;
    my $sum = 0;
    foreach my $value ( @list ) {
        $sum += $value;
    }
    return $sum;
}
```

This function has an explicit return value that is the sum of all the parameters passed into the function. We could have omitted the return keyword and left the last line as $sum. The function would still return the sum because it would return the result of the last statement executed. (Generally, it is good practice to use the return keyword to explicitly denote the return value.)

In fact, if we think of a function as a block of code that returns a result, we can divide functions into two classes: those that are evaluated for their return values, and those that evaluated for their side effects—in other words, for some action the routine performs regardless of the return value. Examples of functions called for their return values are the sqrt() function, which returns the square root of its argument, and the keys() function, which returns a list of the keys of the hash given as an argument. Examples of functions normally called for their side effects are the print() function, which prints its arguments to the specified file handle or STDOUT by default and returns 1 for success and undef for failure, and the chomp() function, which removes trailing newline from its arguments and returns the number of newlines removed.

The return statement causes the function to exit with the expression given. It does not have to be the last statement in the function, and there can be more than one return statement in a given function:

```
sub pos_or_neg {
    my $value = $_[0];
    if ( $value < 0 ) {
        return "negative";
    } else {
        return "positive";
    }
}
```

Here, the function returns the string "negative" if the argument was less than zero. Otherwise, the function returns the string "positive".

Return values are also sensitive to context. Remember context from chapter 4? You can find out the calling context using the wantarray() function. The wantarray() function returns "true" if the calling context is a list context such as @list = my_sub(); or "false" if the calling context is looking for a scalar value:

`$scalar = my_sub();`. Let's say you want a function that returns the length of a string in scalar context or a list of the characters in the string in list context:

```
my $foo = 'Hello World';
my @chars      = get_chars($foo); # called in list context
my $num_chars  = get_chars($foo); # called in scalar context
print "$num_chars : @chars\n"; # prints: 11 : H e l l o   W o r l d

sub get_chars {
    my $string = $_[0];
    if ( wantarray() ) {
        return split(//, $string);
    } else {
        return length($string);
    }
}
```

If `wantarray()` returns a true value, we know our function was called in a list context. We then use the `split()` function with a null regular expression to split the string up into a list of characters and return that list. Otherwise, we simply return the length of the string.

A statement containing only the `return` function returns an empty list in a list context, `undef` in a scalar context, or nothing in a void context. (Void context is simply calling a function without assigning or using its return value.)

7.5 Designing functions

A good function is designed in much the same way as a good program. In fact, it is useful to consider functions as little programs within your program. There are a few additional things to keep in mind, but, before we discuss those, we need to understand why we might want to use functions in the first place.

The most obvious reason for creating and using functions in your programs is simply to avoid duplicate code. Consider the following simple program:

```
#!/usr/bin/perl -w
use strict;
print "enter a number: \n";
chomp( my $number = <STDIN> );
if ( $number < 0 ) {
    my $box = '*' x (length($number)+2);
    print "$box\n";
    print "*$number*\n";
    print "$box\n";
} else {
    my $box = '#' x (length($number)+2);
    print "$box\n";
    print "#$number#\n";
    print "$box\n";
}
```

This program prints out the number entered wrapped up in a "box" of repeated characters, using different characters for positive or negative numbers. For example, input of -12 or 13 would appear as

```
*****
*-12*
*****
####
#13#
####
```

The thing to notice about this program is that each block in the `if/else` statement contains similar code. This duplicate code can be extracted into a function:

```perl
#!/usr/bin/perl -w
use strict;
print "enter a number: \n";
chomp( my $number = <STDIN> );
if ( $number < 0 ) {
    box_print($number, '*');
} else {
    box_print($number, '#');
}

sub box_print {
    my ($number, $char) = @_;
    my $box = $char x (length($number) + 2);
    print "$box\n";
    print "$char$number$char\n";
    print "$box\n";
}
```

Indeed, we can even extract the numeric test itself and place it inside the function definition:

```perl
#!/usr/bin/perl -w
use strict;
print "enter a number: \n";
chomp( my $number = <STDIN> );
box_print($number);

sub box_print {
    my ($number) = shift @_;
    my $char = '#';
    $char = '*' if $number < 0;
    my $box = $char x (length($number) + 2);
    print "$box\n";
    print "$char$number$char\n";
    print "$box\n";
}
```

The benefit here goes beyond merely saving time retyping nearly identical code. First of all, the program is more readable. We can focus on the higher level concept and look up the details in the function definition when necessary. This reduces the complexity of our main program by hiding the implementation (i.e., how the output is being produced) behind the function definition.

A second related benefit is that we won't accidentally make an error—such as forgetting to print the bottom of the box—in one of the versions. When we get the routine right once, it is right every time we call it. This also applies to debugging and maintenance. We only need to make a change in the subroutine's definition, not in several places throughout the program.

Complexity reduction and information hiding are worthy enough benefits to make us use functions even when we would only use the code in one place in the program. Just like our method of designing a program with a top-level description of chunks that are later defined and refined, we can use calls to functions defined elsewhere to give our code similar benefits.

Now that we know some of the benefits of creating and using functions, we can discuss some guidelines that help us achieve those benefits. As I said earlier, the design and style of a good function is similar to that of a program. Function names are subject to the same restrictions as variable names. Therefore, depending on which is the more important purpose of your function, you should choose names that are meaningful either in terms of what the function does or what it returns. For example, the Perl `print()` function is named for what it does (print its arguments), and the square root function (`sqrt()` is named for what it returns (the square root of its argument).

The name you choose should fully describe the intent of the function. Choosing the name is the first thing you should do when designing a function. If you have any trouble coming up with a good, simple, accurate name for the function, it is likely that the function you are trying to create lacks internal cohesion. A function is internally cohesive when it's designed to do just one thing. A function such as `get_input()` is more cohesive than one called

```
get_input_and_search_for_input_in_file_and_print_search_results();
```

Coupling is another factor in function design. We've touched on coupling already when we discussed using copies of parameters rather than relying on global or file-scoped variables. Coupling refers to how much a function relies on other components in a program, such as variables outside of the functions scope, and other functions or file handles. A loosely coupled function is one that does not rely on anything exterior to itself, but it uses only the parameters passed to it in the argument list. A more highly coupled routine might rely on the values of exterior variables and might either call one or more additional functions or be called from other functions in the program. A highly coupled function can be more difficult to maintain because any changes you make to it might affect (or be affected by) other routines in the program including how other routines affect other variables within the program.

7.6 Parameters and references

As we noted earlier, when you pass a list of arguments to a function, that function receives one flat list of all the values of the arguments. So what happens when you want to pass two arrays to a function and be able to distinguish each array separately? For example, if you call a function with two arrays

```
my @list1 = (1, 2, 3);
my @list2 = (4, 5, 6);
some_function(@list1, @list2); # prints: 1 2 3 4 5 6 :

sub some_function {
    my (@array1, @array2) = @_;   # @array1 holds all of @_
    print "@array1 : @array2\n";  # and @array2 is empty
}
```

the function only receives a single flat parameter list of (1, 2, 3, 4, 5, 6). The function can't know where the first array ends and the second begins, or even if two arrays were really passed as arguments. In the assignment to the two lexical arrays in the function, the first array will get the entire parameter list and the second will be left empty. One can get around this by also passing the lengths of the arrays to the function and using them to extract each array (slices of the @_ array) within the function. However, if you recall the brief introduction to references back in chapter 4, you may already realize a simpler way to deal with such issues:

```
my @list1 = (1, 2, 3);
my @list2 = (4, 5, 6);
some_function(\@list1, \@list2); # prints: 1 2 3 : 4 5 6

sub some_function {
    my ($aref_1, $aref_2) = @_;
    print "@$aref_1 : @$aref_2\n";
}
```

Here we have passed in two references to arrays. References are scalar values so the argument list has just two elements. These are assigned to two lexical scalar variables inside the function. We can then use each array reference, and the arrays they reference, separately within the function. It is important to note that these array references still point to the original arrays, so changing the values stored in the referenced array affects the original array variable as well. This is fine for functions designed to change the values of the array arguments as a side effect. (Consider the built-in push(), pop(), shift(), and unshift() functions, for example.) But it would be safer to create new copies if you only require the array values and do not intend to change the original arrays. You can do this by dereferencing each reference within the function and assigning copies of the arrays to new lexical arrays:

```
my @list1 = (1, 2, 3);
my @list2 = (4, 5, 6);
some_function(\@list1, \@list2);

sub some_function {
    my ($aref_1, $aref_2) = @_;
    my @array1 = @$aref_1;
    my @array2 = @$aref_2;
    print "@array1 : @array2\n"; # or do something more complex
}
```

Here we have assigned copies of the arrays to two new lexical arrays. We can manipulate and change these copies in any way we want without affecting the original array variables. Any value can be passed by reference to a function. It is up to you to define the function to do the right thing with its arguments.

7.7 Recursion

Recursion, simply put, is a way of defining something in terms of itself but in a particular fashion that eventually resolves the inherent circularity. The canonical example of a problem that lends itself to recursive solution is calculating factorials. The factorial of a number N (written N!) is just the number N multiplied by (N-1) multiplied by (N-2) and so on until (N-(N-1)). The following table lays out the first five integers and their factorials. (As a special case, the factorial of 0 is 1.)

```
Number          Factorial Calculation        Factorial
  0                       1                       1
  1                     1 * 1                     1
  2                   2 * 1 * 1                   2
  3                 3 * 2 * 1 * 1                 6
  4               4 * 3 * 2 * 1 * 1              24
  5             5 * 4 * 3 * 2 * 1 * 1           120
```

Let's consider a simple function that solves the factorial calculation iteratively:

```
sub factorial {
    my $number = shift @_;
    return undef if $number < 0; # illegal value
    return 1 if $number == 0;
    my $factorial = 1;
```

```
    for(my $i = $number; $i > 1; $i--) {
        $factorial *= $i;
    }
    return $factorial;
}
```

Here we have simply returned the undefined value if the argument was less than zero—since you cannot calculate the factorial of a negative number—or returned 1 if the argument was zero. Otherwise, we calculate the factorial by means of a loop that counts down from $number to 2 and returns the computed factorial.

Let's look at a more mathematical way of defining the factorial of a number N:

```
N! is 1 if N is 0
N! is N * (N-1)!
```

This is a recursive definition of the factorial of a number N. We call this definition recursive because it defines factorials in terms of factorials—but not entirely in terms of itself, since that would be a circular definition. Recursion is more like a spiral definition. Consider the case when N is 5 once again:

```
5! is 5 * 4!
4! is 4 * 3!
3! is 3 * 2!
2! is 2 * 1!
1! is 1 * 0!
0! is 1
```

Using the recursive definition we know that 5! is just 5 * 4!, but then we need to calculate 4!, which is simply 4 * 3!, and so on down to 1!, which is 1 * 0!, and we know by definition that 0! is 1. Once we have found the simplest solution we can then work our way back up the list inserting the value of 1! (1 * 1), calculating the value of 2! (2 * 1) and so on up the list until we have our answer for 5!. Now consider a factorial function that calls itself to do the same thing:

```
sub factorial {
    my $number = shift @_;
    return undef if $number < 0;
    return 1 if $number == 0;
    return( $number * factorial( $number - 1 ) );
}
```

This function performs the same checks for an argument less than zero or equal to zero. But, to calculate the factorial of a number larger than zero, it simply does what the recursive definition asks and returns the number itself multiplied by the factorial of one less than the number.

A recursive function always has two main components: 1) a simple answer for the simplest case (or cases, if the recursion has more than one endpoint); and 2) a recursive call to itself with a slightly simpler case. Incorrectly detecting the simplest case—i.e., the case that should stop the recursion—is a common error when constructing recursive functions. You must always make sure that your recursion has a definite endpoint or you will have what is referred to as an infinite recursion. In other words, you'll have a function that keeps calling itself forever, or at least until the computer runs out of memory.

Many problems lend themselves to recursive solutions, but a recursive solution, even one that appears simpler as in the factorial case, is not always best in terms of efficiency. Consider the recursive factorial function above when N is 5. The function is called initially with a value of 5. It then must call itself with the value of 4, then 3, all the way down to 0 before it can begin to reconstruct the final answer. That amounts to a total of six function calls just to calculate the answer. This is more expensive both in terms of speed and memory than the simple iterative version given earlier.

However, sometimes an iterative solution is not as simple as in the factorial case, and a recursive function provides a much cleaner way of solving the problem. Algorithms that traverse tree-like structures or follow paths on a graph often use simple recursive definitions.

7.8   Putting it together

We haven't covered everything about function syntax at this point. Our discussion of references, in particular, has been minimal, and we haven't discussed prototypes, or declaring functions with certain argument types, at all. We will consider references in much more depth in the next chapter. Prototypes can be confusing and are often not needed by the beginner so I have left them out of this book altogether. As mentioned previously, the *perlsub* pod-page has detailed information on prototypes for those who wish delve into them, but be warned that using prototypes correctly requires knowledge of references and a firm understanding of context. For the remainder of this chapter, we will tackle a couple of problems and put our knowledge of functions to practical use.

7.8.1 Revisiting the mathq program

When we designed and wrote the `mathq` program in chapter 3, we used chunks to break up the code into manageable sections of related code. However, when we finally re-integrated all the chunks back into a single program, we were left with a long while loop containing all of the program logic. While this program did not involve redundant code, it could have benefitted from the use of functions to reduce the complexity within the main loop. One possible rewrite of this program would simply use functions where some of the chunks were defined:

```perl
#!/usr/bin/perl -w
use strict;
print "Welcome to the mathq program\n";
my $quit = 0;
until ($quit) {
    my @tokens = gen_tokens();
    my ($question, $solution) = gen_question(@tokens);
    my $response = get_valid_response($question);

    # test response
    if ($response eq 'q') {
        $quit = 1;
    } elsif ($response == $solution) {
        print "Correct\n";
    } else {
        print "Incorrect: $question $solution\n";
    }
}
print "exiting the mathq program\n";


###### Subroutines
# gen_tokens: generate equation tokens (numbers and operator)
# parameters: none
# returns: first_number, second_number, operator

sub gen_tokens {
    my $first_number  = int(rand(10));    # range: 0 to 9 inclusive
    my $second_number = int(rand(9)) + 1; # range: 1 to 9 inclusive
    # choose random operator code: 0 or 1
    # operator codes: 0 is division
    #                 1 is multiplication
    my $operator      = int(rand(2));
    return ($first_number, $second_number, $operator);
}


# gen_question: generate question and solution strings
# parameters:
#    first_number  (integer in 0-9)
#    second_number (integer in 1-9)
#    operator      (0 => division, 1 => multiplication)
# returns: question, solution

sub gen_question {
    my ($first_number, $second_number, $operator) = @_;
    my ($question, $solution);
    if ($operator == 1) {
        $solution = $first_number * $second_number;
        $question = "$first_number x $second_number = ?";
    } else {
        $solution = $first_number * $second_number;
        ($solution, $first_number) = ($first_number, $solution);
        $question = "$first_number / $second_number = ?";
    }
```

```
        return ($question, $solution);
}

# get_valid_response: obtain user response to question
# parameters:   question (string)
# returns: response

sub get_valid_response {
    my $question = $_[0];
    my $response;
    my $is_valid = 0;
    until ($is_valid) {
        print "$question\n";
        $response = <STDIN>;
        chomp($response);
        # valid input is 'q' or  only digits
        if ($response eq 'q' or $response =~ m/^\d+$/) {
            $is_valid = 1;
        } else {
            print "Invalid: enter an integer or 'q' to quit\n";
        }
    }
    return $response;
}
```

This version contains virtually the same code as the original version in chapter 3, but we've pulled out chunks of related code involved in generating or obtaining values for variables. We have thus made the logic of the main loop more apparent. Notice that we did not turn the final test response chunk of code into a function. This code involves the actual output of the loop—in other words, the goal of the loop—as well as the conditional variable for exiting the loop ($quit). Pulling this code into a subroutine would have made it harder to understand the loop rather than simpler because one would have to look at the subroutine to understand what condition would cause the loop to terminate.

7.8.2 Routine examples

Here are a few additional example routines that need little explanation.

Calculate the area of a circle given its radius:

```
# area_circle: returns the area of a circle
# parameters: radius of a circle

sub area_circle {
    my $radius = shift @_;
    my $area   = 3.14159 * ($radius ** 2);
    return $area;
}
```

A lot of Perl programmers might code the above function much more concisely as:

```
sub area_circle {
    return 3.14159 * ( $_[0] ** 2 );
}
```

However, this kind of conciseness is not always the best way to show off your skills as a Perl programmer. Which routine would you want to read next year? In this case, the name and simplicity of the function make either one reasonably readable, but if you slip into the habit of being overly concise, you risk lowering readability in more complex functions.

Here's one that will reformat a paragraph of text to a new width. You pass the function two arguments: a width and a string containing the paragraph. The function will return a string containing the paragraph wrapped to the given width:

```
# wrap_it: wraps a string to a given width
# parameters: wrap width, string to wrap
sub wrap_it {
    my ($width, $text) = @_;
    $text =~ s/\n/ /g;
    my @new_para;
    while ($text =~ s/^(.{1,$width})(\s|$)//) {
        push @new_para, $1;
    }
    return join("\n",@new_para)."\n\n";
}
```

7.9 Exercises

1 Write a routine, sum(), that returns the sum of all its arguments.

2 Write two routines, max_num() and min_num(), that return the maximum and minimum of their argument lists respectively. For example

```
print max_num(12, 3, 42, 7); # should print: 42
print min_num(12, 3, 42, 7); # should print: 3
```

3 Write a complementary pair of routines, min_str() and max_str(), that return the minimum and maximum strings—minimum and maximum in terms of their location in a sorted list, not in terms of their lengths.

C H A P T E R   8

References and aggregate data structures

Perl's basic structured variables (arrays and hashes) are generalized and useful as they are, but you might be wondering about whether Perl supports slightly more advanced structures such as two dimensional arrays. The answer is yes. Perl supports multi-dimensional arrays as nested arrays—arrays of arrays. In fact, you can build up nested or aggregate data structures of any complexity using Perl. By nested or aggregate data structure I mean a structure that is simply a collection of Perl's basic types such as an array of arrays, or a hash of hashes, or a hash of arrays. (More abstract data structures will be considered in the advanced section of this book.) The key to building nested or aggregate data structures in Perl is references. First, let's consider why we might want a nested data structure. Imagine that you have a class of students. You've recorded their marks for three assignments in a simple text file in the order they were turned in and marked like so:

```
Bill Jones:2:35
Anne Smith:3:41
Sara Tims:2:45
Sara Tims:3:39
Bill Jones:1:42
Anne Smith:1:42
Sara Tims:1:41
Anne Smith:2:47
Bill Jones:3:41
```

We'll assume there are more students and this is just a representative chunk of the data file. Now, each assignment is scored out of 50 and before the final exam, which will count for twenty-five percent of the final mark, you want to generate a report that lists student's name, their scores on each exam, and their total score adjusted for seventy-five percent of the final mark so you can inform each student of his or her standing prior to the final exam.

To accomplish this, we must collect the assignment scores for each student in the class. A hash would be a good idea if we could only store a list for each key rather than just a scalar value. Perhaps you are already thinking of references. References, you may remember, are scalar values even when the reference itself refers to a list value such as an array or a hash. In chapter 4, we briefly demonstrated taking a reference to an array and storing that reference in a scalar variable. In the previous chapter, we even passed two array references to a subroutine. Here, we will use a hash with the student names as keys, and an array reference as the value, thereby creating a hash of lists. First, we need to cover some ground on creating references.

8.1 Creating references

In chapter 4, you learned that you could create a reference to any named variable by using the backslash operator:

```
$scalar = 42;
$sref   = \$scalar;
@array = (1, 2, 3);
$aref   = \@array;
%hash = (a => 1, b => 2, c => 3);
$href = \%hash
```

The backslash operator allows us to create references to variables that already exist. A more useful technique is to create references to anonymous values. An anonymous value is simply a value stored in memory without an associated variable name attached to it. Perl provides two special *constructors* for creating anonymous arrays and anonymous hashes.

An anonymous array can be created using square brackets around a list of scalar values:

```
$aref = [1, 2, 3];
```

Here, $aref contains a reference to an array value that is not associated with an array variable. Figure 8.1 shows a graphical comparison between taking a reference to an array variable and taking a reference to an anonymous array.

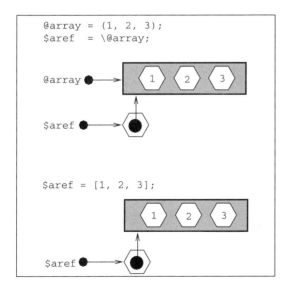

Figure 8.1   A reference to an array variable vs. a reference to an anonymous array

A similar syntax using curly braces can be used to create an anonymous hash value and return a reference to that value:

```
$href = {a => 1, b => 2, c => 3};
```

Figure 8.2 shows a graphical comparison between assigning a reference to a hash variable and assigning a reference to an anonymous hash.

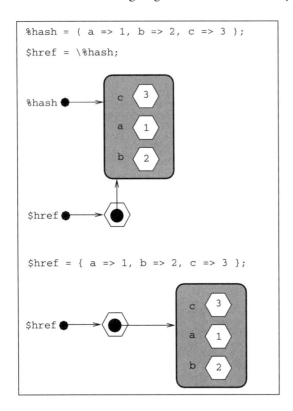

Figure 8.2 A reference to a hash variable vs. a reference an anonymous hash

A few different ways of dereferencing a reference exist to obtain a value from that reference. The first method is to simply prefix a variable symbol of the proper type (either @, %, or $) onto the reference variable. (We saw examples of this in chapter 4):

```
my $aref = [42, 13, 2];
print "@$aref\n";    # prints: 42 13 2
print "$$aref[1]\n"; # prints: 13
```

A more general way is to use curly braces around the intended reference value such as:

```
my $aref = [42, 13, 2];
print "@{$aref}\n";      # prints: 42 13 2
print "${$aref}[1]\n";   # prints: 13
```

Using the braces allows you explicitly to tell Perl what is supposed to resolve to a reference. In fact, in this syntax, the curly braces delimit a block that may contain any number of statements as long as the final value evaluates to a reference.

Another dereferencing syntax is the arrow operator ->, which is used between a reference and a subscript:

```
$aref = [42, 13, 2];
print "$aref->[0]\n"; # prints: 42
```

Now, consider a nested structure of arrays—an array of arrays if you will. (This is actually a reference to an anonymous array of anonymous array references, but that's hard to say five times fast):

```
$aref = [ [42, 13, 2], [1, 2, 3], [7, 8, 9] ];
print "${${$aref}[2]}[0]\n"; # prints: 7
print "$aref->[2]->[0]\n";   # prints: 7
print "$$aref[2]->[0]\n";    # prints: 7
print "$$aref[2][0]\n";      # prints: 7
print "$aref->[2][0]\n";     # prints: 7
```

Notice in the last two print statements we left off the arrow between the subscripts. Perl knows that two subscripts next to each other implies a reference so it automatically supplies the arrow operator for us as a convenience. See how much cleaner the last two print statements are to read.

Another way to create anonymous array or hash values in Perl is by using a scalar as if it was reference. (We could also create anonymous scalars, but anonymous scalars are rarely used in practice.) In other words, if you dereference a scalar variable that did not previously contain a reference to a value, Perl automatically creates an anonymous value of the appropriate type and stores a reference to it in the variable:

```
my $variable;
$variable->[0] = 42;
print "$variable\n";       #prints: ARRAY(0x804a96c)
print "$variable->[0]\n";  #prints: 42
```

Here, the variable $variable did not contain a reference, but when we used it as if it held a reference to an array, Perl automatically created an anonymous array and assigned the value 42 to the first element of that array, storing a reference to that array in the scalar variable. As we saw in chapter 4, printing out a variable containing a reference just prints out its type and memory address.

This way of creating anonymous values is called *autovivification* and can be quite useful. In fact, we will use this method in our solution to the marking problem given above. Here's a top level breakdown of the program:

```
<<scores.pl>>=
#!/usr/bin/perl -w
use strict;
my $data_file = 'scores.txt';
my %students;
<<read file and build data structure>>
<<generate report>>
```

This is all relatively straightforward, so let's jump right into the data structure code. We begin by opening our data file and looping through it to build our hash of arrays. After chomp()'ing the newline off a line, we split() it into array of fields: the first element will be the student name, the second is the assignment number, and the last field is the score for that assignment. We use these fields to build the structure.

```
<<read file and build data structure>>=
open(SCORES, $data_file) || die "can't open file: $!";
while ( <SCORES> ) {
    chomp;
    my @fields = split /:/;
    <<build structure>>
}
```

We are building a hash of arrays where the key for a hash element is the student name. The value will be a reference to an array that will hold scores. This array will have four elements. Elements 1 to 3 will hold the score for the corresponding assignment. This leaves element 0 free for holding the total raw score.

```
<<build structure>>=
$students{$fields[0]}[ $fields[1] ] = $fields[2];
$students{$fields[0]}[0] += $fields[2];
```

We are using the autovivification method to automatically create the array reference if it does not yet exist. We do this by using the student name $fields[0] as the key to the %student hash and treating its value as if it were already an array reference by assigning directly to an element of that array. The first line of this chunk could have also used the following dereference syntax alternatives:

```
${$students{$fields[0]}}[ $fields[1] ] = $fields[2];
$students{$fields[0]}->[ $fields[1] ]  = $fields[2];
```

In fact, the syntax we used was the latter adding the convenience of not needing an arrow between the two subscripts (the hash subscript followed by the array subscript).

We also added the current score (from `$fields[2]`) to the 0'th element of the array, which holds the total score for that student.

To generate the report we simply iterate through the keys of the `%student` hash, print the student's name, and put the total score into a new lexical variable (to make it easier to refer to it later). Then we print the assignment scores by looping over a list of integers from 1 to 3 and use these scores as indices into the array reference. Finally, we report on the total score and the adjusted score.

```
<<generate report>>=
foreach my $name (keys %students) {
    print "$name:\n";
    my $total = $students{$name}[0];
    foreach my $assignment ( 1..3 ) {
        my $score = $students{$name}[$assignment];
        print "\tassignment $assignment: $score\n";
    }
    print "\tTotal score: $total\n";
    print "\tAdjusted score: ",$total/2," out of 75%\n\n";
}
```

Because it is sometimes hard to communicate references in words, figure 8.3 shows graphically what the `%students` hash looks like after the program processes the first line of the data file, and again after the second line, and, finally, after the whole example data file has been read.

Now that we've seen an example in action, let's return to the basics once again and consider a few simple nested structures.

8.1.1 Nested or multi-dimensional arrays

A two-dimensional array can be thought of as an array of arrays, or, in simpler words, a table of rows and columns. Such a structure is easy to create in Perl using references. Consider the following table:

```
3   7   5
8   6   1
4   2   9
```

To store such a table we can use an anonymous array for each row and store the references to these row arrays in another array:

```
my @twoD = (
                [3, 7, 5],
                [8, 6, 1],
                [4, 2, 9],
            );
```

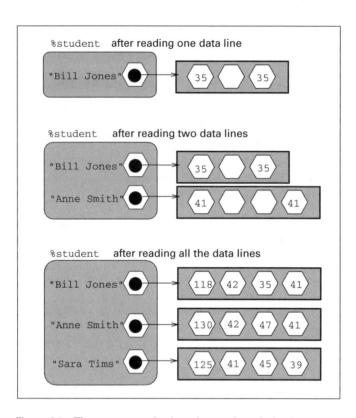

Figure 8.3   The %students hash at three points during its construction

Here, each element of the array @twoD is a reference to an anonymous array. You can print out any given element, or an entire row using the basic dereferencing syntax given earlier:

```
print $twoD[0][1];    # prints: 7
print $twoD[2][2];    # prints: 9
print "@{$twoD[1]}";  # prints: 8 6 1
```

We could also have created the entire structure as a reference to an array of arrays:

```
my $twoD_ref = [ [3, 7, 5], [8, 6, 1], [4, 2, 9] ];
print "$twoD_ref->[0][1]"; # prints: 7
print "@{$twoD_ref->[0]}"; # prints: 3 7 5

$twoD_ref->[1][1] = 'X';   # changes: row 2 element 2
print "@{$twoD_ref->[1]}"; # prints: 8 X 1
```

8.1.2 Nested hashes

A simple hash of hashes can be represented in a similar fashion to the previous array of arrays. Consider a list of employee IDs and the corresponding essential attributes you need to know about that employee:

```
my %employees = ( asmith => { name => 'Anne Smith',
                              age  => 35,
                              beer => 'Pale Ale',
                            },
                  bjones => { name => 'Bill Jones',
                              age  => 21,
                              beer => 'Dark Ale',
                            },
                  stims  => { name => 'Sara Tims',
                              age  => 32,
                              beer => 'Wheat Ale',
                            },
                );
foreach my $id (keys %employees) {
    print "$employees{$id}{name} drinks: $employees{$id}{beer}\n";
}
```

This snippet of code produces the following output:

```
Sara Tims drinks: Wheat Ale
Bill Jones drinks: Dark Ale
Anne Smith drinks: Pale Ale
```

8.1.3 Mixed structures

Some languages provide a special data type for a variable that can contain a mixed collection of other basic data types—for example the "record" in Pascal or the "struct" in C. Perl's nested structures give you complete flexibility over the kinds of things you can nest. We've already seen one mixed structure with the hash of arrays used for the student's assignment scores. Consider a more elaborate kind of record for each employee than that used in the example above. We will consider just a single employee record here, but the hash could contain a multiple number of records, just as the example above does:

```
my %employees = ( asmith => { name => 'Anne Smith',
                              age  => 35,
                              children => ['Amanda', 'Amy'],
                              beer => ['Pale Ale', 'Lager'],
                            }
                );
print "@{$employees{asmith}{children}}\n"; #prints: Amanda Amy
```

8.2 Scope and references

You know that a lexical variable only exists during its current scope (i.e., its immediate enclosing block). So what happens when we take a reference to a variable and that variable goes out of scope (i.e., no longer exists)? Well, when Perl sets aside memory to hold a value, it also stores some extra information about that value. Most importantly, it maintains a count of how many things are pointing at that particular value. This is called a reference count, and it is how Perl determines whether a value stored in memory is still needed by the program or if that memory can be released and used for something else. Let's consider the simplest of cases:

```
my $outer;
{
    my $inner = 42;
    $outer = \$inner;
}
print "$$outer\n"; # prints: 42
```

Now, you might be thinking, "Hey, how can $outer still refer to $inner after $inner has gone out of scope?" That's a good question. The answer is that $outer never referred to $inner, it referred to $inner's stored value. Remember, the variable $inner itself is just a name associated with a particular memory location that holds a value. When we take a reference to a variable we get a reference to the memory location to which is associated, not the to variable name itself. Figure 8.4 depicts graphically what is going on before, during, and after the inner scope. The reference count is depicted by how many arrows are pointing at a value.

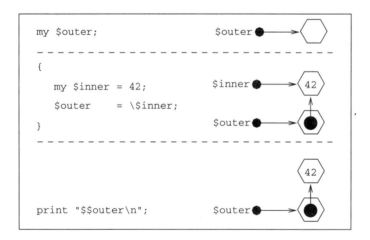

Figure 8.4   Reference to a variable going out of scope

This ability to have a reference to a variable going out of scope is useful when you want to create a reference within a subroutine and store it in a lexical variable while you work with it before returning this reference back to main program.

```
my $foo = get_ref();
print "@$foo\n";      # prints: 1 2 3

sub get_ref {
    my $temp = [1, 2, 3];
    return $temp;
}
```

In this example, the function creates an anonymous array and stores a reference to it in a lexical variable. Even though the lexical variable goes out of scope when the function exits, the anonymous array still exists. You may imagine that the return statement takes the arrow from $temp and hands it to the variable $foo in the assignment statement that called the function.

A more realistic example would be to use a function to turn a line of data into a hash of keys and values and to return a reference to that hash.

```
my @records;
while ( <DATA> ) {
    chomp;
    push @records, make_record($_);
}

foreach my $rec ( @records ) {
    print "$rec->{name} drinks $rec->{beer}\n";
}

sub make_record {
    my @fields = split /:/, $_[0];
    my %record = ( name  => $fields[0],
                   age   => $fields[1],
                   beer  => $fields[2],
                 );
    return \%record;
}
__DATA__
Anne Smith:35:Pale Ale
Bill Jones:21:Dark Ale
```

Each time this function is called, it creates a brand new lexical hash variable called %record that is completely unrelated to any such variable it might have already created in a previous call. A reference to the value of this hash is returned from the function and pushed onto the @records array. The variable went out of scope but the value in memory is retained because something still points to it—that is, its reference count is not zero.

8.3 References to functions

You are not limited to taking references to variables in Perl. You can take references to functions, or create anonymous functions as well. Before we consider why we might want to do either one, let's consider the syntax for a few simple cases.

To take a reference to an existing subroutine, you use the backslash operator against the subroutine name prefixed with the & symbol:

```perl
my $sub_ref = \&foo;
```

To use this reference—in other words, to call the subroutine pointed to by this reference—you may use one of two syntactical constructs, both of which are similar to methods of dereferencing variables:

```perl
my $sub_ref = \&foo;
&{$sub_ref}('one way');
&$sub_ref('same way without braces');
$sub_ref->('arrow syntax');
sub foo {
    print "$_[0]\n";
}
```

To create an anonymous subroutine, you use the sub keyword followed immediately by the block of code that will serve as the subroutine:

```perl
my $sub_ref = sub {
                    my $arg = shift @_;
                    print "$arg\n";
                  };
$sub_ref->("I'm anonymous");
```

References to subroutines are convenient for a variety of things, but the most popular usage is probably for creating *dispatch tables* by creating a hash of function references. Consider an interactive program that asks the user for a command to execute:

```perl
my %dispatch_table = ( foo  => sub { print "You chose 'foo'\n" },
                       bar  => sub { print "You chose 'bar'\n" },
                       quit => \&quit,
                       q    => \&quit,
                       help => \&help,
                     );
print "Enter a command (or 'q' or 'quit' to exit): ";
while (<STDIN>) {
    chomp;
    my $command = $_;
    if ( $dispatch_table{$command} ) {
        $dispatch_table{$command}->();
```

```
    } else {
        print "Illegal command: $command\n";
    }
    print "Enter a command (or 'q' or 'quit' to exit): ";
}

sub help {
    print "The available commands are:\n";
    foreach my $com ( keys %dispatch_table ) {
        print "\t$com\n";
    }
}

sub quit {
    exit 0;
}
```

Here we have two different keys in the hash referring to the same `quit` function. This is not only allowed, since a "thing" can be referenced any number of times, but encouraged. The alternative would have been make a duplicate anonymous function for both the `q` and `quit` keys in the hash. In other words, Perl would have to create and store two separate, but identical, function references when only one was really necessary.

8.3.1 Closures

When you create an anonymous subroutine in Perl it is deeply bound to its current lexical environment. Such a subroutine is called a *closure*. Another way to say this is that an anonymous subroutine carries its lexical environment around with it even when that environment is no longer in scope. This is best shown by example:

```
sub speak {
    my $saying = shift;
    return sub { print "$saying $_[0]!\n";};
}
my $batman = speak('Indeed');
my $robin  = speak('Holy');
$robin->('mackerel'); # prints: Holy mackerel!
$batman->('Robin');   # prints: Indeed Robin!
```

Here, the subroutine `speak()` makes a new lexical variable `$saying` and assigns it the first element of the parameter list passed to it. It then returns a new anonymous subroutine that uses that lexical variable along with the first parameter of whatever will be given to it as an argument. Both `$batman` and `$robin` are assigned the anonymous subroutine from `speak()`, but with different values of `$saying`. These anonymous subroutines are then called using the arrow dereference syntax. Each still contains the original value of `$saying` with which they were created. Thus, even though the referenced subroutines are called in a different scope than where they were created, they act—in terms of any lexical variables used within them—as if they were still within the same scope in which they were created.

The kinds of things closures are good for are somewhat specialized, but we will consider one particular usage here: creating a stream based on a particular mathematical function.

You may or may not be familiar with a mathematical series of numbers called the Fibonacci numbers. The first two Fibonacci numbers are 0 and 1. The next number in the series is obtained by adding together the two previous numbers. So the third number, the result of 0 + 1, is also 1, and the fourth, the result of 1 + 1, is 2. The first ten Fibonacci numbers are

```
0, 1, 1, 2, 3, 5, 8, 13, 21, 34
```

We can envision a recursive definition for the nth Fibonacci number in the sequence: for any position n in the sequence, the Fibonacci number at that position is

```
fibo(n) = n                       if n == 0 or n == 1
fibo(n) = fibo(n-2) + fibo(n-1)   if n > 1
```

We can translate this definition into a simple recursive subroutine that calculated the Fibonacci number for a given position in the sequence. We could also create an iterative type routine that accomplished the same task but more quickly. But what if we wanted to be able to print out the first five such numbers, then do some other things, then print out the next five numbers in the sequence. A subroutine that calculates the Fibonacci number for position n would have to be called at least five times—more if it's a recursive function—once for each position in the list. Then, the program would have to store its position in the sequence in order to continue the sequence later. And, still, each time it calculated the next position in the sequence it would be repeating a lot of computational work already performed.

One answer—probably the best in this case—is to create a separate storage array, a *cache,* for numbers that have already been computed and have the subroutine utilize this array to continue the sequence from where it left off.

An alternative is to use closures to provide a steady stream of Fibonacci numbers that can be continued at any time:

```perl
# fibonacci stream generator:
sub new_fib_stream {
    my ($current, $next) = (0, 1);
    return sub{
                my $fib = $current;
                ($current, $next) = ($next, $current + $next);
                return $fib;
            };
}
```

```
# create two new fibonacci streams
my $fib_stream1 = new_fib_stream();
my $fib_stream2 = new_fib_stream();

# print out first 5 fibonacci numbers from stream 1
foreach (1..5) {
    print $fib_stream1->(), "\n";
}

# print out first 10 Fibonacci numbers from stream 2
foreach (1..10) {
    print $fib_stream2->(), " ";
}
print "\n";

# print out next 5 fibonacci numbers in stream 1
foreach (1..5) {
    print $fib_stream1->(), "\n";
}
```

When the `new_fib_stream()` function is called, it creates a new scope and defines two lexical variables within that scope. It then defines (and returns) an anonymous subroutine that uses those lexical variables. Calling the generator function again creates an entirely new scope with its own lexical variables and also returns a new closure that uses those variables. In this way, you can set up as many completely independent Fibonacci stream closures as you want.

Closures are something of an advanced topic, so we are only introducing the concept here.

8.4 Nested structures on the fly

Imagine a file of employee data, with one employee record per line recording employee ID number, first name, last name, department, and type (full or part time):

```
142a13:John:Doe:Sales:pt
971a22:Jane:Doe:Operations:ft
131b21:Amanda:Smith:Sales:pt
119d17:Frank:Cannon:Support:pt
123a12:Ron:Gold:Support:pt
666s66:Lucy:Kindser:Operations:ft
777q42:Bob:Norman:Sales:ft
```

If we wanted to read this file and create an array of arrays, we could simply loop through it, splitting each line on the colons to produce an array. We could then push a reference to that array into our main array:

```
#!/usr/bin/perl -w
use strict;
open(FILE,'employee.dat') || die "can't open file: $!";

# build structure my @employees;
while( <FILE> ) {
    chomp;
    my @fields = split /:/;
    push @employees, \@fields;
}

# print info from structure
foreach my $person (@employees) {
    print "Name: $person->[1] $person->[2], ";
    print "Department: $person->[3]\n";
}
```

This can be simplified further by using the `split` function inside an anonymous array constructor:

```
my @employees;
while( <FILE> ) {
    chomp;
    push @employees, [ split(/:/) ];
}
```

You can use any expression inside an anonymous array (or anonymous hash) constructor, and the expression will be evaluated in a list context. The result of the evaluation will be the contents of the new anonymous array.

In the case of data of this sort, a hash of arrays may be a better choice for a structure:

```
#!/usr/bin/perl -w
use strict;
open(FILE,'employee.dat') || die "can't open file: $!";

# build structure my %employees;
while( <FILE> ) {
    my @fields = split /:/;
    my $id     = shift @fields;
    $employees{$id} = [@fields];
}

# print info from structure
foreach my $id (keys %employees) {
    print "ID = $id, Name = $employees{$id}->[0]\n";
}
```

Or maybe you'd like to read the data into a hash of hashes so that each field could be accessed by a field name:

```perl
#!/usr/bin/perl -w
use strict;
open(FILE,'employee.dat') || die "can't open file: $!";

# build structure
my @field_names = qw(fname lname dept type);
my %employees;
while( <FILE> ) {
    chomp;
    my ($id, @fields) = split /:/;
    @{$employees{$id}}{@field_names} = @fields;
}

# print info from structure
foreach my $id (keys %employees) {
    print "$id: $employees{$id}{fname} $employees{$id}{lname}\n";
}
```

Another way to structure this data to generate a report would be to create a hash using department names as the primary key pointing to a hash of ID number keys, which, in turn, each point to a hash of the rest of the record fields. To give you an idea of the structure, here is what part of it would look like to build manually:

```perl
%departments = (Sales => {'142a13' => {fname => 'John',
                                       lname => 'Doe',
                                       type  => 'pt',
                                      },
                          '131b21' => {fname => 'Amanda',
                                       lname => 'Smith',
                                       type  => 'pt',
                                      },
                         },
                Support => {'119d17' => {fname => 'Frank',
                                         lname => 'Cannon',
                                         type  => 'pt',
                                        },
                           },
               );
print "$departments{Sales}{'131b21'}{lname}\n"; # prints: Smith
```

And here is one way we could build such a hash of hashes of hashes on the fly:

```perl
#!/usr/bin/perl -w
use strict;
open(FILE,'employee.dat') || die "can't open file: $!";

# build structure
my %departments;
my @field_names = qw(fname lname type);
```

```perl
while( <FILE> ) {
    chomp;
    my @fields = split /:/;
    my %record;
    @record{@field_names} = @fields[1,2,4];
    $departments{$fields[3]}{$fields[0]} = {%record};
}

# print employee data by department
foreach my $dept (keys %departments) {
    print "$dept:\n";
    foreach my $id (keys %{$departments{$dept}}) {
        my $record = $departments{$dept}{$id};
        print "\t$id: $record->{fname} $record->{lname} ";
        print "($record->{type})\n";
    }
}
```

8.5 Review

Reference Creation

```perl
$scalar = 42;
$sc_ref1  = \$scalar; # explicit reference to $scalar's location.
$$sc_ref2 = $scalar;  # implicit creation of new scalar location
                      # holding value of $scalar (autovivification)

@array    = (42, 13, 2);
$a_ref1   = \@array;   # explicit reference to @array's location.
$a_ref2   = [@array];  # explicit creation of new array location
                       # holding copy of @array.
@$a_ref3 = @array;     # implicit creation of new array location
                       # holding copy of @array.

%hash     = (a => 42, b => 13);
$h_ref1   = \%hash;    # explicit reference to %hash's location.
$h_ref2   = {%hash};   # explicit creation of new hash location
                       # holding copy of %hash.
%$h_ref3 = %hash;      # implicit creation of new hash location
                       # holding copy of %hash.
```

Dereferencing

```perl
print "$$sc_ref2";     # prints: 42
print "@$a_ref3";      # prints: 42 13 2
print "${$a_ref2}[1]"; # prints: 13
print "$a_ref2->[1];   # prints: 13
my @ary = keys %$h_ref2;
print "@ary"           # prints: a b
print "${$h_ref3}{b};  # prints: 13
print "$h_ref3->{b}";  # prints: 13
```

8.6 Exercises

1 Write a routine that reads the following table into a two-dimensional array, such as an array of arrays or a matrix:

```
one    two    three
four   five   six
seven  eight  nine
```

Then have the routine transpose the rows and columns to produce the following output:

```
one    four seven
two    five eight
three  six  nine
```

C H A P T E R   9

Documentation

At this point you have acquired the tools and concepts for creating both simple and sophisticated programs using the Perl language. However, unless you document your programs they are incomplete. Some would even consider them "broken." With each program you write, you need to supply both user documentation and source documentation.

User documentation is simply the instruction manual for using your program. Source documentation is the documentation you or another programmer will want when maintaining, revising, or just trying to understand code you or someone else has written. We discussed techniques for source documentation back in chapter 2: trying to make the source code as self-documenting as possible by using good formatting, choosing good variable names (which applies to choosing good names for subroutines and filehandles as well), and by using informative comments. Sometimes all this is not enough. Later in this chapter we will discuss other ways of documenting your source code using Literate Programming (LP) techniques. First, however, we will cover creating user documentation using Perl's standard Plain Old Documentation (POD) format.

9.1 *User documentation and POD*

User level documentation is, as its name implies, intended for the user of the program or module. For programs, this documentation should cover the essentials of running the program: what arguments it expects, what options it might take, and what outputs it produces. For modules (discussed in parts 3 and 4), the intended user is another Perl programmer. Documentation in that case should cover the programmer interface to the module: the availability of functions and/or methods as well as the calling interface and return values of each of those functions or methods.

The current standard way to provide user level documentation for your Perl programs or modules is to embed the documentation directly in the Perl source code file using the POD markup language. POD is a simple markup language that the Perl compiler understands just well enough to ignore—which means you can use it within your script and not worry about it. These two benefits shouldn't be underestimated. Learning to use POD is easy and means your documentation will be available in a standard form since all of the standard documentation included in the Perl distribution is written in POD format. Using POD to include your documentation within your program means that any user of your program or module automatically has the documentation. You may be more likely to properly update your documentation when it is right there in the same file as the code rather than in a separate text file.

Let's consider POD on its own before we discuss embedding it in Perl source code. POD is a way of marking up plain text so that another program (a translator utility such as pod2html or pod2latex) can convert the pod-source into source code for one or another formatting programs. The utility of POD is that you can write your document using just one set of formatting tags. You can then use the various utility translators to produce LaTeX files, HTML files, PostScript, manpages, or something else for which there is a translator. The set of tags is small and is covered in the *perlpod* pod-page. We will just consider the basic elements here.

The first tags we'll consider are structural tags, that indicate headings, lists, and items within a list:

```
=head1  This is a level 1 heading

This is a small paragraph of text below the
level 1 heading.

=head2  This is a level 2 heading

And this is a paragraph of plain text below the
second level heading

=over 4

=item *

first bulleted list paragraph
=item *

second bulleted list paragraph

=back

=cut
```

The =head1 and =head2 tags are fairly self explanatory, they create headings and sub-headings. The =over 4 tag starts a list, the number implying a indent size for some formatters. Each item in the list is tagged with an =item tag which, if followed by an asterisk, produces a bulleted list item. A numbered list can be created simply by using increasing digits in place of the asterisk. The =back tag ends the list and the =cut tag ends the current section of POD until another =xxx style of tag is encountered.

All the POD command or structure tags need to start at the left margin. Plain paragraphs also need to flush to the left margin and need to be separated by blank lines. (Note, though, that seemingly blank lines containing spaces can cause problems.) Within a plain paragraph, several formatting tags can be used:

CHAPTER 9 DOCUMENTATION

```
=head1 Simple Formatting
```

```
Within a plain paragraph some text might be tagged as I<italic text>
or B<perhaps bold> or as C<literal code> (presumably formatted in
fixed width font). The S<This contains non-breaking spaces> tag
means that the text inside the tag delimiter should not be broken
across lines at the spaces.
```

```
You can enclose filenames in an F<filename> tag, index entries using
X<index>, and links with the L<> tag. Links are for manpage
references, and a tag like: L<blah(1)> would translate to "the blah
manpage" but this added text can be controlled (see L<perlpod(1)>
for further information).
```

```
=cut
```

Aside from structural elements and plain paragraphs, you can also create "verbatim" paragraphs—where what you write should get typeset as it is with no wrapping, no interpretation of tags, etc. You create verbatim paragraphs by indenting each line:

```
=head2 Verbatim Example
```

```
This is a plain paragraph that might be wrapped by the formatter and
will have B<tags> interpreted in the process. A I<verbatim>
paragraph, perhaps showing a code example can be achieved by indenting:
```

```
    #this is a verbatim paragraph
    my $foo = "nothing B<interpreted> in here";
    print $foo;
```

```
=cut
```

And that's most of what it takes to write simple POD documents. The added bonus of POD is that everything between an =command type tag and an =cut tag is ignored by the Perl compiler. Therefore, it is simple to write your user documentation (in a manpage format we will discuss next) directly within your program or module. By keeping your documentation inside your program you are more likely to remember to update it to reflect changes and new features, and you are always sure that anyone who receives your program also receives the documentation. This user can then use one of the many translators to produce a nicely formatted document for viewing or printing. Or the user can view the document using the perldoc utility included with the Perl distribution. (Some distributions of Perl may not include the perldoc utility: the MacPerl distribution, for example, comes with a viewer called shuck.)

The standard convention for writing embedded POD documentation is to supply at least the minimum sections of a standard Unix-like manpage. The minimal level-1 sections that you should include for a program called `foo` that solves the world's problems are shown in table 9.1.

Table 9.1   Sections to include in POD documentation

Section	Description
NAME	The name of the program or module and a few words about what it does.
SYNOPSIS	A brief usage example of the program showing its calling syntax, or a representative sample of the functions within the module.
DESCRIPTION	A more extended discussion of the program, possibly with subsections using =head2 tags.
OPTIONS	If any, put them in a list here, or perhaps under the description above. If you choose the latter option, omit this section.
FILES	A list of the files used by the program. If none, leave this section out.
SEE ALSO	A list of manpages for related programs and/or documentation.
BUGS	If you have bugs in your program that aren't ironed out yet, list them here or risk being told about them again and again...
AUTHOR	Author's name and contact information, plus any copyright statement you want to include (which also could be under its own level 1 heading).

There are other relatively standard sections you may want to include. (See *perlpod*.) You can and should add any additional headings and information about your program that you deem appropriate.

You may include POD almost anywhere within your program. The basic rule is that if the compiler reads a POD tag directive when it is looking for a new statement, it will ignore everything up to and including the next =cut directive it finds. Some authors put all the POD information at the beginning of the program; some place it at the end, and others mix it throughout the source code. Like many things in Perl, it is a choice left up to the programmer.

9.2   Source code documentation

Source code documentation was discussed to some extent in chapter 2. That chapter was largely about using good style and comments to produce readable, maintainable code. Often those guidelines are all you need. (Some programmers—and I mean well-respected ones, not crackpots—go as far as to say that if your code needs extra comments to be understood, you need to rewrite your code.) Sometimes, however, this is not enough. You may want to include detailed explanations of certain algorithms, provide diagrams, or present the code in an order different from the more linear order the compiler expects. Literate Programming (LP) techniques can be used for such things and more.

LP is neither specific to Perl, nor necessary for programming with Perl, but it can be such a useful tool that I will devote the remainder of this chapter to using LP in your Perl programming.

Literate Programming is a method of programming developed by Donald Knuth in the early 1980s (Knuth, D. E. "Literate Programming." *The Computer Journal* (27)2:97–111 1984). The essence of LP is embodied in a quote from Knuth:

> Let us change our traditional attitude to the construction of programs: Instead of imagining that our main task is to instruct a *computer* what to do, let us concentrate rather on explaining to *humans* what we want the computer to do. (Knuth, 1984.)

The basic concept is that one should be able to write out the program description and the program source code together in a source file. This can be presented in an order suited to explaining the code to humans. The program source can be extracted from the file and *tangled* together into its proper order for the compiler. The documentation, then, is the original file, which is run through a process called *weaving* to produce the description and code in a form ready for typesetting (usually by LaTeX, but other target formats such as HTML can be used by some LP tools).

Quite a few LP systems exist out there. Many are designed for a particular programming language. There are also a few language-independent LP systems. You are already familiar with some of the syntax of one, the noweb system, created by Norman Ramsey. Some Perl programmers use POD as a form of LP, intermixing sections of POD-formatted description within the source code. Personally, I feel that POD is much better suited to documenting the interface of a program than documenting the source code itself. Thus, in this section we will consider the noweb system of LP.

Back in chapter 3 (and again in chapter 5), we used a simple little syntax to name and define chunks of code. That syntax comes from noweb, though we did not use the complete noweb syntax. This syntax allowed us to break our programs up into manageable little units that we could discuss in any order we wished, independent of the order in which the particular lines of code had to be assembled back into the main program (i.e., the root chunk).

The actual syntax to define a chunk of code in noweb begins with double angle brackets enclosing a chunk name, immediately followed by an equals sign (and nothing else on that line). A chunk of documentation is begun with a single @ symbol at the left margin, followed by a space or a newline. A chunk is terminated when a new chunk begins or the end of the file is encountered.

```
@
This is a documentation chunk in which we would explain why the
following code assigns the answer to the universe (42) to the
variable $foo then does other stuff and finally prints out what $foo
divided by 2 is:
<<chunk>>=
my $foo = 42;
<<some other chunk>>
print "$foo / 2 is $bar\n";
@
This is another documentation chunk, in which we would explain the
significance of dividing $foo by 2 if doing so had any significance,
which, of course, it doesn't.
<<some other chunk>>=
my $bar = $foo / 2;
@
```

Now, if the above were to represent a complete (albeit useless) program, saved in a file named *useless.nw,* then running the tangler—in noweb, the tangler is called notangle—on that source as: notangle -Rchunk useless.nw would produce the following output:

```
my $foo = 42;
my $bar = $foo / 2;
print "$foo / 2 is $bar\n";
```

Had the placement of the two chunks been reversed, the tangled output would have been the same. The chunk given on the command line is found and printed, and any referenced chunks are replaced with their definitions. This means you can begin designing your program using high level concepts as chunk names, then design and define each of the chunks in the order that makes the most sense to you—much as we did for the faqgrep and primes programs in chapters 3 and 5 respectively.

A particular chunk definition may also be continued (i.e., not fully specified in one place) by simply using the same chunk name when starting another chunk definition. Continued chunks must occur in the order they are to appear in the final tangled code—notangle simply concatenates all continued chunks together to produce a single chunk:

```
Documentation stuff...
<<chunk>>=
my $foo = 42;
<<another chunk>>
@
More documentation...
<<another chunk>>=
my $bar = $foo / 2;
```

```
@
Yet more documentation..., then we continue defining the original chunk:
<<chunk>>=
print "$foo / 2 is $bar\n";
@
```

Tangling the above version produces the same output as the previous example. All the continued component chunks of chunk are concatenated together and then the chunk is printed. Any embedded chunks are replaced with their definitions in the same manner.

The -R option told notangle which code chunk to use as the root chunk. A root chunk represents a complete program or module or something you want to tangle out into its own file. A given noweb source file might hold more than one root chunk. For example, you may write a library module that defines several functions. You can write such a module as a literate source file. You can also include in the same file the source code for a program whose purpose is to test each of the functions to ensure they are all working. In this way, you could even have each chunk of testing code follow the chunk (or chunks) of module code that it tests, thus keeping related code close together in the literate source file. Then you could tangle out either the module code or the test code or both.

Of course, we may still make errors in our code and Perl will print error messages to the screen, noting the file name and line number where it found the error (or at least where Perl thinks the error might be). The problem is that we've gone to all the trouble of writing our source code in chunks in a file separate from the tangled program that we actually run. Hence, the line numbers and file name will not be correct. Well, this is not really a problem. Many language compilers or interpreters understand special directives that do nothing except tell the compiler what file it is reading and what line number it is on in that file. These are useful for lying to the compiler about what it is reading. We can use them to tell the compiler where the corresponding code is located in the *useles.nw* file. When an error is encountered, the error messages will point to the corresponding code.

In Perl, a line directive takes the form of a special comment that looks like #line 13 "file" by itself on a line. Actually, it will recognize directives matching the pattern

```
/^#\s*line\s+(\d+)\s*(\s"([^"]*)")?/
```

In that pattern, the $1 variable would hold the line number and the $3 variable would hold the file name. The file name is optional. If the file name is not included, Perl uses whatever it currently thinks is the file name.

The tangler in noweb can be given a -L option and it will emit line directives into the tangled code referring to positions in the original *.nw* source file. Using the above *useless.nw* file as an example, a call to

```
notangle -Rchunk -L useless.nw > xxx
```

would produce the following output in a file named *xxx*:

```
#line 3 "useless.nw"
my $foo = 42;
#line 11 "useless.nw"
my $bar = $foo / 2;
#line 5 "useless.nw"
print "$foo / 2 is $bar\n";
```

That is, with the -L option in effect, a line directive is emitted whenever it enters or returns from a code chunk. Now, if there was an error, such as my $bar = foo / 2; (where the $ symbol on $foo is missing), then running the resulting tangled code as perl -w *xxx* would produce the following errors:

```
Unquoted string "foo" may clash with future reserved word at
useless.nw line 11.
Argument "foo" isn't numeric in divide at useless.nw line 11.
```

So we could proceed directly to our original noweb source file to find the problem. We only use the tangled code to run the program. We write, debug, revise, and maintain the literate source.

If that were all noweb (and other LP systems) allowed you to do, it would still be beneficial. The original *.nw* source file would be your program's documentation. However, there is another side of the LP system—"weaving." The noweb system can weave your source file to produce LaTeX or HTML documentation for formatting and viewing. This means you can write the documentation chunks using whatever capabilities the target formatter allows such as: typeset mathematical formulas, diagrams, lists, cross-references, and indexes. Both the LaTeX and HTML backends perform additional formatting and cross-referencing of your actual code chunks, and any identifiers you specify, through the use of command line options to the noweave part of the system.

When you end a code chunk, you may use a special directive to specify a list of identifiers—variables, filehandles, subroutine names, etc.—considered "defined" in that chunk. In the woven version, such identifiers will be cross-referenced and an index can be produced listing all defined identifiers, the chunks where they were defined, and all the chunks that used that identifier. Chunks themselves will also be cross-referenced and indexed for easy reference purposes. You may specify such

identifiers by following the @ symbol that ends the code chunk with a space and the
%def directive, followed by a space-separated list of identifiers on the same line:

```
In a documentation chunk. Here is a code chunk which
includes identifier definitions marked at the end of
the chunk:
<<chunk>>=
my $foo = 42;
my $bar = 13;
@ %def $foo $bar
Now in another documentation chunk...
```

Unfortunately, because this book is not being typeset using LaTeX and the
noweb system, it is not possible to show you here exactly what the typeset documentation actually looks like. However, I have created noweb source files for a more
sophisticated version of the faqgrep program (shown in chapter 13) and the simple
tangler program to be shown later in this chapter. These will be available at *http://
www.manning.com/Johnson/*, where you will find a link to additional online resources
for the book, including source code and PostScript, and Portable Document Format
(PDF) versions of the typeset documentation for the two programs mentioned.

9.2.1 Other uses of LP

One good use of an LP style of programming is the presentation of source code for
teaching purposes, which is exactly why I have used a form of LP when presenting
many of the programs you have encountered thus far in this book.

A couple of related uses arise from the fact that a single literate source file may
contain the source code for more than one program, each with its own root chunk
further elaborated. Of what possible use is this? Consider that you are writing a
program or module with many small components (chunks). You may also wish to
write a comprehensive test program that verifies that each component works correctly. Using LP, you can create two root chunks—one for the program or module,
and one for the test suite—then develop each component of the program, followed by its related testing component. In this way, test code remains close to the
code it is intended to test, and the documentation can deal with issues at the same
time. If a component needs to be fixed or modified, the appropriate test code is
easily adjusted at the same time.

This idea applies to test data as well: you may keep chunks of code that deal
with particular kinds of data next to chunks of data designed for testing that particular chunk of code.

Similarly, a program may read an external configuration file or a file describing a set of parsing rules. As above, the program and the external configuration or
parsing data can be written in the same source file in a parallel fashion.

None of this implies that literate code need be contained in a single file (though our tangling script given below in section 9.3.1 does only operate on one file at time). You are free to use multiple files to create your literate source code for a system. The multiple files do not need to match up with the multiple files ultimately produced by the tangling process. Instead, you might choose to break your literate sources into files along chapter or section boundaries or whatever works best for presenting the source code in a logical fashion. Like Perl, LP is about giving you more freedom and flexibility in how you approach both code design and documentation.

9.3 Tangling code

The following section presents a simple tangle-like program that will work with the noweb syntax we've just described. We call the presentation only partially literate because it lacks all the formatting and cross-referencing that would be available in the real typeset version. (When the literate program is typeset—using noweb and LaTeX—such cross reference material is automatically added.) We will include a few identifier definition markers so you can see what they look like. Remember, the full plain text source and typeset versions of the following program are available for download at *http://www.manning.com/Johnson/*. The following program will allow you to try out writing literate source code without fetching and installing the actual noweb system. It will also serve to tie together many of the things you've learned in the previous chapters, and introduce a couple of new functions you haven't seen yet.

9.3.1 A simple tangler

Now that we know what the chunk definition and the reference syntax are, we can build a limited tangler program to allow us to write our Perl programs using noweb's syntax, intermixing code chunks and documentation chunks (we are in a documentation chunk right now) throughout the source file.

We want our tangler to operate similarly to notangle, allowing a -R option to specify the root chunk and a -L option to include line directives. We add two differences. The notangle program simply prints the tangled code to STDOUT so you have to redirect it to a file yourself. We assume that the root chunk name is also the file name you want to use for the tangled code. So, running our tangler program with a root option of -Rblah creates a file named *blah* and writes the tangled code to it. The second difference is that, if no -R option is given, our program will automatically find all root chunks and print them to their respective files based on their chunk names. A root chunk is any chunk not used inside another chunk definition.

We call our tangler pqtangle for Perl Quick Tangler and write it in a file named *pqtangle.nw*. Our initial program outline (i.e., our root chunk) looks like

```
<<pqtangle>>=
#!/usr/bin/perl -w
use strict;
<<declare variables>>
<<get options>>
<<open and parse file for chunks>>
<<make array of root chunks>>
<<print root chunks>>
<<subroutine definitions>>
@
```

We need variables to reflect the two options our program can accept—the -R and -L options, for a root chunk and to turn on line directives, respectively:

```
<<declare variables>>=
my $Root;    # root option
my $Line_dir; # format option
@ %def $Root $Line_dir
```

We've used the %def syntax on the chunk-ending line to mark these two variables as defined in this chunk. These def lines are ignored by the tangler, but we have to recognize them if we want to recognize general noweb syntax. Also, we may as well use them so that we can weave our documentation—if you obtain noweb—and have cross-referenced information available. We will consider other variables shortly.

A simple technique exists for extracting options and their potential arguments from the command line arguments. Recall that all command line arguments are in the @ARGV array when the program runs. We can simply use a while loop to pull the first item out of this array if it starts with a dash, then test that the option is valid—in this case, whether the option begins with either -R or -L—and set our option variables appropriately: for the root option, we simply capture everything following the -R into the $1 variable and assign it to the $Root variable; for the line directive, we assign a generic string to the variable containing placeholders for the line number, file name, and newline that we will substitute in as needed during the program:

```
<<get options>>=
while ($ARGV[0] =~ m/^-/) {
    $_ = shift @ARGV;
    last                        if m/^--$/;
    $Root    = $1               if m/^-R(.*)/;
    $Line_dir = '#line %L "%F"%N' if m/^-L/;
}
@
```

The convention for command line options is that they must all come before any other arguments and that anything after a -- argument is not to be treated as an option. This allows you to pass other arguments that start with a dash but are not options.

We need a few more variables declared at the file scope to allow us to store bits of information relating to the chunks we find. We need an array to hold the list of all the root chunks we find, a hash to mark the chunks used in other chunks, and a hash of arrays to store file and line number information where each chunk starts in the source file:

```
<<declare variables>>=
my (@roots, %used, %chunks, $file);
@
```

The next thing we need to do is open the source file and parse it for chunks. In other words, we need to read through the source file and identify chunks according to the rules of what a chunk looks like. As we parse, we record information about each chunk we find:

```
<<open and parse file for chunks>>=
<<open the source file>>
while ( <FILE> ) {
    <<find and parse chunks>>
}
@
```

This is a simple tangling program. We only allow one source file to be specified on the command line. Now that we have already pulled out any options from @ARGV, we can simply test this array to make sure there is still at least one more item (the file name) in it , store that value in our $file variable, and open the file:

```
<<open the source file>>=
unless (@ARGV) {die "no file given for processing\n"}
$file = $ARGV[0];
open(FILE,$file)||die "can't open $file $!";
@
```

We declare two additional lexical variables to be used during our parsing loop on the file, one to hold each line in turn and one to hold the current line number. (Actually, the latter lexical variable will hold the current line number plus 1 so that, if we find a chunk definition, the line number points to the first line of code immediately following the chunk tag.)

```
<<find and parse chunks>>=
my $line = $_;
my $line_no = $. + 1;
if ($line =~ m/^<<([^>]+)>>=\s*$/) {
    <<parse chunk>>
}
@ %def $line $line_no
```

The regular expression above finds lines that match the chunk definition tag and captures the chunk name into the $1 variable. This expression assumes that a > will not be part of the chunk name and that no chunk name will be entirely empty.

The first thing we do when parsing a chunk itself is record the position in the file where the chunk begins. We do this using the tell() function. This function returns the current *byte offset* into the file represented by the file handle. Later we can use this value to seek() directly to this position in the file when we actually tangle out the code. Then we can continue looping through the chunk—as long as the current line does not match either a single @ or one followed by a %def list of identifiers. Inside this loop, we grab the next line of the file, and see if it contains a reference to another chunk. If it does, we use that chunk name as a key in our %used hash and add one to its value. This hash will thus be a record of every chunk that was used inside of another chunk:

```
<<parse chunk>>=
my $begin_offset = tell FILE;
while (($line !~ m/^(\@\s*$|\@\s*\%def)/)) {
    $line = <FILE>;
    $used{$1} += 1 if $line =~ m/^\s*<<([^>]+)>>\s*$/;
}
push @{$chunks{$1}}, "$begin_offset:$file:$line_no";
@
```

When we finished reading through the chunk, we used the autovivification syntax to push a string containing the byte offset, file name, and line number information of the chunk we just parsed. In other words, the %chunks hash contains keys that are chunk names and keys values hold an array of offset/information strings for every location where that chunk's definition is continued throughout the file. The $1 variable here is the one matched in the outer if statement. The one matched inside the inner while loop was localized to that block which is now out of scope.

At this point, we know the byte offset location where every chunk definition starts in the file and the line number of the first code line in that chunk definition. We also have a record of every chunk used in another chunk and, hence, every chunk that cannot be a root chunk. We now populate our @roots array with the root chunks we need to extract. If we were given the -R option, we will only store that one root chunk name in this array. If that option was not given, we will want to extract all the root chunks. We can do this by looping through the keys of the %chunks hash since the keys are all the chunk definitions encountered and pushing them onto the @roots array if they were not used (i.e., if they are not seen in the %used hash):

```
<<make array of root chunks>>=
if ($Root) {
    @roots = ($Root);
```

```
} else {
    foreach my $key (keys %chunks) {
        push @roots, $key if not $used{$key};
    }
}
@
```

Printing out the root chunks is simply a matter of opening a file for writing for each root chunk name and printing out the tangled version of that chunk. We do this using a function called `print_chunk()`:

```
<<print root chunks>>=
foreach my $root (@roots) {
    open(PROGRAM, ">$root") || die "can't open $root: $!";
    print_chunk($root,'');
}
close PROGRAM;
@
```

The `print_chunk()` subroutine takes two arguments, the name of the chunk to print and a string representing the current indentation level (which is empty for the beginning of root chunks). We will discuss this indentation argument shortly.

Now we can start defining our chunk of subroutine definitions, which at the moment has only one:

```
<<subroutine definitions>>=
<<sub print_chunk>>
@
```

The subroutine for printing the chunk begins by assigning the two arguments to lexical variables. This function will be called recursively to print out any chunks contained within the current chunk being printed. For this reason, we need to ensure that the current chunk name is actually defined in the %chunks hash. There may have been, for instance, a typo in the name of an embedded chunk reference. Then we may print the chunk:

```
<<sub print_chunk>>= sub print_chunk {
    my ($chunk,$whitespace) = @_;
    <<make sure chunk is defined>>
    <<print the chunk>>
}
@
```

Testing whether the current chunk is defined is a simple matter of checking its name in the %chunks hash. If we do not find it, we issue a warning and return from the function. We should probably use die() here, but by using a warning we can continue and perhaps find other such errors that the user can fix all at once.

```
<<make sure chunk is defined>>=
unless (exists $chunks{$chunk}) {
    warn "undefined chunk name: <<$chunk>>\n";
    return;
}
@
```

Printing out the chunk is a fairly complex task. We need to break this down into more manageable units before proceeding. First, we assign the list of chunk information strings—that is, offsets and line numbers for chunk definitions—into a lexical array variable. Then we seek to the position in the file where the chunk begins, set a shebang line *flag* (we will discuss this shortly), set up and print the line directive if necessary, and tangle out (print) the current chunk:

```
<<print the chunk>>=
my @locations = @{$chunks{$chunk}};
foreach my $item (@locations) {
    <<get location info and seek to offset>>
    <<set flag for shebang line>>
    <<set and print line directive>>
    <<tangle out current chunk>>
}
@
```

Remember that each chunk was assigned a list of strings, each of which was a colon-separated list containing the offset into the file, the file name itself, and the line number. We split such a string at the colons into three lexical variables and then seek() to the offset in the file where the chunk definition begins (or is continued). The seek() function takes three arguments: a file handle to seek on, a byte offset position, and a third argument that tells seek to move to the position relative to a certain point. (0 means "move directly to that position," 1 means "move that many bytes forward from the current position," and 2 means "move to byte position given relative to the end of the file"—in which case it usually only makes sense to use a negative byte offset.) We use only the 0 flag for the third argument. The seek() function returns 1 if successful and 0 if it failed, so we can test it and die() just as we do for a call to the open() function:

```
<<get location info and seek to offset>>=
my ($offset, $filename, $line_number) = split /:/,$item;
seek(FILE, $offset,0) || die "seek failed on $filename: $!";
my $line=<FILE>;
@
```

In a Perl program, you often use a shebang line as the first line in the program. This line must be the first line in the file so we don't want a line directive emitted before this line. Instead, we would like to emit a line directive immediately following the shebang line and pointing to the next line in the code chunk. Here we merely test if the current code line is a shebang line and set a flag if it is:

```
<<set flag for shebang line>>=
my $shebang_special = 0;
$shebang_special = 1 if $line =~ m/^#!/;
@
```

At this point, we need to create a formatted line directive, substituting the correct information for the placeholders we used in the $Line_dir variable. We format this line directive in a separate function. Then we need to print out this line directive, but only if the current line is not a shebang line, or an embedded chunk reference. In those cases, we would want to print a line directive when processing that chunk.) We use a simple set of logical ORs that terminates at the first true expression, and thus only prints out the line directive when needed:

```
<<set and print line directive>>=
my $line_dir;
if ($Line_dir) {
    $line_dir = make_line_dir($line_number,$filename);
    $line =~ m/^\s*<<.*?>>\s*$/ ||
            $shebang_special   ||
            print PROGRAM  "$line_dir";
}
@
```

Since we have just used the make_line_dir() function, we should go ahead and define it here. This example also illustrates the point about being able to write our literate source in the order that makes sense for discussion. First, let's add to the subroutine definitions chunk:

```
<<subroutine definitions>>=
<<sub make_line_dir>>
@
```

Now the function to format our line directive is a simple set of substitution operations. The function is passed parameters for the current line number and the file name, which we immediately assign to lexical variables. We then declare a new lexical $line_dir variable and assign it the value of our file-scoped $Line_dir variable, which holds the line directive string with placeholders. Finally, we simply replace the placeholders with their proper values and return the value of the $line_dir variable:

```
<<sub make_line_dir>>=
sub make_line_dir {
```

```
        my ($line_no,$file) = @_;
        my $line_dir = $Line_dir;
        $line_dir =~ s/\%L/$line_no/;
        $line_dir =~ s/\%F/$file/;
        $line_dir =~ s/\%\%/%/;
        $line_dir =~ s/\%N/\n/;
        return $line_dir;
    }
@
```

In order to tangle out our chunk, we use a loop similar to that used when parsing the chunks in the first place. That is, we continually loop as long as the current
line does not match a chunk terminating line. We must make sure we read in
another line in both blocks of the `if/else` statement or we would be looping forever on the same line. Inside the loop, the current line might be an embedded
chunk reference, in which case we need to tangle out that embedded chunk. Note,
we are capturing the leading whitespace if there is an embedded chunk reference, as
well as the chunk name—this way we can call the `print_chunk()` routine and pass
it a string representing the current indentation level so our tangled code has the
appropriate indentation. If the line does not contain a chunk reference, we will print
the code line (and print out a line directive following it if it was a shebang line):

```
<<tangle out current chunk>>=
while ($line !~ m/^(\@\s*$|\@\s\%def)/) {
    if ($line =~ m/^(\s*?)<<([^>]+)>>\s*$/) {
        <<tangle out embedded chunk>>
    } else {
        <<print out line>>
        <<take care of shebang line>>
    }
}
@
```

To tangle out an embedded chunk, we first get the current offset into the file
and calculate our new indentation level. Then we make a recursive call to the
`print_chunk()` function to deal with the embedded chunk. Following that, we
reset our indentation to its previous value, `seek()` back to where we left the file,
and read in a new line from the file. We also have to print a new line directive indicating our position in the file again:

```
<<tangle out embedded chunk>>=
my $offset = tell FILE;
my $addedspace = $1;
$whitespace = $addedspace.$whitespace;
&print_chunk($2,$whitespace);
$whitespace = substr($whitespace,length($addedspace));
seek(FILE,$offset,0) || die "can't seek on $filename: $!";
```

```
$line_number += 1;
$line = <FILE>;
<<add returning line directive>>
@
```

We need to add a new line directive to indicate that we have returned back to the position in the current chunk. We need only do this if the current line is not another chunk reference:

```
<<add returning line directive>>=
if ($Line_dir) {
    $line_dir = make_line_dir($line_number,$filename);
    print PROGRAM $line_dir if $line !~ /^\s*<<.*?>>\s*$/;
}
@
```

If the current line is not a chunk reference, we simply need to print it out with the correct amount of leading whitespace, read in another line from the file, and increment our line number counter.

```
<<print out line>>=
print PROGRAM $whitespace,$line;
$line = <FILE>;
$line_number += 1;
@
```

Finally, if the current line is a shebang line, we want to add a line directive directly after it and reset the shebang flag to 0:

```
<<take care of shebang line>>=
if ($Line_dir && $shebang_special) {
    $line_dir = make_line_dir($line_number,$filename);
    print PROGRAM "$line_dir" if $line !~ m/^\s*<<[^>]+>>\s*$/;
    $shebang_special = 0;
}
@
```

That concludes the `pqtangle` program. The whole program is about ninety-five lines of code and won't be listed here. Of course, you already have enough experience reading the chunk syntax to assemble it yourself from the literate listing above. If you do not wish to enter the code manually, the tangled script is available at *http://www.manning.com/Johnson/*.

9.4 *Further resources*

A complete description of POD can be found in the *perlpod* pod-page. Some additional information is located near the end of the *perlsyn* pod-page. You can also read about the various included translator utilities—included at least in the standard source distribution—such as pod2man, pod2html, pod2text, and pod2latex by using the `perldoc` utility to read their respective pod-pages.

Further information on LP can found here:

- *http://www.cs.virginia.edu/~nr/noweb*
  The `noweb` homepage contains information about the system, links to download the package, additional tools and filters for use with the system, and some examples.

- *http://shelob.ce.ttu.edu/daves/faq.html*
  The LP FAQ is available here and contains discussions of LP as well as a reference list of various LP programming tools.

In addition, the following two articles contain introductions to the `noweb` system of literate programming.

- Johnson, Andrew L. and Johnson, Brad C. "Literate Programming using Noweb." *Linux Journal* 42 (Oct 1997).

- Norman Ramsey. "Literate Programming Simplified." *IEEE Software* 11(5):97–105 (Sept. 1994).

Practical elements

C H A P T E R   1 0

Regular expressions

Regular expressions (singular regex or plural regexen) are a powerful device for general text processing. Perl's particular brand of regular expression language is more powerful and rich in features than almost any other flavor of regular expression. Unfortunately, this additional power comes with a price of additional complexity. In this chapter, we will examine Perl's regular expression language in some detail, starting with just the basics and moving on to discuss most of the features of the regex language in recent versions of Perl. (We won't, however, cover some new features in Perl's version 5.005 that are at an experimental stage.) We will explore the match and substitution operators, as well as a few additional string functions in chapter 11.

10.1   The basic components

Figure 10.1 provides a table of most elements of Perl's regex language that we will consider in this chapter. These are presented here simply for reference purposes and to give you an idea of what's to come. By the end of this chapter, you should have a good idea of what all this funky punctuation actually means. Even then, as with any language, it will take some time and practice before these elements become familiar. (For a full look at Perl's regular expressions, see the *perlre* pod-page).

Quantifiers		Grouping
`* + ? {n} {min,} {min, max}`		`(...)`
`*? +? ?? {n}? {min,}? {min,max}?`		`(?...)`

Character Class	Anchors	Alternation
`[...]`	`^ $ \A \Z \G \b \B`	<code>|</code>
`[^...]`		

Double Quote Sequences		Lookahead Lookbehind
`\b \t \n \r \f \a \e \num \xnum \cchar`		`(?!...)`
		`(?=...)`
`\L \l \U \u \Q \E`		`(?<!...)`
		`(?<=...)`

Backreferences	Class Sequences	Dot
`\1, \2, \3 ...`	`\s \w \d \S \W \D`	`.`

Figure 10.1   Perl's regular expression elements

We took a limited look at using regular expressions and Perl's pattern matching and substitution operators back in chapter 6. In this chapter, we will start afresh and present most of the regular expression language elements available in recent versions of Perl. To begin with, we will consider five simple concepts that we are already familiar with from chapter 6 and then use these to demonstrate how pattern matching works. Then we'll go on to consider the more sophisticated regex elements.

The five simple concepts we need to begin with are:

1. Concatenation: This is an implicit concept that simply allows us to combine two or more simple patterns into a larger pattern. For example, `m/f/` is a simple pattern, and `m/o/` is a simple pattern; the pattern `m/foo/` is a concatenation of three simple patterns to form a larger pattern.

2. Alternation: The meta-character (`|`) is the alternation operator that allows us to specify a choice among two or more patterns. For example, `m/foo|bar/` will match if it finds `foo` or `bar` starting at any position in the target string.

3. Grouping: Parentheses provide a grouping mechanism that allows us to create subpatterns that can be treated as a unit. The pattern `m/f(u|oo)bar` is a concatenation of the elements `f`, `(u|oo)`, and `bar`. The parentheses also provide a limiting scope for the alternation operator. Parentheses are also used to capture matched substrings into the special `$1, $2, $3 ...` variables as explained in chapter 6 (we will present a special form of grouping parentheses that do not capture matched text in section 10.6).

4. Iteration: The star operator (`*`) is an iterative or repetitive construct that matches zero-or-more of the previous pattern element, if it is a single character or a subexpression delimited by parentheses. For example, `m/fo*/` will match an `f` followed zero-or-more `o` characters. The pattern `m/(foo)*/` will match zero-or-more strings of `foo`. When I say zero-or-more, the behavior is to match as many as possible while letting the remainder of the regex match.

5. Dot: The dot (`.`) is a wildcard operator that will match any single character except a newline character. (This operator can be modified with the `/s` modifier, as we will see in the next chapter.) Thus, the pattern `m/f.o/` will match an `f` followed by any character followed by an `o`.

Using just these five constructs, we can create patterns of surprising utility and complexity. In fact, many of the other regex constructs are shorthands (and possibly optimizations) for patterns you can create with these simple constructs.

To get the most out of regular expressions, one requires an understanding of the kinds of things that go on during a pattern match. For the next few pages, we will construct simple patterns using the elements above to step through the processes of matching a pattern. The explanation here does not describe the underlying machinery that actually performs the match but, instead, provides a description of how that machinery walks through a string to find a match.

To begin with, we will look at what happens during a match of m/foo/ against the string fofoo. Although, in actuality, when a literal string is the pattern, an optimized search can be performed, here we will describe it here as a regular expression search.

Figure 10.2 shows a graphical depiction of the steps required for our simple pattern. At each step, the target string is above the regular expression. At step 1, the regex is lined up below the beginning of the target string with a pointer representing the current position in both the regex and the target string. The first regex component is checked against the first position in the string. A match is found so the pointer moves ahead one position. The second position also matches the second regex component, and the pointer moves ahead again. Now the third regex component fails to match at the current position in the string. The pointer is returned to the beginning of the regex, and the whole regex is bumped ahead one position in the string (step 4), and the process repeats. The regex immediately fails and is bumped ahead again (step 5). Finally, the first component of the regex matches the current position so the pointer moves ahead again. The second and third components match in turn, and the pointer arrives at the end of the regex indicating a successful match.

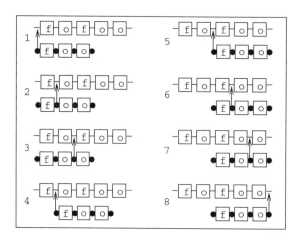

Figure 10.2 Stepping through a simple pattern match

This all seems relatively straightforward perhaps—and a long way to describe a simple match sequence that we could have performed in our head at a glance— but looking at these little steps will help us later when constructing more complex regular expressions.

Let's consider a slightly more complex pattern: m/f(u|oo)bar/ on the string foobar. We will only consider the grouping and alternation aspects here, not the capturing behavior. Again, we can easily see the match right away, but Perl will have to tackle the operation in simple steps once again. Figure 10.3 represents the steps taken in searching for this pattern. Here I have placed the second alternative below the first with connecting lines to show where it belongs in the regex sequence (if it is needed). The process begins as before. The first component matches at the first position in the target string, so the pointer moves ahead one position. Now the second component fails at the current position. The underlying search machinery sees that it has an alternative component to try here so it tries again with the second alternative in place. Now the two sub-components of the second regex element match in turn, as do the remaining components, and the pointer progresses to the end of the regex indicating success again.

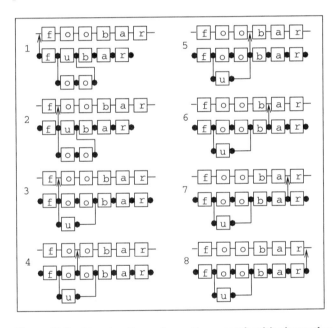

Figure 10.3   Stepping through a pattern match with alternation

Finally, let's consider a simple case that utilizes the star (repetition) and the dot (wildcard) elements. Here we will use a pattern of m/f.*bar/ against the target string afoobar. Figure 10.4 represents the steps taken in this matching process.

Here we see the failure at step 1. The regex bumps ahead to position 2 in the string. The first component matches here so the pointer moves ahead. Now, the dot can match anything, and the star says to match zero-or-more, so this component stretches right to the end of the string (step 4) leaving markers (i.e., the stars

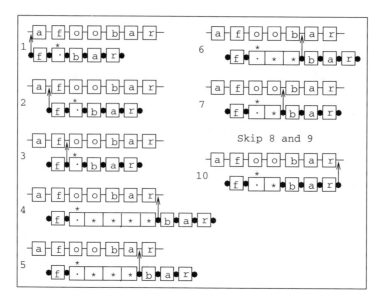

Figure 10.4   Stepping through pattern match with iteration

inside the boxes within this component) at each position . Now, the regex realizes it cannot match the next regex component because it is at the end of the string. So it returns to the second component, .*, backs up one marker, and tries the third component once again (step 5). This backstepping (backtracking) continues until step 7 when the third component does match. After this, the remaining components match in turn (steps 8 and 9, not shown) until we reach the end of the regex and have a successful overall match.

This might seem like an odd way for the star operator to work, grabbing as much as it can, then releasing one step at a time and testing the remaining components. This is what is commonly referred to as a "greedy" or "maximal" matching quantifier. In section 10.4, we will introduce a non-greedy equivalent that first tries taking zero positions in the string and tests if the rest of the regex matches. If that fails, it takes one position from the string and tests the remaining regex components and so on until the match either succeeds or fails overall.

Now that we have a sense of the process of matching, we can begin to introduce the remaining regular expression elements shown in figure 10.1.

10.2   The character class

Another common feature of Perl's regex language is the character class. In simple terms, a character class is just an easy way of providing a list of characters from which to choose a match for a given position in the string. A character class consists of a set of square brackets enclosing the list of character choices. For example, the pattern m/f[uo]bar/ would match either fubar or fobar, but not fuobar or fbar. Think of this pattern as equivalent in meaning to m/f(u|o)bar/. In reality, a character class is optimized and generally much more efficient than an alternation sequence. So, while the above two patterns mean the same thing in terms of what gets matched, the character class version will run more quickly.

You can specify a range of characters within a character class by using a dash between two characters. The character class [a-f] will match one lower case letter from a to f inclusive. If you want to include a dash (as a character not an operator) within a character class, you should place it first or last in the class: [a-z-] matches one character that is either a lower case letter or a dash.

A useful variation of the character class is the negated character class, which matches one character not in the list of characters in the class. To create a negative character class, you use the ^ character as the first character within the class: [^a-z] will match one character that is not a lower case letter. If you place the ^ anywhere but at the beginning of the character class, it is not special and simply becomes one of the characters in the list that may be matched.

10.2.1 Search and replace: capitalize headings

So far we've been using examples that make it easy to demonstrate a point but are somewhat removed from real world use. Here we will look an example that addresses more typical usage of regular expressions—searching and replacing text in a file.

Let's say we have written or been given a lengthy file containing the source for a lengthy HTML document. The author of this document only capitalized the first word in each heading, and the boss wants us to edit the file so that every word in a heading is capitalized. A typical heading appears as

```
<H1> A typical heading </H1>
```

Luckily, in this case, the headings are all short and every heading (and its beginning and end tags) are located on individual lines in the file (we will consider cases of matching across multiple lines later in this chapter). The headings used in the document come in three levels marked by tags of <H1>, <H2>, and <H3>, although the author sometimes used lowercase (<h2>) versions of the tags.

We want to find every line containing a heading and capitalize each word within the heading. Before we do this, we need to review some of the special escapes that can be used within a double-quoted string. These can also be used in the replacement portion of a substitution operation and will greatly simplify our task. (These are listed in table 10.1 and were presented previously in chapter 4's table 4.1.) The sequence we want in this case is the \u sequence, which uppercases the following letter:

```
print "here \uis an ex\uample"; # prints: here Is an exAmple

my $string = 'foobar';
$string =~ s/(b)/\u$1/;
print $string;                    # prints: fooBar
```

The other thing we need to briefly introduce is the /g modifier, which causes the match or substitution operator to repeatedly search for the pattern throughout the target string. In the case of the substitution operator, it finds every occurrence within the string that matches the given pattern, and it replaces the matching text with whatever is in the replacement portion of the operator:

```
$string = 'foobar baz blob';
$string =~ s/(b)/\u$1/g;
print $string;                    # prints: fooBar Baz BloB
```

Now we can tackle our main problem, capitalizing every word within a heading in the document. A simple way to do this is to search for a line containing an opening heading tag, then find the first letter of each word. Any word will start right after a space character except the first word that might begin right after the opening tag as in <H1>This is the heading</H1>. We already know that the first word is capitalized so we only need worry about the rest. The expression that performs the task is simply

```
s/ ([a-z])/ \u$1/g
```

This says to find a space followed by a lowercase letter—which is captured into the special $1 variable—and replace the matched text with a space, followed by the same letter in uppercase. Let's assume the document is in a file called *article.html*. We can simply rename this file as *article.html.bak* and use the following program to create a new version of *article.html*:

```
#!/usr/bin/perl -w
use strict;
open(INPUT, 'article.html.bak') || die "can't open file: $!";
open(OUTPUT, '>article.html')   || die "can't open file: $!";
while(<INPUT>) {
    if ( m/<[Hh][1-3]>/ ) {
        s/ ([a-z])/ \u$1/g;
    }
    print OUTPUT $_;
}
```

CHAPTER 10   REGULAR EXPRESSIONS

A more general version of this program would simply read a file given on the command line and print the resulting output on standard output so that it could be redirected to another file:

```perl
#!/usr/bin/perl -w
use strict;
while( <> ) {
    if ( m/<[Hh][1-3]>/ ) {
        s/ ([a-z])/ \u$1/g;
    }
    print;
}
```

If you named this program cap_heads, you could run it from the command line like this:

```
perl cap_heads article.html.bak > article.html
```

This way you can use it to modify other such documents without having to edit the program to replace the filenames.

10.2.2   Character class shortcuts

There are three special escape sequences that stand for commonly used character classes. Each of these has a variant to stand for the corresponding negated character class. We saw each of these and some examples of their use in chapter 6. We repeat them here for review:

Table 10.1   Escape sequences for commonly used character classes

Escape sequence	Description
\w	equivalent to: [a-zA-Z0-9_], a word character any letter or digit or an underscore character
\W	equivalent to: [^a-zA-Z0-9_], a non-word character any character that is not a letter, digit, or underscore
\d	equivalent to: [0-9], any single digit
\D	equivalent to: [^0-9], any non-digit character
\s	equivalent to: [\n\f\r\t], a whitespace character a space, newline, formfeed, return, or tab character
\S	equivalent to: [^ \n\f\r\t], a non-whitespace character

10.3   Greedy quantifiers: take what you can get

Another greedy quantifier that operates similarly to the star is the plus (+) quantifier. This one matches one-or-more of the previous components. You can think of m/f(o+)bar/ as being the same as m/f(oo*)bar/, in that matching one-or-more is the same as matching one thing, then zero-or-more of the same thing. The pattern m/fo*bar/ would match against the string fbar, matching and f then zero o characters followed by bar. The pattern m/fo+bar/ would not match against fbar because there isn't at least one o following the f in that string.

The star is an indeterminate quantifier that can match any number of characters. The plus is only slightly determinate in that it must match at least one thing, but could match any number of additional characters. Perl also offers a few other greedy quantifiers with varying degrees of indeterminacy. These are listed in table 10.2 along with their meaning and an example with an equivalent formulation using constructs we already know:

Table 10.2 Greedy quantifiers

Quantifier	Description
?	match zero-or-one time
m/fo?bar/	equivalent to m/f(ol)bar/
{n}	match exactly n times
m/fo{2}bar/	equivalent to m/foobar/
{min,}	match min-or-more times
m/fo{2,}bar/	equivalent to m/foo+bar/
{min, max}	match at least min times, but at most max times
m/fo{2,4}bar/	equivalent to m/f(ooooloooloo)bar/

In the first example above, the equivalent m/f(o|)bar/ might seem strange. All the grouped alternation means is match an o or match nothing. Also, if the ordering of the alternatives in the last example surprised you, remember that these are all greedy quantifiers and will first try to match as much as possible (or as much as they are allowed) before trying lesser amounts.

10.4 Non-greedy quantifiers: take what you need

Often, greedy quantifiers are simply too greedy for your intended purpose. Consider trying to match and capture all the text on a line up to the first occurrence of a15:

```
$line = "one two three a15 four five six a15 seven\n";
$line =~ m/(.*)a15/;
print "$1\n"; # prints: one two three a15 four five six
```

What happened? The star is greedy and matched all the way to the end of the string and then backtracked until an a15 could match. What we need is something that will match as little as possible and then check the rest of the expression to see if it matches yet. All of the greedy quantifiers have a non-greedy form that is simply the quantifier followed by a question mark. A revised version of our example above now using a non-greedy star quantifier would be

```
$line = "one two three a15 four five six a15 seven\n";
$line =~ m/(.*?)a15/;
print "$1\n"; # prints: one two three
```

The `(.*?)` tries to match zero characters followed by an a15, then one character followed by an a15, and so on until it finally matches fourteen characters one two three and succeeds in finding a following a15. The other non-greedy versions of the quantifiers are given in figure 10.1 and operate in a similar manner.

10.5   Simple anchors

An anchor is a form of zero-width assertion. This means it matches not a character, but a position with certain properties. You have already seen two such elements in chapter 6: the ^ (caret) can be used to match at the beginning of a string, and the $ can be used to match the end of a string. Another anchor type regex element that you've already seen is the word-boundary element \b. This matches at a position between a word character (\w) and a non-word character (\W.) or between the beginning or end of a string and a \w character. To get an idea of what it means to match a position rather than a character, let's consider another simple example depicted graphically.

In figure 10.5 we step through running the pattern m/\bfoo\b/ against the strings foo bar and foodbar. At step 1, \b matches at the start of the string (between the start of the string and the f character) in both cases. Because this is a zero-width assertion, the pointer remains pointing at the same position in the target string. In order to show the regex components in the place where they match on the string, we advance the pointer to the next regex component but drop the first component down below the regex. This is simply my way of showing that the \b and the f regex element both are successful at the first position in the string.

The pointer then advances along in the usual manner in each string until we hit the final \b. In the first case, there is again a match because the position between the o and the space is a word-boundary position. Thus the regex succeeds at step 6. In the second string, the position lies between an o and a d, which are both word characters, so the regex fails at this point. (Note: although not shown in the figure,

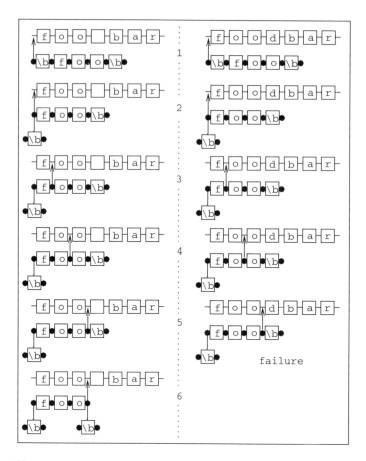

Figure 10.5 Stepping through a pattern match with anchors

the pointer would return to the beginning and the whole regex would repeatedly attempt to match the first component against every position in the string.)

The word-boundary anchor has a complement, the \B anchor, which matches at a position in a string between two word characters or two non-word characters.

When the /m modifier (we will discuss modifiers in the next chapter) is used on a match or substitution operator it means that the ^ and $ anchors can match at the start and end of lines within a multi-line string. The \A and \Z anchors match only the beginning and end of a string respectively, regardless of whether it is a multi-line string or not.

The final simple anchor is the \G anchor, which works in conjunction with the /g modifier and anchors the match to the last position matched in a repeated match operation.

10.6 Grouping, capturing, and backreferences

Until now we have only used plain parentheses for grouping subexpressions. The disadvantage of this technique is that anything matched by the parenthesized subexpression is captured and assigned to a special variable based on the position of the parentheses in the overall expression. This takes extra time and memory for the regex machinery, and, often, you are only interested in grouping a subpattern, not capturing its matching text. A form of parenthesization that will only group an expression is the `(?:subexpression)` form. For example, if you are not interested in capturing the matched text, the earlier example using `m/f(u|oo)bar/` would be better written as `m/f(?:u|oo)bar/`.

When capturing parentheses are used, the captured text is stored in a set of special variables (`$1`, `$2`, `$3` ...) where the digits reflect the order of occurrence of the subexpressions themselves counting from left to right. If the pattern `m/(foo(bar)baz)(xyz)/` did match against a target string, then `$1` would contain the string `foobarbaz`, `$2` would contain the string `bar`, and `$3` would contain the string `xyz`. These variables may be used within the replacement part of a substitution or in statements following a successful pattern match. These special variables are global, but automatically localized within their immediate enclosing block. They will retain their values until either another pattern match successfully matches or the current scope or block is exited. This is useful for extracting particular bits of data from within strings of text. (We saw examples of this sort of thing in chapter 6.)

Using capturing parentheses in a pattern also makes the captured text available later within the same pattern using the `\1`, `\2`, `\3` ... escape sequences. These are called backreferences because they refer back to previously matched text. A simplistic approach to searching a file for double words would be to use a pattern such as `m/\b(\w+)\s+\1\b/i`. This would match something resembling a word followed by one-or-more whitespace characters, followed by whatever word was matched by the capturing parentheses. The `/i` modifier tells the match operator to ignore case so we can catch doubled words that might differ in case. If used on multi-line strings—such as when the special `$/` variable is set to an empty string to read a file by paragraphs instead of line by line—we can still catch double words even if one is at the end of one line and the other is at the beginning of the next line. This is possible because we used the `\s` sequence instead of just a space. Remember that the `\s` sequence represents the character class `[ \n\f\r\t]` so the two words may be separated by one or more of any of those characters. Also note that we placed a word boundary following the backreference. This ensures that the backreferenced text here is not simply the beginning of a larger word such as in the perfectly logical string `This thistle is bristly`.

A program that makes use of this pattern to locate paragraphs containing doubled words and to highlight them somehow can be as simple as

```
#!/usr/bin/perl -w
use strict;
$/ = ";  # read files in paragraph mode
while( <> ) {
    print if s/\b(\w+)(\s+)(\1)\b/*$1*$2*$3*/gi;
}
```

We captured the first occurrence of the word, the intervening whitespace, and the second occurrence of the word into three separate variables so we could replace the text with a few asterisks inserted to make the doubled words stand out. We also used the /g so that we could highlight multiple occurrences of doubled words within a paragraph. Jeffrey Friedl gives a more involved version of this program in his book[1] that allows an intervening tag such as an HTML tag between the doubled words, uses ANSI escapes to highlight the text, and prints out only highlighted lines rather than the whole paragraph. You are encouraged to add similar improvements to the above version of the program.

10.6.1   Prime number regex

Back in chapter 5, we developed a program to list all the prime numbers from 2 to N (where N was a number entered by the user of the program). That program was straightforward and relatively efficient. Here we will show another program to list prime numbers, one that is neither straightforward nor efficient, but nonetheless a marvelous example of something (of what we're just not sure).

If you visit *http://www.dejanews.com* and search the *comp.lang.perl.misc* archives for the terms "Abigail" and "prime," you'll eventually find a rather surprising usage of regular expressions to determine if a given number is prime. Abigail is a frequent poster to the *comp.lang.perl.misc* newsgroup and this example originated (as far as I know) as a clever little one-line program in one of Abigail's sign-off signatures. Since then, it has been commented on within the group on a few occasions and with a few variations, so you are sure to find quite a few articles when you search the archives. The following is an extended version that lists all the primes from 2 to N (where N is an argument to the program):

```
#!/usr/bin/perl -w
use strict;
my $N = shift @ARGV; # get the number
```

---

1 Friedl, Jeffrey. *Mastering Regular Expressions*. Sebastopol, CA: O'Reilly and Associates, 1997.

```
for (my $number = 2; $number <= $N; $number++) {
    my $string = '1' x $number;
    print "$number is prime\n" if $string !~ m/^(11+)\1+$/;
}
```

Saving this program as *reprimes.pl* and running it from the command line produces the following results:

```
[danger:ajohnson:~]$ perl reprimes.pl 20
2 is prime
3 is prime
5 is prime
7 is prime
11 is prime
13 is prime
17 is prime
19 is prime
```

But as I said earlier, this program is not very efficient—especially if you start trying larger values for N. For example, timing this program using a value of 1000 for N took 4.38 seconds compared to our chapter 5 "sieve" program, which took only 0.10 seconds to produce the same list.

Still this program does demonstrate backtracking and backreferences. In fact, all the real work is done using these mechanisms in the regular expression. Let's take a closer look at what the main part of the program is doing. Each time through the loop, we have a new value of $number to be tested for primality. We do this test in two steps:

```
my $string = '1' x $number;
print "$number is prime\n" if $string !~ m/^(11+)\1+$/;
```

First, we create a string of $number characters (any character will do; we use the 1 character here) using the repetition operator (see chapter 4). So if $number is 5, our string is 11111. Then we use the regex against the string to test if it contains a prime number of characters. Let's look just at the regex itself, separated into its main components:

```
^       match the start of the string
(11+)   match 2 or more '1' characters and save in \1
\1+     try to match one or more of whatever we matched in \1
$       match the end of the string
```

The first thing to notice is that the pattern describes an entire string from beginning to end. The parentheses capture two or more characters, and the backreference attempts to match one or more of the same text matched in the parentheses. If this match is successful, it means that the number of characters in the string is evenly divisible by some integer greater than 1 and, hence, is not prime. So we use the negated form of the binding operator !~ to say that the number is prime if it does not match the pattern.

10.7 Other anchors: lookahead and lookbehind

Perl's regex language has two additional, and very powerful, zero-width assertion mechanisms: lookahead assertions (negative and positive) and lookbehind assertions (negative and postive). The lookahead assertions have been available for quite some time, but the lookbehind assertions were introduced only in recent versions of Perl (5.005). The idea is similar to any other anchor—match a given position (not a character) in the string if the assertion is true.

Lookahead and lookbehind assertions come in two forms:

```
(?=subexpression)   positive lookahead
(?!subexpression)   negative lookahead

(?<=subexpression)  positive lookbehind
(?<!subexpression)  negative lookbehind
```

The positive lookahead assertion is true when the subexpression matches from the current position in the string, but, like the other anchors, it does not advance the pointer in the string—it merely tests to see if it would match. Similarly, a negative lookahead is successful when the subexpression does not match from the current position in the string.

```
m/ab(?=c)/;    #matches 'ab' only if followed by c
m/ab(?!c)/;    #matches 'ab' only if not followed by c
m/(?<=f)ab/;   #matches 'ab' only if preceded by an 'f'
m/(?<!f)ab/;   #matches 'ab' only if not preceded by an 'f'
```

Do not confuse the negative examples with a negative character class. If the target string is flab, then m/ab[^c]/ will fail because [^c] must match one character (just not a c). The pattern m/ab(?!c)/ will match against flab, however, because it contains an ab that is not followed by a c. Furthermore, a character class can only match one character from a list, but a lookahead can test any arbitrarily complex expression. Lookbehinds are not quite so powerful. The subexpression in a lookbehind subexpression must be a fixed-width lookbehind. It cannot contain any indeterminate quantifiers. The subexpression must describe a fixed-width substring.

10.7.1 Inserting commas in a number

One frequently asked question is how to insert commas into a number—for example, how to change "123456789" into "123,456,789." This is not quite as easy as it may seem. The FAQs do provide a couple of answers. Before we look at the FAQ solution that uses lookahead assertions, let's consider another example from Jeffrey Friedl's book. In this example, we also introduce the /x modifier, which allows us to write the regex pattern over multiple lines and insert comments. When the /x modifier is used with either a match or substitution operator, all whitespace within the pattern is ignored unless it is escaped with a backslash. Comments begin with the # character and continue to the end of the line:

```
$_ = 123456789;
s/                      # begin substitution operator
    (\d{1,3})           # match and capture one-to-three digits
    (?=                 # if they are followed by:
        (?:\d\d\d)+     # one-or-more groups of three digits
        (?!\d)          # that are not followed by a digit
    )                   # end lookahead assertion
/$1,/gx;                # /g = perform substitution repeatedly
print;     #prints: 123,456,789
```

The /x modifier makes the above expression much more readable than the equivalent s/(\d{1,3})(?=(?:\d\d\d)+(?!\d))/$1,/g. This may require a little while to digest—take your time.

One limitation with the expression above is that the number cannot have a decimal portion: 123456.654321 would get transformed into 123,456.654,321. If you want to insert commas correctly into decimal numbers, you first need to split the number at the decimal before you just commify the first portion and join the two sections again.

I came up with one of the FAQ answers to this problem shortly after reading Jeffrey's book when I needed to create reports out of large sets of simulation data. This version not only handles numbers with decimal portions; it can be used to commify all the numbers in a large block of text in one go. To achieve the results I wanted, I realized I would need something like a lookbehind assertion. At the time, Perl did not have them. Even now, Perl's lookbehind are fixed-width only, so they still will not solve the problem. The next best thing is to reverse the string itself and think about the problem backwards—a technique I call "Poor man's lookbehind." This is simple to do because Perl has a built-in reverse() function that can be used to reverse a string:

```
$_ = '123456.789123 and 3.14159 and $15000.00';
$_ = reverse $_;
# now $_ contains: '00.00051$ dna 95141.3 dna 321987.654321'

s/
    (\d\d\d)    # match 3 digits
    (?=\d)      # if they are followed by a digit
    (?!         # and they are not followed by
```

```
        \d*         # zero-or-more digits
        \.          # followed by a decimal point
    )               # end negative lookahead
/$1,/gx;
$_ = reverse $_;
print $_; # prints: 123,456.789123 and 3.14159 and $15,000.00
```

The way this works is fairly simple. First, let's consider an integer number such as 1234567. If we reverse this string, the number appears as 7654321. In this direction, we want to place commas after every three digits, but only if those three digits are followed by another digit. (How many doesn't matter, just as long as there is a least one additional digit.) A pattern of `s/(\d\d\d)(?=\d)/$1,/g` would first match 765 and then test for a following digit (which exists) and replace 765 with 765,. Because of the `/g` modifier, the regex would continue to try to match the pattern again and would find 432, which is also followed by a digit, and so another comma is inserted. There are no remaining groups of three digits, so the operation is completed, and reversing our number string provides us with the correctly formatted result.

Handling decimal numbers in a reversed string only requires one extra preventive measure. Given a number such as 1234.5678, the reversed form is 8765.4321. We know that any set of digits followed by zero-or-more digits and a decimal point is on the wrong side of the decimal point and should be ignored. All we need to add is another zero-width assertion—a negative lookahead in this case—to ensure that no set of digits on the left side of a decimal point will be matched. Our new pattern is `(\d\d\d)(?=\d)(?!\d*\.)`. Running this as the pattern in our substitution against the reversed number 8765.4321 would first match 876, test for a following digit (which succeeds), and then test again to see that that digit is not followed by zero-or-more digits and a decimal point. It is, and this assertions fails, so the regex moves ahead to try 765, which also fails the negative lookahead. The regex moves ahead until it can match three digits again with 432, which is followed by a digit and is not followed by zero-or-more digits and a decimal point. This succeeds, and a comma is correctly inserted.

The version in some earlier FAQs is in the form of a subroutine and has a slight error that will be noticed only when the subroutine is called in a list context, such as when it is used as an argument for the `print()` function. The correct subroutine version should be:

```
sub commify {
    my $input = shift @_;
    $input = reverse $input;
    $input =~ s<(\d\d\d)(?=\d)(?!\d*\.)><$1,>g;
    return scalar reverse $input;
}
```

10.8 Exercises

1 Will the pattern `m/(.*)(\d\d?)/` match the string `foo12bar`? If so, what will `$1` and `$2` contain? What would change if the pattern were `m/(.*)(\d\d)?bar/`?

2 Write a regex that will match a target string only if it contains only an integer number (all digits). Write one to match if the string is an integer or decimal number. Write one to match if the string is a positive or negative number including numbers in scientific format (i.e., `3e12`). See the *perlfaq4* page if you have difficulty.

C H A P T E R   1 1

Working with text

String manipulation, text processing, data munging—whatever you want to call it, Perl can do it. In chapter 6, we introduced regular expressions, matching, and substitution. In chapter 10, we took a more in-depth look at Perl's regular expression language. In this chapter, we return to the match and substitution operators and describe them and their modifiers in more detail.

While regular expressions are perhaps the heart of Perl's text processing capabilities, there are a few other vital string things in Perl's toolbox. We've seen a few of these already—split(), join(), and reverse(), for example. This chapter will also introduce you to the index() and rindex() functions for finding the position of substrings within strings and the substr() function for changing or extracting substrings within strings. We will also cover the often neglected translation operator tr///, which can be used to substitute, delete, or squash lists of characters within strings.

11.1 The match operator

We have used the match and substitution operators and some of their modifiers in previous examples without giving a full treatment of the modifiers and how these operators behave under scalar and list contexts. This section, and the one that follows, will provide a brief reference style overview of the operators and the modifiers that govern their behavior.

The match and substitution operators have the following single character modifiers in common:

```
i   Case insensitive matching
m   Multi-line mode
s   Single-line mode
x   Extended layout syntax
o   Compile pattern only once
g   Match globally
c   Conserve reset
```

The first four affect how the regular expression is interpreted by the regex engine. The /i modifier tells the regex engine that the pattern is to be treated as case-insensitive:

```
my $a = 'blah foo bar';
my $b = 'blah FOO bar';
my $c = 'blah FoO bar';
foreach my $string ($a,$b,$c) {
    print "$string: Yes to m/foo/\n" if $string =~ m/foo/;
    print "$string: Yes to m/foo/i\n" if $string =~ m/foo/i;
}
__END__
this example prints:
```

```
blah foo bar: Yes to m/foo/
blah foo bar: Yes to m/foo/i
blah FOO bar: Yes to m/foo/i
blah FoO bar: Yes to m/foo/i
```

The /i modifier applies to the entire pattern, and a match operation of m/foo/i is equivalent to m/[fF][oO][oO]/.

The /m modifier tells the regex engine that the string to which it is being applied is to be treated as a multi-lined string—that is, a string with embedded newlines. Normally, the ^ and $ anchors only match at the beginning and end of a string regardless of whether embedded newlines exist in the string. Using /m allows these anchors to match at the beginning and end of embedded newlines as well:

```
my $string = "this is\na string\nwith embedded newlines";
if ( $string =~ m/^a string$/ ) {
    print "No /m, this won't match\n";
}
if ( $string =~ m/a string/m ) {
    print "This matches with /m\n";
}
```

Here we see that with the /m modifier, the pattern is allowed to match the beginning and ends of an embedded "line" within the string. The \A and \Z anchors are unaffected and will still only match at the beginning and ends of the entire string when the /m modifier is in effect. If you are not using these anchors in your pattern, the /m modifier is not needed and should not be used (even if the string is a multi-line string).

The /s modifier puts the string into what's called single line mode and has the effect of allowing the dot (.) to match newlines (which means that dot now matches anything). Often, these last two modifiers are combined as /ms to allow the dot to traverse over embedded newlines and allow the ^ and $ to match at embedded line boundaries. You can see the effects of these modifiers in the following:

```
$_ = "foo\nbar\nbaz";
s/^.*bar$/blah/;       # doesn't match, string unchanged

$_ = "foo\nbar\nbaz";
s/^.*bar$/blah/s;      # doesn't match, string unchanged

$_ = "foo\nbar\nbaz";
s/^.*bar$/blah/m;      # string is now: "foo\nblah\nbaz"

$_ = "foo\nbar\nbaz";
s/^.*bar$/blah/ms;     # string is now: "blah\nbaz"
```

As with the /m modifier, you should use the /s modifier only when using a dot in your pattern and the string has the potential of being a multi-line string.

We saw examples using the /x modifier in the previous chapter, but we didn't explicitly say how the modifier works. This modifier allows us to write a regex across multiple lines and to include comments. It works by ignoring unescaped whitespace unless inside a character class—for example, m/f oo ba r/x is the same as m/foobar/—recognizing the # symbol as a comment marker, and ignoring everything following up to a newline or a match delimiter. This last point means you cannot include a match delimiter in a comment

```
$_='blah';
m/
    blah # comment /
/x;
```

The above causes a syntax error because Perl finds the / in the comment and assumes it is the final match delimiter. Perl then finds another /x;, which, by itself, is not legal syntax. You can avoid such problems by choosing a match delimiter that doesn't conflict with any characters you might use in your comments.

A match or substitution operator does double quotish interpolation of the given pattern, allowing you to use a variable within the pattern. Thus, part of a script that searches an array for lines matching a user-specified pattern might be

```
print "Enter pattern to search for: ";
chomp( my $pattern = <STDIN> );
foreach my $line ( @file ) {
    print $line if $line =~ m/$pattern/;
}
```

However, when a variable is used within a pattern, Perl has to compile the pattern into its own internal format each time it executes the statement because it does not know if the contents of the variable have changed. Sometimes you want this behavior; other times, as in the above example, it is just extra work because the variable never changes while the loop is running. The /o modifier tells Perl that this particular match (or substitution) pattern should be compiled only once and reused each time the expression is executed:

```
print $line if $line =~ m/$pattern/o;
```

If a pattern does not contain a variable, it is compiled only once anyway and the /o modifier does nothing. Do not make the mistake of using /o when the variable does change. Sometimes you want to check each line against a list of patterns as in:

```
while ( <FILE> ) {
    foreach my $pattern (@patterns) {
        print if m/$pattern/;
    }
}
```

If you used the /o modifier here, then Perl would compile the first pattern in the list patterns and reuse it for the duration. You would then not be testing if a line matched any of the other patterns in the list. (See *perlfaq6* for a way to match many regular expressions more efficiently than the above example.)

The /g modifier means "match globally, or repeatedly throughout the string." This operator interacts with the context of the match operation, so we will discuss it in conjunction with an explanation of the match operator's return values in scalar and list context.

11.1.1 *Context of the match operator*

In scalar context, the match operator returns either true or false (a 1 or an empty string respectively in this case) if the match succeeded or failed, respectively. In a list context, if there are no capturing parentheses used in the pattern, the match operator returns the list (1) on success or the empty list () on failure. If capturing parentheses are used in the pattern, the match operator returns the list of captured substrings ($1, $2, ...) on success or the empty list on failure.

When the /g modifier is used in scalar context, the match operator returns true each time it finds the next match and false when it finally fails. It remembers where the last match ended and begins matching from that point the next time it is used:

```
$_ = '12 and 3.14159 and 130.2';
my $match_count = 0;
while ( m/\d+(?:\.\d+)?/g ) {
    $match_count++;
}
print "found $match_count numbers\n";
```

In a list context without capturing parentheses, the m//g operator returns a list of each matched string. When capturing parentheses are used, it returns a list of all the captured substrings throughout the string.

The built-in function pos() returns the position after the current match in a string. The /g modifier sets the current match postion in a string each time the pattern matches and resets it to the beginning of the string on failure:

```
$string = '12 and 3.14159 and 130.2';
while ($string =~ m/(\d+(?:\.\d+)?)/g ) {
    print "$1 ends at: ", pos($string), "\n";
}
```

The /c modifier (useful only in conjunction with /g) prevents this "reset on failure" from occurring. This modifier can be used in combination with the \G anchor, which matches the position where the last match left off, to work your way through a string using several different regular expressions. This example attempts to divide the string into substrings of sets of characters:

```
$_ = 'ja9#HR d+122';
{
    print "$1:\tlc\n"      and redo if m/\G([a-z]+)/gc;
    print "$1:\tuc\n"      and redo if m/\G([A-Z]+)/gc;
    print "$1:\tdigit\n"   and redo if m/\G(\d+)/gc;
    print "$1:\tw-space\n" and redo if m/\G(\s+)/gc;
    print "$1:\tsymbol\n"  and redo if m/\G(\W+)/gc;
    print "$1:\tunknown\n" and redo if m/\G(.)/gc;
}
```

This example makes use of the fact that a bare block is considered a loop with respect to the loop control statements (next, last, and redo; see chapter 5). Without the /c modifier, this block would loop forever because, when any regex failed, the string position would be reset to the beginning. The final "unknown" pattern, which matches any single character except a newline, would always ensure at least one success to redo the block.

11.2 The substitution operator

All of the match operator modifiers discussed above also apply to the substitution operator. However, the return value of the substitution operator is always the number of substitutions performed, regardless of the context, capturing parentheses, or the /g modifier. This is much simpler than the match operator's return value interactions.

In addition to the modifiers mentioned above, the substitution operator can also take a /e modifier. This modifier tells Perl that the replacement side of the operator is to be executed as standard Perl code rather than as a double-quoted string. Consequently, you can make function calls within the replacement using the $1, $2,... variables as arguments:

```
$_ = 'It is 2.7 miles from here to there';
s/(\d+(?:\.\d+)?)\s*miles/miles_to_km($1) . ' kilometers'/e;
print;

sub miles_to_km {
    my $miles = shift;
    my $km = sprintf("%.2f",$miles / 0.6);
    return $km;
}
```

This makes use of the sprintf() function for formatting numbers—in this case formatting a fractional number to a maximum of two decimal places. (See perldoc -f sprintf for all the ways you use this function to format data.)

11.3 Strings within strings

Regular expressions are powerful. Once you become familiar with them, it is easy to see every string manipulation problem as a regular expression problem. But not every problem requires a regex solution. If you just want to test if a given substring (not a pattern) is in a string, then Perl offers the index() function, which has the following form:

```
index TARGET, SUBSTRING, OFFSET
```

The TARGET is the string you want to search; SUBSTRING is the string you are looking for; and the optional OFFSET argument gives a character position in the target string from which to begin searching. This function returns the position in the target string where the first occurrence of substring begins. The beginning of a string is position 0 by default unless the $[variable has been set to something else—generally not a good idea. (See perldoc perlvar for information on $[.) If the substring is not found, then the function returns -1:

```
$target = 'blahfooblah';
print rindex($target, 'foo');      # prints: 4
print index($target, 'blah', 2);   # prints: 7
print index($target, 'oops');      # prints: -1
```

Similarly, the rindex() (reverse index) function can be used to find the position of the last occurrence of a substring. This also returns -1 on failure.

```
$file_path = '/home/ajohnson/devel/sim/simpn2.c';
print rindex($file_path, '/'); # prints: 24
```

By themselves, these functions can be quite useful for testing for the existence of a given substring within a string or, in larger routines, comparing the relative positions of substrings in a string. A third string function, the substr() function, makes these functions even more useful. The substr() function may be used to extract chunks of text from a string (whose position might be obtained from one of the above two functions). This function can also be used to replace or insert a chunk of text into a string. It has the following general form:

```
substr TARGET, OFFSET, LENGTH, REPLACEMENT
```

The REPLACEMENT and LENGTH arguments are optional. This function returns a chunk of text from the TARGET, starting from the position given by the OFFSET argument and extending for LENGTH characters. If the LENGTH is omitted, it returns everything from the OFFSET position to the end of the string. If the REPLACEMENT argument is given, then the TARGET string is actually changed by replacing the specified chunk with the string given by the replacement argument:

```
$target = 'blahfoobar';
print substr($target, 4, 3); # prints: foo
print $target;               # prints: blahfoobar

substr($target, 4, 3, 'something');
print $target;               # prints: blahsomethingbar
```

The `substr()` function may also be assigned instead as an alternative to using the four-argument form:

```
$target = 'blahfoobar';
substr($target, 4, 3) = '-';
print $target;    # prints: blah-bar
```

As you can see in the examples above, neither the replacement argument nor the assigned string needs to be the same size as the chunk of text each replaces—the target string will grow or shrink as needed. To insert a string into a target at a given position without replacing any text, you can just specify a zero-length argument:

```
$target = 'foobar';
substr($target, 3, 0) = 'd';
print $target:    # prints: foodbar
```

Here the zero-length chunk of text is replaced by the assigned string. Using `substr()` along with the two functions above, we can parse a full file pathname into its directory path and its file-name components:

```
# assuming unix style file paths
$file_path = '/home/ajohnson/devel/sim/simpn2.c';
($dir_path, $filename) = fname_parse($file_path);
print join("\n", $dir_path, $filename);

sub fname_parse {
    my $file = shift;
    my ($dir, $pos);
    unless ( ( $pos = rindex($file, '/') ) < 0 ) {
        $dir = substr( $file, 0, $pos + 1, '' );
    }
    $dir ||= './'; # default initial path
    return ($dir, $file);
}
```

Of course, this can be done easily with regular expressions as well:

```
$file_path = '/home/ajohnson/devel/sim/simpn2.c';
($dir_path, $filename) = fname_parse($file_path);
print join("\n", $dir_path, $filename);
```

```perl
sub fname_parse {
    my $fullname = shift;
    my ($dir, $file) = ( $fullname =~ m<^(.*/)?(.*)$> );
    $dir ||= './'; # default initial path
    return ($dir, $file);
}
```

This version is much simpler overall. A quick benchmark shows that the first version is a little faster (around 18%) than the regex version. So unless you were going to be doing a large number of such operations, the simplicity of the regex version probably outweighs any efficiency concerns your program might have.

The substr() function is also commonly used to pick apart fixed column data files—files where each field of data starts in the same column position and is the same width for every line (or record) in the file. (The unpack() function might be a better choice this type of task though.) In the following example, we have some fixed column data with a few missing fields. The data consists of a four-character group designation followed by measurement data with field widths of 2, 3, 3, 2, 3, 2, 2, 2, 2, and 3. We have already identified fields where missing data occurs. Now we simply want to extract only the columns of complete data, which we will print as comma-separated data for use in another program:

```perl
#!/usr/bin/perl -w
use strict;
while (<DATA>){
    chomp;
    my @fields = (substr($_, 0, 4),  substr($_, 4, 2),
                  substr($_, 9, 3),  substr($_, 14, 3),
                  substr($_, 17, 2), substr($_, 21, 2),
                  substr($_, 25, 3)
                 );
    print join(',', @fields);
    print "\n";
    }
__DATA__
120B2212110622116953136322101
220b26   1021911793 3929090
220b29125111 118952934  096
220b181231182811596233630093
140D2611810821112882831  092
140D23   1062011291293833096
```

An interesting thing happens when you take a reference to the substr() function: you do not get a reference to the literal substring itself, but to the given region of the string:

```perl
my $string = 'foobar';
$ref = \substr($string, 1, 4);
print "$$ref\n";                  # prints: ooba
```

CHAPTER 11 WORKING WITH TEXT

```
$string = 'scoolly';
print "$$ref\n";              # prints: cool
```

Here, the reference in $ref is not to the particular substring ooba, but to the four-character slice of $string, starting at position 1 (the second character). So, after we assign a new string to $string, our reference now refers to the four-character slice of this new string.

11.4   Translating characters

Another situation that often arises and seems like a good choice for a substitution operation is translating characters. Assume you want to change all spaces in a string into underscores. One obvious method is to use the substitution operator with the /g modifier:

```
$_ = 'this is a string';
s/ /_/g;
print;              # prints: this_is_a_string
```

The translation operator (tr//) accomplishes the same task:

```
$_ = 'this is a string';
tr/ /_/;
print;              # prints: this_is_a_string
```

The first thing to realize about the tr// operator is that it does not treat the first part as a regular expression: it treats both portions as lists of characters. The first part is a list of characters for which to search, and the second part is a corresponding list of replacement characters: tr/SEARCHLIST/REPLACEMENTLIST/. By default, it operates on the $_ variable, but it can be bound to any variable using the binding operator:

```
tr/abc/cab/;      # replace a with c, b with a, and c with b.
tr/a-z/A-Z/;      # replace lower case letters with corresponding
                  # uppercase letters.


$string =~ tr/A-Z/Z-A/; # replace upper case letters in $string
                        # with their counterparts in a reversed
                        # alphabet.
```

You can use this as an easy method of doing ROT13 encoding—a simple encoding scheme where the alphabet is divided into two halves and swapped so that a maps to n and b maps to o and vice versa. You can call the following rot13() function to encrypt a string, then call it again on the encrypted string to get the original text back:

```
sub rot13 {
    my $string = shift;
    $string =~ tr/a-zA-Z/n-za-mN-ZA-M/;
    return $string;
}
```

The `tr//` function returns the number of characters in the search list that it found. When the replacement list is empty and no modifiers are used, the search list is replicated as the replacement list. This allows you to count characters in a string:

```
$count = tr/a//;            # $count gets number of 'a'
                            # characters in $_
$count = tr/aeiouAEIOU//;   # $count gets number of vowels in $_
```

When the replacement list is shorter than the searchlist, then the last character of the replacement list is repeated to equalize the two lists:

```
tr/a-z/ABC/;    # a to A, b to B, c to C and all other lowercase
                # letters translate to C as well
```

Three modifiers may be used with the `tr//` operator, in the same way that modifiers are used with the match and substitution operators: `/c`, `/d`, and `/s` (which stand for complement, delete, and squash, respectively).

The `/c` modifier means that the searchlist is taken as a complement—in other words, the list of all characters not in the given searchlist. The `/d` modifier means that, instead of replicating the last character in the replacement list until it is the same size as the searchlist, all matching characters that do not have a counterpart in the replacement list are deleted from the target string. The `/s` modifier means to squash consecutive matching characters with one copy of the replacement character.

```
tr/aeiou/*/c;   # replace all non-vowels with an asterisk
tr/aeiou/x/d;   # replace a with x and delete all other vowels
tr/aeiou//cd;   # delete all non-vowels
tr/ / /s;       # replace consecutive spaces with a single space
```

I would like to stress again that the `tr//` operator does not use regular expressions. The expression `tr/a*b/xyz/` does not replace zero-or-more a characters in a row followed by a b with xyz. It replaces each a with an x, each asterisk with a y, and each b with a z.

11.5 Exercises

1 Write a function that returns a list of all doubled words (two words repeated such as: "The the way to…") in a string. A doubled word may have different case and be separated by any amount of whitespace including an embedded newline.

2 Write a regex to substitute every occurence of the word `apple` with `orange` only if is followed by a space and the word `peel`. Do not change the `apple` in `pineapple`.

3 Write a function that prints out a summary of the frequencies of each vowel in a string. For example, if passed the string `This is the winter of our discontent`, it would print:

```
a    0
e    3
i    4
o    3
u    1
```

C H A P T E R   1 2

Working with lists

Lists are an important and powerful feature of the Perl language, so it should come as no surprise that, just as with strings, Perl has a few list manipulation tools up its sleeve. In earlier chapters, we've seen the essential built-in functions for working with arrays and hashes—push(), pop(), shift(), unshift(), keys(), exists(), to name a few—as well as a few functions and operators for making or joining lists—the range operator, and the split() and join() functions. In this chapter, we will examine a few built-in functions designed explicitly for processing list data: the map(), grep(), and sort() functions. We will also consider more uses of the reverse() function.

12.1 *Processing a list*

The standard way to process a list of data, or to perform some action on each element of a list, is to iterate through the list in a foreach loop:

```
foreach my $item ( @list ) {
    # do something with $item
}
```

This should probably be your first choice when you need to process a list of data, but it does have certain limitations. Consider a simple case where you want to create a new array that contains the value of each element of an existing array multiplied by a factor of two:

```
my @list = (1, 2, 3);
my @new_list;
foreach my $item ( @list ) {
    push @new_list, $item * 2;
}
print "@list\n";      # prints: 1 2 3
print "@new_list\n"; # prints: 2 4 6
```

The map() function allows us write the preceding code more directly as a list assignment from one list to another:

```
my @list = (1, 2, 3);
my @new_list = map $_ * 2, @list;
print "@list\n";      # prints: 1 2 3
print "@new_list\n"; # prints: 2 4 6
```

The map() function has two basic forms:

```
map BLOCK LIST
map EXPR, LIST
```

The block or expression is evaluated once for each element in the list argument, and the return of the function is the list of each such evaluation's results. Each time the block or expression is evaluated, the $_ variable is set to the current value in the list. (Actually, $_ is an alias to the element in the list, but changing it is not recommended under most circumstances.)

When a block is used as the first argument (a series of statements enclosed in curly braces), the return value of each evaluation is the value of the last statement in the block. Also, you do not use a comma between the block argument and the following list:

```
@new_list = map {$_ * 2} @list;
```

The map() function may also be used to transform a list in place. Consider how you might do this with a foreach loop (remembering that the loop variable is an alias to the current element in the list):

```
my @list = (1, 2, 3);
foreach my $item ( @list ) {
    $item *= 2;   # same as: $item = $item * 2;
}
print "@list\n"; # prints: 2 4 6
```

It is not wise to use this "aliasing" feature too much because it can tend to hide the real object of the code in the indirection. The map() function allows a more direct assignment that is unmistakably changing the contents of the array:

```
my @list = (1, 2, 3);
@list = map {$_ * 2} @list;
print "@list\n";    # prints: 2 4 6
```

In this version, it is perfectly clear that @list is being assigned a new list value that is a modification of its previous list value.

The map() isn't limited to returning just a single element for each element it receives in the list; it can return a scalar or a list value. Consider initializing a hash from an array where each array element is taken to be a key and given a value of 1:

```
@key_list = qw/one two three/;
my %hash  = map { $_ => 1 } @key_list;
```

This also has the effect of filtering out any duplicate elements in the key list array because there can be only one of each key in a hash.

12.2 Filtering a list

Often we don't want to process a list; we want to filter it—that is, get all the elements that meet some criteria. Another function, similar in syntax to map(), is the grep() function:

```
grep BLOCK LIST
grep EXPR, LIST
```

Unlike the map() function, which returns a value (or a list of values) for every element in the list, this function returns the list of elements for which the block or expression evaluates to true. (Again, the $_ variable is assigned to each value in the list in turn.) This function is commonly used with a regular expression as its first argument:

```
my @list = qw/one two three four/;
my @new_list = grep m/^t/, @list;
print "@new_list\n";    # prints: two three
```

Think of grep() as a filter that allows through only things that pass a test. In the case above, only those elements for which the regex m/^t/ is true—those elements that start with a t—are passed through to the new list.

grep() is by no means limited to using a regex as a first argument. Here's one of the standard FAQ answers for extracting the unique elements in an array:

```
my @array = qw/one two two three four three two/;
my %seen;
my @unique = grep {! $seen{$_}++} @array;
print "@unique\n";
```

Here we use the block form and create a hash to count occurrences of each element. The grep() filter here allows only those elements that we have not seen already.

12.3 Sorting lists

Perl's built-in sort() function is versatile, allowing you to supply a function (or block) that performs the comparisons or simply to use the default comparison routine, which uses stringwise comparisons. The basic form of the function is

```
sort SUBNAME LIST
sort BLOCK LIST
sort LIST
```

To sort an array of strings, you can simply use the default sorting routine:

```
@list = qw/one two three four five/;
@list = sort @list;
print "@list\n";  # prints: five four one three two
```

When you want to provide a different sorting method you need to realize how sorting is accomplished. Any sorting method must compare two elements at a time to each other and determine if the first element is larger than, smaller than, or equal to the second element. While sorting the list, the sort() function takes care of figuring out which pairs of elements need to be compared at any given time. When you supply a comparison method, the sort() function places these pairs of elements into the localized variables $a and $b. Your comparison function must return -1 if the first element is smaller, 0 if they are equal, and 1 if the first element is larger (remember the cmp and <=> operators). For example, to duplicate the default sort method using stringwise comparison, you could use

```
@list = qw/one two three four five/;
@list = sort { $a cmp $b } @list;
print "@list\n";
```

And, to do it as a subroutine, you could use

```
@list = qw/one two three four five/;
@list = sort stringwise @list;
print "@list\n";

sub stringwise {
    $a cmp $b;
}
```

To sort a list numerically, you would use

```
@list = (3, 4, 2, 9, 1);
@list = sort { $a <=> $b } @list;
print "@list\n";   # prints: 1 2 3 4 9
```

To reverse the sense of the sort order, you simply swap the two special sort variables:

```
@list = (3, 4, 2, 9, 1);
@list = sort { $b <=> $a } @list;
print "@list\n";   # prints: 9 4 3 2 1
```

As you know, the keys in a hash are not stored in any particular order, but you often want to retrieve them in some sorted fashion:

```
my %family = ( Andrew => 35, Sue => 39, Joseph => 14, Thomas => 7 );
foreach my $key (sort keys %family) {
    print "$key is $family{$key}\n";
}
__END__
this prints:
Andrew is 35
Joseph is 14
Sue is 39
Thomas is 7
```

But what if we wanted to list the family members in descending order by age? We can supply a block that sorts by value, instead of by key:

```
my %family = ( Andrew => 35, Sue => 39, Joseph => 14, Thomas => 7 );
foreach my $key (sort{$family{$b} <=> $family{$a}} keys %family) {
    print "$key is $family{$key}\n";
}
__END__
this prints:
Sue is 39
Andrew is 35
Joseph is 14
Thomas is 7
```

Sometimes, there is more than one field in the data that you wish to sort. Consider a colon-separated data file of first names, last names and ages. We want to sort by last name, then by first name (if the last names are equal), and, lastly, by age (if all else is equal):

```
#!/usr/bin/perl -w
use strict;
my @data = <DATA>;
my @sorted = sort myway @data;
print @sorted;

sub myway {
    (split /:/, $a)[1] cmp (split /:/, $b)[1]
                    ||
    (split /:/, $a)[0] cmp (split /:/, $b)[0]
                    ||
    (split /:/, $a)[2] <=> (split /:/, $b)[2]
}
__DATA__
Sue:Johnson:39
Andrew:Johnson:35
Bill:Jones:37
Bill:Jones:36
Mike:Hammer:45
```

This makes use of a list facility that we have not discussed yet: you can subscript (or take a slice of) a list just as you can with an array. The example above also makes use of the || (logical OR) operator. The entire function is a single Perl statement made up of three expressions that are OR'd together. First, we split the data into lists at the colons and compare the second elements of that pair of lists. If they are equal (cmp returns zero), the expression is false, and we do the next expression to compare the first elements of the pair of lists (the first names). Again, if they are equal, we go on to numerically compare the third element of the pair of lists (age). The || operator short circuits (see chapter 5) so this subroutine returns the result of the first comparison that does not return zero or returns zero if all comparisons are equal.

This is not a very efficient way to perform such multiple field comparisons. For every pair of elements that need to be compared (which can be a large number of comparisons), we are performing between two and six splits on the data. We can greatly improve this if we split the data once into anonymous arrays, then sort by each element of those arrays:

```
#!/usr/bin/perl -w
use strict;
my @data = <DATA>;
my @sorted;
@sorted = map { [$_, split /:/] } @data;
@sorted = sort myway @sorted;
@sorted = map { $_->[0] } @sorted;
print @sorted;

sub myway {
    $a->[2] cmp $b->[2] ||
    $a->[1] cmp $b->[1] ||
    $a->[3] <=> $b->[3];
}
__DATA__
Sue:Johnson:39
Andrew:Johnson:35
Bill:Jones:37
Bill:Jones:36
Mike:Hammer:45
```

In this example, we've first used the map() function to create an anonymous array for each line of data. This anonymous array contains the actual line of data as the first element, and the list of fields (the result of splitting the line of data) as the next three fields. The resulting list of anonymous arrays is assigned to the @sorted array. We then sort this array of anonymous arrays in the myway() sub, dereferencing each particular field we want to compare. Finally, we extract just the first element of each anonymous array (the data line itself) in another map() function so that the final @sorted array contains just the lines of data now in the sorted order we wanted.

12.4 Chaining functions

One of the most famous Perl idioms is called the "Schwartzian Transform," named after Randal Schwartz. The Schwartzian Transform implements the sorting idea above in a more compact fashion by chaining the three map, sort, map operations together into a single statement. Before we tackle that particular idiom, let's consider what chaining is in the first place.

Chaining is simply using the results of one operation or function as the input into another operation or function. Try to work through the following simple example:

```
#!/usr/bin/perl -w
use strict;
my @unique;
my %seen;
while( <DATA> ) {
    chomp;
    push @unique, grep !$seen{$_}++, split ' ';
}
print "@unique\n";
__DATA__
this is one line of data
this is another line of data
this is the last line of data
```

You might have guessed that this program creates an array of all the unique words in the given data. But do you see how it works? We have chained together three list functions in a single statement. Parentheses may help to make the chained statement more understandable for a first reading:

```
push( @unique, grep( !$seen{$_}++, split( ' ') ) );
```

Looked at this way, the push() function has two arguments: the array to push into and a list of things to push into that array. The second argument is the list resulting from the grep() function. The grep() also has two arguments: the conditional expression and a list. The list argument to the grep() function is the list resulting from the split() function (using the special case of splitting on whitespace).

Most often you will not see chained functions with all those parentheses, let's look at the original version again:

```
push @unique, grep !$seen{$_}++, split ' ';
```

The way to understand chained functions is to read them from right to left one function at a time. Here we could read this in English as "split the line into a list of words, filter that list through the grep() function, and push the resulting list onto the @unique array."

Now let's consider the Schwartzian Transform and the last sorting method given above:

```
#!/usr/bin/perl -w
use strict;
my @data = <DATA>;

my @sorted = map { $_->[0] }
             sort myway
             map { [$_, split /:/] } @data;
print @sorted;

sub myway {
    $a->[2] cmp $b->[2] ||
    $a->[1] cmp $b->[1] ||
    $a->[3] <=> $b->[3];
}
__DATA__
Sue:Johnson:39
Andrew:Johnson:35
Bill:Jones:37
Bill:Jones:36
Mike:Hammer:45
```

Notice how we have reversed the order of the map() calls because the chained series is evaluated from right to left. First, each element of @data is turned into an anonymous array, then the resulting list of these anonymous arrays is sorted myway, and the sorted list is passed to the leftmost map() function, which simply returns the first element of each anonymous array. We could have even done the whole sorting chain using a block instead of a named subroutine:

```
my @sorted = map { $_->[0] }
             sort {
                   $a->[2] cmp $b->[2] ||
                   $a->[1] cmp $b->[1] ||
                   $a->[3] <=> $b->[3];
                 }
             map { [$_, split /:/] } @data;
```

12.5 Reverse revisited

The `reverse()` function is context sensitive. While we've only used it thus far to reverse a scalar, you should be aware that it takes a list as its argument. We have only used it like this:

```
$string = 'halb';
$string = reverse $string;
print $string;     # prints: blah
```

Here, the function is taking `$string` as a one element list. It does what we expect because we called it in a scalar context. In scalar context, this function concatenates all of its arguments into a single string and reverses that string. Consider the following:

```
@array = ('blah');
@array = reverse @array;
print "@array\n";   # prints: blah
```

In a list context, such as this example, the `reverse()` function reverses the order of the list, leaving each element unchanged. With a one element list such as this, the resulting list is unchanged:

```
@array  = ('one', 'two', 'three');
@array  = reverse @array;
print "@array\n";  # prints: three two one
$string = reverse @array;
print "$string\n"; # prints: enoowteerht
```

But what do you suppose the following will produce?

```
$string = 'halb';
print reverse $string;
```

The `print()` function takes a list—i.e., provides a list context—so the `reverse()` is performed in a list context, and the single element list (`$string`) is printed in reverse order. This explains the bug I mentioned previously regarding the `commify()` subroutine in chapter 10. To get the intended meaning, you need to use the `scalar()` function to explicitly put the `reverse()` into scalar context:

```
$string = 'halb';
print scalar reverse $string;
```

The `reverse()` function can be used to print a file in reverse order (by lines):

```
print reverse <>;
```

It can also be used to invert a hash (so long as the values of the hash are unique) to create a new hash that has the values of the former hash as its keys and the keys of the former as the values:

```
%mon2num = ( Jan => 1, Feb => 2, Mar => 3, Apr => 4, May => 5,
             Jun => 6, Jul => 7, Aug => 8, Sep => 9, Oct => 10,
             Nov => 11, Dec => 12 );
%num2mon = reverse %mon2num;
print "$mon2num{Mar}, $num2mon{3}\n"; # prints: 3, Mar
```

12.6 Exercises

1 Write a function that, when given a hash, returns the list of hash values sorted by the hash keys. Write the same thing in one line using a map() function.

2 Modify the one-line version above to also filter out any value less than 25.

C H A P T E R   1 3

More I/O

In chapter 6, we covered the basics of reading from and writing to a file using the built-in open() function. This is not the only way for your programs to read or write data. You can also capture the output of external programs, run external programs (which might write data to files or elsewhere), and open directories and read their contents. This chapter takes us on a brief foray through these alternate I/O mechanisms.

13.1 Running external commands

Running an external program may not seem like an I/O operation, especially if you are not sending that program data or receiving its output. Nevertheless, you are communicating with the world outside your program, causing programs to be run and, perhaps, data to be read from a file or printed to files or the console.

Perl has two mechanisms for running external commands or programs when you are not immediately interested in capturing the output of those commands: the system() and exec() functions. Each of these will run an external program. The difference between the two is that the exec() function causes the external program to replace the currently running Perl program while the system() function spawns another shell process to run the given program and waits for it to complete before continuing.

```
system('ls'); # runs the 'ls' command and waits for it to complete
print "Still running\n"; # will print when 'ls' finishes

exec('ls');   # substitutes 'ls' command for current running script
print "Still running\n"; # will only print if 'ls' failed
```

We can detect failure in a manner similar to our tests of the open() call, but with one significant difference: the system() returns 0 for success (a false value) and an error code for failure. To test for failure, you need to use the logical && operator with the die statement:

```
system('ls') && die "hmm, 'ls' command failed\n";
```

So, what happens to the output from the command? In both cases, the standard filehandles are inherited from the Perl program, and the output goes to STDOUT. In the second example above, as indicated in the comments, the print statement will not be executed if the exec() was successful. Because the new process has completely replaced the current Perl program, nothing after the exec() call can be executed.

Why would you want to run external programs using these functions? Well, even though you can write routines in Perl to do pretty much anything an external command could do, it is sometimes simpler to just use the external commands. On Unix systems, there are a variety of command line utilities exist that are often used for such things as sorting, searching, and finding files. Perhaps your program has just collected and printed to a file a large amount of data that you would now like to sort and remove duplicate elements from before exiting the program:

```
# code that writes lots of raw data to  $tmp_file # ...
exec("sort $tmp_file | unique > $final_file");
```

Or, similarly, say you wanted to do the same thing to an existing file before reading it, in which case you would use the `system()` function so your program could continue after running the given command. The perldocs offer a little more detail regarding these functions and how they process their arguments (see `perldoc -f system` and `perldoc -f exec`). More often you want to capture or read the output of external commands. Let's look at some aspects of these last operations.

13.2 Reading and writing from/to external commands

Perl also provides mechanisms to run external commands, to collect or read their output, or to send data from your Perl program into the standard input of an external command.

Backtics are the simplest mechanism for collecting data from an external program. The syntax is to simply enclose the external command in reverse (or opening) single quotation marks, also referred to as backtics (``):

```
$listing = `ls`;  # $listing has output as single string
@listing = `ls`;  # @listing has output as array of lines

$listing = `dir`; # same as above on DOS
@listing = `dir`; # same as above on DOS
```

In scalar context, backtics collect and return the output of the given command as a single string. In list context, the output is returned as a list of lines (where the meaning of "line" is dependent on the current value of the special `$/` variable).

Alternately, you can open a file handle onto an external process using the `open()` function by giving an external command followed by a pipe as an argument:

```
open(DIR, 'ls |') || die "can't fork: $!";
while() {
    chomp;
    print "$_" if -s $_  5000;
}
close DIR || die "failed $!";
```

Here we open the `ls` process and pipe it into our file handle so we can read one line at a time and print only the names of files that are over 5000 bytes in size (see section 13.4). Note, catching open pipe failures is not straightforward—please see *perlfaq8* for a solution to this problem.

We can also open up a whole pipeline of processes, such as the one we used in the `exec()` example above:

```
open(SORTED, "sort $tmp_file | uniq |") || die "can't fork: $!";
while( <SORTED> ) {
    print;
}
close SORTED || die "problem with SORTED: $!";
```

Here we have opened the `sort` program on the file `$tmp_file`, piped its output to the `uniq` utility to remove duplicate lines, and, finally, piped that output to our file handle so we can read it line by line.

This piping mechanism works either way but only one way at a time. We can write data to an external process as well by using a leading pipe symbol:

```
open(OUT, "| sort | uniq > $final_file") || die "can't fork: $!";
while ( <> ) {
    print OUT;
}
close OUT || die "problem with OUT: $!";
```

In this case, we are sending our data to the `sort` command, then to the `uniq` utility, and finally redirecting it to a file. These are standard utilities on Unix systems. The utilities available on your system may differ.

13.3 Working with directories

Although we gave a few examples above of using external commands (`ls` or `dir`) to obtain directory listings, Perl also has a built-in set of functions for opening, reading, and closing directories (directory handles) and reading their contents.

```
opendir(DIR, '/home/ajohnson') || die "can't: $!";
my @listing = readdir DIR;
closedir DIR;
```

And, if you wanted to print out all the files with a .txt extension, you could use the `grep()` function to filter the output of the `readdir()` function:

```
opendir(DIR, '/home/ajohnson') || die "can't: $!";
my @listing = grep /\.txt$/, readdir DIR;
closedir DIR;
```

One thing to remember though is that the directory entries produced by readdir() do not contain leading path information, just the actual entries themselves. Thus, you couldn't try to just open one of the files because chances are it doesn't exist in your current directory.

```
my $dir = '/home/ajohnson/public_html';
opendir(DIR, $dir) || die "can't: $!";
my @listing = grep /\.html$/, readdir DIR;
closedir DIR;
foreach my $file ( @listing ) {
    # open(FILE, $file) || die "can't: $!"; # won't work
    # must use full pathname to the file
    open(FILE, "$dir/$file") || die "can't: $!";
    # more stuff...
}
```

Of course, how do we really know if the $file in the example above is really a file. It might be a directory (or a FIFO or a socket). The filetest operators are often used in conjunction with reading directories to determine what kind of entity a particular directory entry really is.

13.4   Filetest operators

There are several filetest operators that can be used to find out information about a particular directory entry. Table 13.1 on page 230 shows many of the commonly used such tests. (See perldoc perlfunc for the complete list of file test operators.)

Most of these return a simple true or false value and are often used in conditional expressions or grep() expressions. If a filename or file handle is not given, then the test is performed against the filename contained in the default variable ($_):

```
$dir = '/home/ajohnson/bin';
opendir(DIR, $dir) || die "can't: $!";
my @listing = grep -f "$dir/$_", readdir DIR;
closedir DIR;
```

The -M, -A, and -C tests return an age in days (fractional) relative to the start of the current program. Therefore, to test if a file was created after the program started, you could test if (-M 'filename' < 0).

As a simple example, here's a small script that will print out how many directories and how many plain files exist under a given directory. It uses a grep !/ ^(\.|\.\.)$/, readdir DIR expression so as not to include "." and ".." entries in the summary:

```
#!/usr/bin/perl -w
use strict;
my $dirname = shift @ARGV if @ARGV;
$dirname ||= '.';

opendir(DIR, $dirname) || die "can't: $!";
my @entries = map{"$dirname/$_"} grep !/^(\.|\.\.)$/, readdir DIR;
closedir DIR;

my $num_files = grep -f, @entries;
my $num_dirs  = grep -d, @entries;

print "$num_dirs Directories under $dirname/\n";
print "$num_files Files under $dirname/\n";
```

Table 13.1 Common filetest operators

Operator	Description
-e	file exists
-z	file exists with zero size
-s	file exists and is non-zero in size: size is returned
-f	file is plain file
-d	file is a directory
-l	file is a symlink
-p	file is a FIFO: a named pipe
-S	file is a socket
-r	file/directory is readable
-w	file/directory is writable
-x	file/directory is executable
-T	file is a text file
-B	file is a binary file
-M	days since last modified (relative to script start time)
-A	days since last access (relative to script start time)
-C	days since inode change (relative to script start time)

13.5 *faqgrep revisited*

Our first incarnation of the faqgrep program only allowed us to search for a single word or phrase and showed us which *perlfaq* files contained the matching questions. That version also had us specify the names of all the FAQ documents contained in the FAQ directory. In this version, we read the contents of the FAQ directory to obtain the names of the FAQ files. We also allow for a search of more than one pattern. We provide an option to search for questions containing any of the keywords given—the default will be to show questions containing all the keywords given—as well as an option to show particular FAQ entries so that users don't have to open and search through particular *perlfaq* themselves.

To begin with, first outline the overall structure of the script:

```
<<faqgrep>>=
#!/usr/bin/perl -w
use strict;
<<initialize_variables>>
<<read_in_perlfaq_filenames>>
<<search_and_print>>
@
```

The first thing we need to do is initialize some variables. In particular, we need a variable to hold the location of where the FAQ files can be found, we need variables for our two options, and we need a variable to hold our search pattern. For options, we use a -f option to print found entries and the -or option to perform an OR'd search on the keywords:

```
<<initialize_variables>>=
# set $faqdir to point to your installed pod files:
my $faqdir = '/usr/local/lib/perl5/5.00502/pod';
my($opt_f,$opt_or,$pattern);
<<get_options>>
<<create_keyword_pattern>>
@
```

We use a simple method to extract our command line options and die() with a usage statement if we get an unrecognized option:

```
<<get_options>>=
while($ARGV[0]=~/^-/){
    $_ = $ARGV[0];
    if ( /^-or$/ ) { $opt_or = 1; shift @ARGV; next }
    if ( /^-f$/ )  { $opt_f = 1;  shift @ARGV; next }
die<<HERE;
illegal option: $_
usage: faqgrep [-f] [-or] [keywords...]
HERE
}
@
```

Now that we have removed any options from the command line arguments, we do a quick check for remaining keywords. (Why bother running the programming if there are no keywords to search for?) To create a pattern in the case of the -or option, we join all the keywords together with the | alternation operator preceded by a wildcard pattern. This is somewhat inefficient, but it serves for the present task. For the default search, we use a series of lookaheads, one for each keyword, which must all be found for the pattern to succeed:

```
<<create_keyword_pattern>>=
die "no keywords specified\n" unless @ARGV;
if($opt_or){
    $pattern = '.*(?:' . join('|',@ARGV) . ')';
}else{
    $pattern=join('',map{"(?=.*$_)"}@ARGV);
}
@
```

In our previous version, we supplied all the FAQ file names in an array. In this version we will simply read the FAQ directory for all filenames containing FAQ:

```
<<read_in_perlfaq_filenames>>=
opendir(FAQDIR,$faqdir) || die "can't open $faqdir $!";
my @faqs = grep /faq/,readdir FAQDIR;
close FAQDIR;
@
```

We then perform our search of the FAQ files in a manner similar to our first version of the program. The only catch is that we also print the entire answer if the -f option was given:

```
<<search_and_print>>=
foreach my $faq (@faqs) {
    open(faq,"$faqdir/$faq")||die "can't $!";
    while (<FAQ>) {
        if (s/^=head2($pattern)/$1/io) {
            print "$faq:$_" ;
            <<print_answer_if_-f_option>>
        }
    }
    close FAQ;
}
@
```

To print the answer, we just keep printing lines until we hit another =head2 line that does not contain our search pattern or until we hit the end of the current file:

```
<<print_answer_if_-f_option>>=
if ($opt_f) {
    while(<FAQ>){
        last if m/^=head(?!$pattern)/io;
        print;
    }
}
@
```

The program above is a little more useful than the original version because it allows multiple keywords and will print the answers directly if we want. Consider the case of wanting to print a random line from a file:

```
[danger:ajohnson:~]$ faqgrep random
perlfaq4.pod: Why aren't my random numbers random?
perlfaq4.pod: How do I shuffle an array randomly?
perlfaq4.pod: How do I select a random element from an array?
perlfaq5.pod: How do I randomly update a binary file?
perlfaq5.pod: How do I select a random line from a file?
```

We can see from this list of matching entries that it is the last one we want to view, so we can then invoke fagrep with the -f option and an extra keyword so that only the entry we want is given:

```
[danger:ajohnson:~]$ faqgrep -f random line
perlfaq5.pod: How do I select a random line from a file?

Here's an algorithm from the Camel Book:
    srand;
    rand($.) < 1 && ($line = $_) while <>;

This has a significant advantage in space over reading the whole
file in.  A simple proof by induction is available upon
request if you doubt its correctness.
```

13.6 Exercises

1 Write a program that uses the system() function to run an external command such as (ps) to list all currently running processes owned by the user given as a command line argument

2 Write a similar program that reads from the ps command and lists the processes being run by the user given as a command line argument.

3 Extend the last chapter's filetest program example to summarize all the file types (files, directories, sockets, FIFOs, and symlinks) under the given directory.

4 Modify the program from the previous exercise to also state which files are readable, writable, and/or executable files.

C H A P T E R   1 4

Using modules

One of the greatest benefits of programming with Perl is not having to do much programming to get the job done. This is due to features we have already seen: powerful and flexible variable types (arrays and hashes) that can grow dynamically, references and anonymous data structures you can generate on the fly, integrated regular expressions and string operations…the list goes on. But the single most valuable resource for the lazy programmer—lazy in a good way by not wasting time doing things that have already been done—is the large body of existing publicly available code that you can reuse. This body of code is the previously mentioned Comprehensive Perl Archive Network (CPAN). CPAN is a well organized archive of hundreds of *modules*, libraries, and scripts contributed by countless members of the Perl community at large. (Well, okay, a countable number of contributors does exist, but *I'm* not going to count them. The number would change before this book hits the market anyway.)

If you haven't already done so, point your browser at *www.perl.com*, follow the CPAN link, and do some exploring. You can view the modules grouped by category or listed individually. The end of this chapter lists the main category headings for modules with a brief description of what kinds of things can be found under each category.

If you are using the ActiveState version of Perl, it comes with a ppm program for installing packages built for use with this version. You can get these packages by using the ppm program or, manually, by pointing your browser at *www.ActiveState.com/packages/zips/*. (There are currently around 150 modules listed at this site.)

Modules do not have to be written in Perl; in fact, many modules are implemented in C or have components implemented in C to truly extend Perl in ways that would be difficult using just Perl itself. These modules require you to have a C compiler to make them, unless you are using the ActiveState port and a ppm version of the module is available. (Remember, if there is a ppm version, you can use the ppm program to get and install these modules.)

If you are using MacPerl, a relatively new module-porters page contains links to several modules along with installation instructions at *http://pudge.net/mmp/*. If the module you want isn't listed here, then chances are that the standard version of the module already works fine with MacPerl.

An easy way to search for modules is by way of the CPAN search engine housed at: *http://theory.uwinnipeg.ca/search/cpan-search.html*. Many modules also require other modules in order to work correctly, and it can be a frustrating exercise downloading a module only to find that it requires another module you don't yet have, and so on, and so on. The theory site has a dependency listing for most modules available on CPAN. This listing can be viewed at *http://theory.uwinnipeg.ca/*

CPAN/depend.html. This can be a great help in finding out everything you need to obtain in order to successfully install a new module.

Another simple way to access CPAN is to use the *CPAN.pm* module. This module gives you an interactive shell to work with to query CPAN for modules and bundles, download modules, and even automatically build and install them. (The module can often handle dependencies during the building process.) You can fire up a CPAN shell using the following command at your command line prompt:

```
perl -MCPAN -e shell
```

This will leave you with a `cpan>` prompt where you can type in commands—enter `h` for a list of commands. For further infomation regarding this module, see `perldoc CPAN`.

14.1 Installing modules

The standard way to install modules (not using `ppm` or the CPAN module) is to simply download and unpack the module *.tar.gz* or *.zip* file and `cd` into the resulting directory and type

```
$ perl Makefile.PL
$ make
$ make test
$ make install
```

ActiveState users can obtain a version of `make` called `nmake` from *ftp:// ftp.microsoft.com/Softlib/MSLFILES/nmake.exe.* Another version of `make` called `dmake` can be found at *http://www-personal.umich.edu/~gsar/.* (To use this one, you must make changes in your *Config.pm* for Perl.)

After that, you should be able to view the documentation for the module using `perldoc ModuleName`. (Some systems may also add the documentation to the installed set of HTML documentation.) If all is successful, then congratulations! You've just added features and/or functions to your bag of Perl tools.

If you are using Perl on a Unix machine where you don't have permissions to install modules in the standard places, you can install modules into your own private library in your home directory. Section 8 of the Perl FAQs addresses this capability. Essentially, you create a directory to serve as your private module directory and then use that directory as a prefix when you do the `make` process. For example, I might set up a private Perl library directory in my home directory and call it *myperllib.* To build and install modules into this directory, I would use the following:

```
perl Makefile.PL PREFIX=/home/jandrew/myperllib
```

Then I would run the `make/make test/make install` sequence as above, and the appropriate subdirectories will be built and the module installed into my private library.

14.2   Using modules

To use an installed module, all you need to do is put a `use Module_Name` statement in your script (generally right near the top). This statement causes the Perl interpreter to search a special set of directories for the module and to load it when it is found. The particular directories searched are configured into Perl when it is compiled. They are then available in the special built-in array named `@INC` (the include array).

You can tell Perl to search other directories in addition to those in the `@INC` array by placing a `use lib 'path/to/other/libs';` statement prior to the `use ModuleName;` statement. A third way to tell Perl to search other directories for modules is by setting the PERL5LIB environment variable to point to a directory you wish to be in the include search path. You will need to use one of these two techniques to use modules that you have installed into a private Perl library. Setting the environment variable is probably the easiest method.

Some modules are simply collections of functions imported into your program. You can call them just like any other function you might have defined. Which functions get imported depends on how the module was written. Some modules don't import any functions into your program by default. You have to supply a list of functions that you want to import. Others automatically import some or all of their functions. Running `perldoc ModuleName` should provide you with all you need to know to use a module and to access or import its functions.

Other modules are written in an object-oriented (OO)—or OOP for object-oriented programming—fashion and do not import any functions directly into your program. Instead, you call a constructor method in the module to create an object. You then use this object to access the *methods*—the OO way of saying functions—that the module provides. Some modules provide both a procedural (functions) and an OO interface. Which you choose to use is a matter of preference.

```
use SomeModule;  # imports whatever default functions and variables
                 # the module provides
# -----------
use SomeModule 'func1 func2';  # imports func1 and func2 from the
                               # module 'SomeModule'
# -----------
use SomeOOmod;           # nothing imported
my $foo = SomeOOmod->new; # calls new() method in someOOmod
                          # new() returns an object into $foo
```

```
$foo->blah;   # calls method blah() in SomeOOmod module on
              # object $foo
```

If this seems like a lot to think about, don't worry. The documentation included with most modules is pretty good and usually gives several examples of how to use the module and its functions or methods. We will be taking a much more in-depth look at modules in chapter 16 and later chapters. For now, we are only concerned with using them as black boxes that do what we want (though you are always encouraged to peek at the source code for the module to learn how it works).

14.3   File::Basename

Many modules are included as part of standard distribution and should already be installed and available on your system. For our first example, we reconsider the file basename problem and solution given in chapter 11. There we showed two solutions: one involving the `rindex()` and `substr()` functions; and the other using a regular expression. Your Perl distribution already includes a module that accomplishes the task using regular expressions—`File::Basename`.

```
#!/usr/bin/perl -w
use strict;
use File::Basename;

my $fullname = '/devel/sim/simpn2.c';
my $filename = basename($fullname);
my $dirname  = dirname($fullname);

print "$dirname : $filename\n"; # prints: /devel/sim : simpn2.c
```

There is also a function to parse the fullname into parts all at once:

```
my ($filename, $dirname) = fileparse($fullname);
```

You can supply a list of suffixes to try to match, and if one matches, the suffix will be extracted separately as well:

```
#!/usr/bin/perl -w
use strict;
use File::Basename;
my @suffs = ('.pm', '.c');
my $fullname = '/devel/sim/simpn2.c';
my ($filename, $dirname, $suffix) = fileparse($fullname, @suffs);
print "$dirname\n";  # prints: /devel/sim/
print "$filename\n"; # prints: simpn2
print "$suffix\n";   # prints: .c
```

Now, using one of the short little functions we created in chapter 11 might not seem like such a big deal. But those functions dealt only with Unix-style pathnames. `File::Basename` handles pathnames from most operating systems and, thus, is a far more portable solution.

14.4 Command line options

We have already written a couple of example programs that use command line options (in chapters 9 and 13). In these, we used a simple `while` loop to parse the command line arguments in the `@ARGV` array for things that look like options (or switches). If we found them, we removed them from the array and set some variable to indicate the option had been passed to the program.

The `Getopt::Std` module (part of the standard distribution) provides easy but powerful ways to extract options, and options with parameters, from the command line arguments. Before we look at using this module, let's take a simple example and process options the old way once more. This program merely accepts certain options (any or all of -a, -b, or -c) and displays them, followed by any remaining command line arguments:

```
#!/usr/bin/perl -w
use strict;
my %opts;
while($ARGV[0] =~ m/^-/){
    $_ = shift @ARGV;   # remove option from @ARGV
    m/^-([abc])$/ and $opts{$1} = 1 and next;
    print "illegal option: $_\n";
}
foreach my $option (sort keys %opts){
    print "$option:$opts{$option}\n";
}
print "remaining arguments: @ARGV\n";
```

This is a fairly simple way to parse out the command line options and set values in a hash. It suffices for simple option parsing, as in the following example runs:

```
$ perl simpopt.pl -a foo
a:1
remaining arguments: foo

$ perl simpopt.pl -a -c foo
a:1
c:1
remaining arguments: foo
```

```
$ perl simpopt.pl -a -c -b foo
a:1
b:1
c:1
remaining arguments: foo

$ perl simpopt.pl -x -b foo
illegal option: -x
b:1
remaining arguments: foo
```

The single character options above are usually referred to as switches because they do not take any parameters. In other words, they are thought of as being either on or off. (In the Unix world, it is common for programs to accept such switches in clusters. For example, to turn on three such switches one might simply invoke the program as `perl simpopt.pl -abc`. This won't work with the above program.)

A second difficulty arises when dealing with options that take parameters (i.e., specific values that the program needs to know about). The example above doesn't handle such cases either (but the `pqtangle` program in chapter 9 handled a case of one option taking a parameter). Handling these cases is certainly possible, but, depending on the complexity, it requires some care to do it right.

Enter the `Getopt::Std` module. This module provides two functions for dealing with command line options. Here we will consider only one of them—the better one, in my opinion. Before we discuss this function let's see what a version of the preceding program looks like using this module's `getopts()` function:

```
#!/usr/bin/perl -w
use strict;
use Getopt::Std;
my %opts;
getopts('abc',\%opts);
foreach my $opt (sort keys %opts){
    print "$opt:$opts{$opt}\n";
}
print "remaining arguments: @ARGV\n";
```

The `getopts()` function takes a string of characters representing the switches as its first argument and a reference to a hash as its second argument. Any option then sets a corresponding key in the hash. This function already allows for clustering the switches so calling it with an option of -abc sets all the options:

```
$ perl getopt.pl -abc blah
a:1
b:1
c:1
remaining arguments: blah
```

If you want an option to take a parameter, you simply add a colon after that character in the first argument:

```
#!/usr/bin/perl -w
use strict;
use Getopt::Std;
my %opts;
getopts('ab:c',\%opts);
foreach my $opt (sort keys %opts){
    print "$opt:$opts{$opt}\n";
}
print "remaining arguments: @ARGV\n";
```

Now the -b option expects a parameter to follow it on the command line. The hash value for this option is set to that parameter:

```
$ perl newopt.pl -ac -b param blah
a:1
b:param
c:1
remaining arguments: blah
```

More powerful option processing, such as using long names for options and requiring specific parameter types, is available in the Getopt::Long module. This module is also part of the standard distribution. (See perldoc Getopt::Long for details on using this module.)

14.5 The dating game

Manipulating dates is a fairly common task, but that does not make it a simple task. How would you tell if one date was earlier than another? Consider the dates January 12, 1999 and March 17, 1999. Certainly you can just glance at them and tell which one comes first, but how do you tell the computer to sort them out? How would you find out how many days were between those dates? How many business days?

Sorting dates is not so terribly difficult. If you change the month name into a numeric code (Jan = 00, Feb = 01, ...), then you can just concatenate the year, month, and day and do numeric comparisons:

```
19990012  is less than 19990317
```

So let's try to compare two dates given in MM/DD/YYYY format and print out the earlier date:

```
#!/usr/bin/perl -w
use strict;
my $date1 = '01/29/1998';
my $date2 = '02/01/1997';
```

```
my $new_date1 = $date1;
my $new_date2 = $date2;

$new_date1 =~ s<^(\d\d)/(\d\d)/(\d\d\d\d)$><$3$1$2>;
$new_date2 =~ s<^(\d\d)/(\d\d)/(\d{4})$><$3$1$2>;

if ( $new_date1 == $new_date2 ) {
    print "dates are the same\n";
} elsif ( $new_date1 < $new_date2 ) {
    print "$date1 is earlier than $date2\n";
} else {
    print "$date2 is earlier than $date1\n";
}
```

That's not so hard right? But what if we were getting the dates from a file and they were in a few different formats (Jan-2-1999, 01-02-1999, January 2, 1999, 1st Saturday in Jan 1999,...)? And remember, we still don't know how many days lie between these two dates. Which months have 31 days? When is leap year? Enter Date::Manip, a Perl module for manipulating and calculating dates in a variety of formats. Date::Manip is available on CPAN and is written entirely in Perl, so you won't need a C compiler to install it. Let's answer some questions about a couple of dates:

```
#!/usr/bin/perl -w
use strict;
use Date::Manip;
my $first_date = 'last Friday in Jan 1998';
my $second_date = 'Feb 20th 1998';

my $date1 = ParseDate($first_date);
my $date2 = ParseDate($second_date);

if ( $date1 lt $date2 ) {
    print "$first_date is earlier\n";
} elsif ( $date1 gt $date2 ) {
    print "$second_date is earlier\n";
} else {
    print "the dates are the same\n";
}
my $err;
my $delta = DateCalc($date1, $date2,$err,1);
$delta = Delta_Format($delta,2,"%dt");
print "$delta days from $first_date to $second_date\n";

$delta = DateCalc($date1, $date2,$err,2);
$delta = Delta_Format($delta,2,"%dt");
print "$delta business days from $first_date to $second_date\n";
```

We have used the ParseDate(), DateCalc(), and Delta_Format() functions from the Date::Manip module. All of the functions this module provides to your program are documented in the POD documentation included with the module. (See `perldoc Date::Manip` for explanations of the above functions and others that the module provides.)

14.6 Fetching webpages

Let's face it, the reason many of you decided to learn to program with Perl was to do some Internet programming, either Web-Client or CGI programming (or more likely, both). The first web program I wrote was a simple thirty-line script that fetched a webpage using the `Socket` module, sending the necessary HTTP headers, retrieving the response, and printing it on STDOUT. If thirty lines of code seems fairly small for such a task, you should know that I can do the same thing now, including asking the user to enter a URL, (without needing to know any of the lower level `socket()` calls nor the HTTP protocol) in just a handful of code lines:

```
#!/usr/bin/perl -w
use strict;
use LWP::Simple;
print "Enter url to fetch: ";
chomp(my $url = <STDIN>);
getprint("http://$url");
```

Of course, I am really using much more than six lines of code. I am using all the code in the `LWP::Simple` module, which itself use several other modules in the `LWP` package, simplifying everything down to the provided `getprint()` function. But I don't have to think about all that. That's one of the benefits of using modules. The `LWP::Simple` module is part of a large package of web-related modules distributed as the `lib-www` package on CPAN and also available as a `ppm` package at the ActiveState site.

14.6.1 Stock quotes and graphs

In this section, we are going to use the `LWP::Simple` module to fetch stock quote data from Yahoo's website. We will just be fetching the data as comma-separated values (csv format) and writing it to a simple text file data base, one data file for each stock in which we are interested. We will then use this data to create graphs in `gif` format using the GIFgraph package (available on CPAN and as a `ppm` on the ActiveState site).

Although you can use your browser to view stock information and charts directly, and even set up a portfolio at the Yahoo site, we will be doing everything ourselves. One reason you might want to do such a thing yourself is to customize the information to suit your own purposes. Another might be to retrieve the data overnight so the information is ready for you in the morning. (Some Internet

Service Providers—ISPs—offer cheaper hourly rates at night, so using a scheduler such as cron on Unix to run information collecting programs overnight can save you money.)

We will not be doing anything complex here, just setting up a basic framework which you can build on later. Our goal will be to merely update our stock database and to create a chart in gif format for each stock. You can write these gif files to your own web directory and include them in a webpage of your own design. Each morning when you view your page, the charts will have been updated with the latest information.

The first thing we need to do is layout our top-level view of the program. We need to include the LWP::Simple module to fetch the stock quote data and the GIFgraph::mixed module to create our charts. The GIFgraph::mixed module is part of the GIFgraph package and allows us to create a multiple chart. We will use the noweb syntax again, including the single @ to signify the end of a chunk. In this way, I can run my *pqtangle* directly on my chapter—which is a plain text file—to extract the program and check it for errors.

```
<<stocker.pl>>=
#!/usr/bin/perl -w
use strict;
use LWP::Simple;
use GIFgraph::mixed;
<<initialize variables>>
<<read list of stock symbols>>
<<fetch stock data and create charts>>

<<define subroutines>>
@
```

We need a variable to hold the path to the directory where we store our data files, and we need a configuration file to list the stock symbols we want to check. You should set these according to your own needs. We also need an array to hold our list of stock symbols:

```
<<initialize variables>>=
my $root_dir = '/home/ajohnson/STOCK/portfol';
my $stock_file = "$root_dir/stock.conf";
my @Symbols;
@
```

Before proceeding, we need to figure out what format we want use for our configuration file ($stock_file). Here is the layout we use:

```
Symbols:
CODE    MNCb.TO
CODE    TMF
```

```
Purchases:
#BUY/SOLD    symbol   date        price   quantity
BUY          MNCb.TO  11/2/1998   36.00   100
BUY          TMF      11/2/1998    7.00   100
BUY          TMF      12/4/1998    6.375  100
BUY          MNCb.TO  1/11/1999   46.00   100
SELL         TMF      1/5/1999     6.625  100
```

The stock symbol codes are given in the first section. Just substitute the stock codes you want to track. (The *http://quote.yahoo.com/* contains a symbol lookup feature page you can use to find the symbols for the stocks you want to track.) The second section is a (fake) record of purchase and sales data for your stocks. We won't use this data here; it is only included to suggest other information you might include. Later you can develop your stock tracking system to include charts of total investment worth if you desire.

If you are just starting to track stock data, you can link to and download historical data in csv format for any stock by replacing the symbol in the URL *http://chart.yahoo.com/d?s=MNCb.TO* with the symbol of your choice. When we collect our data, we will use the same csv format as the historical data.

Now that we have a stock symbol file set up, we need to read through it to obtain a list of the stock symbols:

```
<<read list of stock symbols>>=
open(STOCK, $stock_file) || die "can't open file: $!";
while( <STOCK> ) {
    last if m/^Purchases:/;
    chomp;
    push @Symbols, $1 if m/^CODE\s+([\w\.]+)/;
}
close STOCK;
@
```

The above loop exits as soon as we hit a line starting with Purchases:. We don't need to read below that line. The loop pushes each symbol onto our array using a simple regular expression to extract the symbol name from each CODE line.

Next, we can simply loop through each symbol and fetch the csv data and append it to the appropriate data file, then read our data file and create our chart:

```
<<fetch stock data and create charts>>=
foreach my $symbol (@Symbols) {
    my $quote = fetch_quote($symbol);
    write_quote($symbol, $quote);

    my @data  = read_data($symbol);
    make_gif($symbol, @data);
}
@
```

Of course, all the real work is done in the four subroutines:

```
<<define subroutines>>=
<<sub fetch_quote>>
<<sub write_quote>>
<<sub read_data>>
<<sub make_gif>>
@
```

The first subroutine merely has to use the get() function supplied by the LWP::Simple module to fetch the quote using the appropriate URL for Yahoo's quote CGI program. The format string used asks for just those fields returned by the historical data page mentioned earlier:

```
<<sub fetch_quote>>=
sub fetch_quote {
    my $symbol = shift;
    my $format = 'd1ohgl1v';
    my $url    = 'http://quote.yahoo.com/d/';
    my $quote  = get("$url/quotes.csv?s=$symbol&f=$format&e=.csv");
    $quote =~ s/\s+$/\n/; # replace line ending with newline
    return $quote;
}
@
```

The routine to append the quote to the data file is straightforward. We open the data file for append (using the >> syntax), write the quote to the file, and close the file:

```
<<sub write_quote>>=
sub write_quote {
    my ($symbol, $quote) = @_;
    open(DBASE, ">>$root_dir/$symbol.csv") || die "can't: $!";
    print DBASE $quote;
    close DBASE;
}
@
```

Reading the data is a little more complicated. The plot_to_gif() function we use later (supplied by the GIFgraph module) requires an array of array references with each array reference being the x-axis and y-axis data sets. In our case, we supply two y-axis data sets, one for the closing price and one for the volume traded. We implicitly create our array references using techniques shown in chapter 8. First, we open the data file and throw away the first line. (The downloaded historical data includes a first line that gives all the field names for the data.) We then collect the data we want and use a `map()` function on the x-axis data (the dates) to remove the quotes that surround this field:

```
<<sub read_data>>=
sub read_data {
    my $symbol = shift;
    my @data;
    open(FILE, "$root_dir/$symbol.csv")||die "can't open file: $!";
    $_ = <FILE>; # throw out first line
    <<collect data>>
    close FILE;
    @{$data[0]} = map{s/^"|"$//g;$_} @{$data[0]};
    return @data;
}
@
```

Collecting the data is simply a matter of pushing the value of the appropriate field onto the appropriate array reference. The first array reference is the x-axis data and consists of the dates; the second is the first y-axis data consisting of the last price for a given day; and the second y-axis data is the volume traded on a given day:

```
<<collect data>>=
while ( <FILE> ) {
    my @fields = split /,/;
    push @{$data[0]},$fields[0];
    push @{$data[1]},$fields[4];
    push @{$data[2]},$fields[5];
}
@
```

The routine to create the `gif` chart is long, but most of it is simply setting a series of options for the graph. The `GIFgraph` modules are object-oriented and do not export any functions into our program. Instead, we create a graph object using a fully qualified module name to that modules `new()` function. This `new()` function returns an object that we then use to call the other methods to set options in the graph and to write the graph to a `gif` file:

```
<<sub make_gif>>=
sub make_gif {
    my($title, @data) = @_;

    my $graph = GIFgraph::mixed->new();
    $graph->set_legend('Close Price', 'Volume Traded');

    $graph->set(
        title              => $title,
        two_axes           => 1,
        types              => ['lines', 'bars'],
```

```
    x_label            => 'Date',
    y1_label           => 'Close Price',
    y2_label           => 'Volume Traded',
    y_min_value        => 0,
    x_label_position   => 1/2,
    x_labels_vertical  => 1,
    x_label_skip       => 5,
    t_margin           => 10,
    b_margin           => 10,
    r_margin           => 10,
    l_margin           => 10,
    legend_placement   => 'BC',
    );
    $graph->plot_to_gif("$title.gif", \@data);
}
@
```

This creates a mixed chart that consists of a line chart for the first y-axis (closing price) and a bar char for the second y-axis (volume traded). The chart is written to a filename consisting of the symbol name with a *.gif* extension.

All of the methods and options used above are well described in the GIF-graph documentation. The object-oriented syntax may seem a bit strange at first, but it isn't hard to get used to. Just think of the object $graph above as a reference with its own methods (functions). You create the object and then use the object to call its functions. We will go into more detail about objects in the advanced section of this book. For now, we merely have to make use of the OO calling syntax, which is straightforward. All OO modules should provide examples of using them in their documentation.

That's the extent of the program. You can place all of these files—the script itself, the *stock.conf* file, and the csv data files—in a directory in your personal web directory (*public_html* on many systems) and change the first two variables in the script to point to this location. Then you can set up a scheduler program, such as cron, to log you onto your ISP and run this program every weeknight at midnight or 4 A.M. before logging you out. If you also create a static HTML page in this directory that sources the gif files with an <IMG SRC="..."> tag, then every morning you can load that page in your browser and have up-to-date charts (without having to log on first to your ISP). For example, here is a minimal HTML page to display the two charts used in the above example data:

```
<HTML>
<HEAD>
<TITLE> Stock Tracker </TITLE>
</HEAD>
<BODY>
```

```
<H1 align=center> Latest Stock Charts </H1>
<CENTER>
<IMG SRC='MNCb.TO.gif'>
<IMG SRC='TMF.gif'>
</CENTER>
</BODY>
</HTML>
```

You can certainly build quite a bit of customization from this framework. You can make use of the additional purchase data shown above in the *stock.conf* file to create a running chart of total investment value, or you can have the program itself write out the HTML page, including a table of currently owned shares and values, and profits or losses for each stock. You could even have the program inform you when your stocks attain or fall below a certain value.

14.7   CGI.pm

Although Perl has been around a lot longer than the Internet, and is used for an incredible variety of tasks, it is probably an interest in Internet and CGI programming that draws most newcomers to the language. Perl is well suited for this particular niche. We will not attempt to describe or explain the protocol that CGI programs use, nor will we discuss the HTML markup language and all the details of form creation. What we will do in this section is make use of the CGI.pm module included with the standard distribution to create a simple web-based CGI version of our faqgrep program.

This program will be used to search the HTML documentation. (See perldoc installhtml to install a set of HTML formatted documentation on your system if one is not already installed for you.) You will need to know where the HTML docs are installed on your machine to make use of this script. You will also need a webserver and permission to install and execute CGI programs on your system— not a problem if you are using your own machine, but it might be a problem if your only access to Perl is on an ISP's system.

The CGI.pm module takes care of the details of speaking the protocol. You can even have it write most or all of the HTML markup for your pages and forms. However, if you intend to focus your Perl skills on CGI programming, you need to familiarize yourself with these details as well as the details of various webservers and client software.

The CGI.pm module provides both an OO interface and a procedural (function) interface. Because our script here is simple, we use the function interface and import the standard functions this module provides by including an argument to use Module call to tell it we want the standard functions. Our top level script is

```
<<faqgrep-cgi.pl>>=
#!/usr/bin/perl -w
use strict;
use CGI qw/:standard/;
<<config variables>>
<<print start of page>>
<<print form>>
<<search FAQs if a pattern is supplied>>
<<print end of page>>
<<subroutine to search FAQ questions>>
@
```

We need to set a couple of configuration variables to point to the absolute path to the HTML documentation files and a root path to use for setting up hyperlinks to any questions we find:

```
<<config variables>>=
my $faqdir = '/usr/local/etc/httpd/htdocs/nperl/nmanual/pod';
my $root   = 'nperl/nmanual/pod';
@
```

Printing out the correct headers to start off your page is a simple matter of using the provided functions. We also print out a level one heading at the top of the page, followed by a brief explanation of the search tool:

```
<<print start of page>>=
print header(),
      start_html('Perl FAQ-finder'),"\n",
      h1('Perl FAQ-Finder'), "\n";
print<<EOF;
<P> This is a limited tool for grepping through the Perl FAQs. Simply
enter a search term (or list of terms) into the entry box below
and hit the search button. A list of links to all the questions
containing any of the search terms will be returned.
</P>
EOF
@
```

Next, we create the form, providing a method and action argument to the start_form() function, followed by a prompt to enter the search terms, a textfield element, the submission button, and the end of the form:

```
<<print form>>=
print start_form(-method => 'post',
                 -action => 'http://localhost/cgi-bin/faqgrep-cgi.pl'),
      "Enter a Keyword: ",textfield('pattern'), "\n",
      submit(),
      end_form();
@
```

That's all there is to creating the initial page with the query form. The rest of the program handles what takes place if the `pattern` parameter contains actual data—as it would once a search term was entered in the textfield and the submit button was pressed.

```
<<search FAQs if a pattern is supplied>>=
if (param('pattern')) {
    <<set up variables>>
    <<read the faqdir for FAQ documents>>
    <<retrieve, sort, and print the search results>>
}
@
```

Here we just set up variables to hold the keywords passed in and the pattern we construct from those keywords:

```
<<set up variables>>=
my $keywords = param('pattern');
my $pattern  = join('|', split ' ', $keywords );
@
```

That last line splits the string of keywords into a list of words and rejoins that list with the regex alternation operator in between. This gives a pattern of alternations so we can search for any of the terms supplied.

Using the `opendir/readdir/closedir` functions from the previous chapter, we quickly get a list of all the files in the FAQ directory that have the pattern `m/faq/` in them:

```
<<read the faqdir for faq documents>>=
opendir(FAQDIR,$faqdir)||die "can't open $faqdir: $!";
my @faqs=grep /faq/,readdir FAQDIR;
close FAQDIR;
@
```

We will retrieve the relevant FAQs using a modified `grep_faq_heads()` routine, which returns a single string of all the results and a count of how many FAQ entries were found. Each result in this string contains a score of how many times the pattern matched against the particular entry so we can sort our results with the highest scoring results first. We use a Schwartzian Transform type of sort routine (from chapter 12) to do this. Finally, we print out the sorted list of results, which are already formatted as hyperlinks to the actual FAQ entry in the HTML documents:

```
<<retrieve, sort, and print the search results>>=
my ($result,$count)=grep_faq_heads($pattern, @faqs);
$result = join("\n",map  {$_->[0]}
                    sort {$b->[1]<=>$a->[1]}
                    map  {[$_,m/^<li>(\d+)/g]}split /\n/,$result);
```

```
print "Keywords '$keywords' returned $count hits:<br>",
      "<ul> $result </ul>";
@
```

Printing the end of the page involves a call to the appropriate function imported from the CGI module:

```
<<print end of page>>=
print end_html();
@
```

The routine to search the FAQ heads is quite similar to the one we used in the original faqgrep program. The only differences are that our search pattern must look for level 2 HTML headings rather than the POD headings we used previously; we also need to construct our results as an HTML list of hyperlinks to the appropriate documents and maintain a record of the number of "hits" we got on the search terms:

```
<<subroutine to search FAQ questions>>=
sub grep_faq_heads {
    my ($pattern, @faqs) = @_;
    my $count=0;
    my $result='';
    foreach my $faq (@faqs) {
        open(FAQ,"$faqdir/$faq")||die "can't open $faq: $!";
        while (<FAQ>) {
            if (m/^<h2><a name="([^"]+)">(.*?\b(?:$pattern).*)/oi){
                $count++;
                my ($where,$what)=($1,$2);
                my $score = grep {$what=~m/\b$_/i} split /\|/, $pattern;
                my $url    = "http://localhost/$root/$faq#$where";
                $result   .= qq|<li> $score <a href="$url">$what</a>|;
            }
        }
        close FAQ;
    }
    return ($result,$count);
}
@
```

That's the whole program. You can place it in your cgi-bin directory (assuming you have permission) and point your browser to its URL to bring up the initial search page. Enter a term such as "sort," click the submit button, and you should get a new page with the search form (in case you want to do another search), followed by a list of successful hits that you can click on to go directly to the FAQ entry.

For testing and debugging your CGI script—using *CGI.pm* of course—you can run the program from the command line and pass in parameters as arguments to the script. The section of the *CGI.pm* documentation on debugging explains the various ways you can do this. If you plan on running your CGI scripts on your ISP's server—have permission to—I strongly suggest that you obtain one of the many free webservers available and install it on your own machine. This will allow you more freedom to test and debug your script before you upload it to your server.

The Perl FAQs list several other resources you can turn to if you are having problems with your CGI programs. For further information, see the *perlfaq3* page under the question: "Where can I learn about CGI or web programming in Perl?"

14.8 Reuse, don't reinvent

We have barely scratched the surface of the modules introduced above, let alone the many others available on CPAN, but I hope you can see how using modules can greatly simplify your task as a programmer. Remember, CPAN exists for a reason—to help you solve problems and generally make your life easier. These modules have been looked at and used by a large community of Perl programmers on a variety of systems and, consequently, have had the large majority of bugs hammered out.

On the other hand, sometimes a module does far more than you need and using it can consume more resources than is required. For a critical application, you might be better off coding just what you need. Still, you can obtain the module and borrow or modify just the code you need rather than starting from scratch. Another reason you might forego using a module is to simply practice and develop your own coding skills. If a module exists for something you are coding yourself, you can always compare your code to the module code with an eye to understanding any differences in logic or method.

If you want to design and build a new-fangled solar powered car, it doesn't make sense to waste time reinventing the wheel—at least not until you've designed a prototype car and discovered that the current wheels could be improved.

As promised at the beginning of this chapter, we present in table 14.1 a list of main categories for modules on CPAN.

Table 14.1   Main categories for CPAN modules

Category	Description
Perl Core Modules	This category refers to the modules already included in the standard distribution, along with a few that may be included in the future.
Development Support	Modules to assist developers, such as a make replacement and tools to profile code.

Table 14.1 **Main categories for CPAN modules (continued)**

Category	Description
Operating System Interfaces	Modules providing interfaces to various operating specific tools and information.
Networking Devices IPC	Modules implementing various networking protocols, such as Telnet, FTP, and SNMP, among others.
Data Type Utilities	Modules that implement or work with various data types, such as Bit vectors, Dates, and several Math extensions.
Database Interfaces	Interfaces to a variety of database systems, including Oracle, MySQL, and Postgress among others.
User Interfaces	Modules for creating user interfaces, including terminal-based interfaces and many graphical toolkit interfaces.
Language Interfaces	A few modules for using Perl in conjunction with other languages.
File Names Systems Locking	Modules for managing files and to implement file locking procedures.
String Lang Text Proc	Modules for manipulating or parsing text in various data or markup languages, such as SGML, XML, and for performing linguistic/grammatical operations on plain old English.
Opt Arg Param Proc	Modules for processing command line options and configuration files.
Internationalization Locale	Modules for working with character sets other than plain ASCII.
Security and Encryption	Variety of encryption and authentication modules.
World Wide Web HTML HTTP CGI	A large collection of modules for various aspects of web programming. Parse HTML, create web clients, write your own webserver. The tools are here for the taking.
Server and Daemon Utilities	Small collection of server and daemon utilites.
Archiving and Compression	Modules for data compression and archiving as well as some data conversion modules.
Images Pixmaps Bitmaps	Variety of modules for creating and manipulating images in various formats. Summarize your web statistics in a chart in GIF format for your webpage.
Mail and Usenet News	Modules to implement various client software for sending and retrieving News or Mail.
Control Flow Utilities	Small set of modules that handle or extend basic flow of control.
File Handle Input Output	Several I/O modules for doing—what else—I/O.
Microsoft Windows Modules	A few modules dealing with Windows-specific issues/features.
Miscellaneous Modules	A mish-mash of things not classified into the other categories.
Commercial Software Interfaces	An Altavista search development kit seems to tbe only thing in this category.

14.9 Exercises

1 Go to your nearest CPAN mirror site and explore the wealth of modules there. Download, install, and try out any that catch your attention.

C H A P T E R   1 5

Debugging

By this time, you've probably encountered many error and warning statements due to inevitable programming mistakes that resulted in syntax errors or runtime warnings. (For example, using == instead of eq to compare two strings). If you followed the advice given in chapter 3, you have tackled one error at a time, checked the *perldiag* pod-page if you didn't understand the error message, and checked the reported line number carefully (and those preceding it if the line checked out okay). You are probably already quite used to taking care of these minor problems.

This chapter is about tackling subtler kinds of problems, logic errors (or syntax OK errors) that are caused not by faulty syntax but by faulty logic in the code. Errors like these range from using = instead of ==—though this is often caught by the -w switch—to faulty loop boundaries—looping from 0..10 when you meant to loop from 0..9—to simply using bad equations for some formula in your code. Sometimes an actual error message might be emitted, such as a division by zero message, but you are sure the variable being used should be non-zero.

Essentially, two ways exist to track down such problems: manually examining the code and strategically placing print() statements; and using the Perl debugger to walk through your program. We introduce both methods in this chapter.

15.1   Debugging by hand

Usually your first response to a bug—whether detected by you or reported by a user of your program—is a cursory examination of the relevant code, or at least the code you think is relevant. If nothing obvious is readily apparent, it is time to begin debugging in earnest. Make a backup of your current version of the program so you can always return to where you started.

The first thing you need to do in any debugging situation is have a condition or set of conditions—for example, input values or a specific set of events—under which the program repeatedly fails or exhibits the offending behavior. You already have a description of the problem from your own experiments or a bug report. If you can't reliably reproduce the bug, it'll be that much harder to track it down. It also means you may not gain a real understanding of the underlying problem and you may not be able to say with any certainty that you've fixed the problem.

Often, finding a set of conditions under which the program fails to perform its task is often enough to point you to the problem area, but you should strive to find the simplest set of conditions that produce the bug, not just any set of bug-producing conditions.

Sometimes finding these conditions is not as easy as checking input given to the program. You might have a random number generator supplying numbers to part of an equation, and that equation might not produce correct results with a certain range of numbers. In such a case you, may have to write a separate function to replace the random number function, one that outputs a predictable series of numbers. This way you can determine the failure range systematically rather than randomly.

Once you are armed with the problem description and a reliable way to reproduce it, you can begin phase two: isolating the problem code. In fact, at this point, you've probably already narrowed the problem down to a small section of code. Two simple techniques exist to narrow down the search. If the problem produces a warning or error message, you can comment out several lines of code (and function calls) until the message disappears. Then uncomment them slowly until the problem reappears—using your head of course. If you comment out a variable declaration but not another line that uses that variable, you'll wind up with more errors. If the problem is simply bad results being produced from good input data, then you'll have to work out what the intermediary results, if any, should be. Then you can insert print statements to print out the input data, plus additional intermediary data, to locate where the program begins deviating from correct behavior. Let's look at an example.

We have a report that the table being produced by one of our programs is sometimes incorrectly formatted, and we have an example of the badly printed table:

```
142a13   John       Doe       Sales       pt
666s66   Lucy       Kindser   Operations  ft
131b21   Christine  Smith     Sales       pt
119d17   Frank      Cannon    Support     pt
971a22   Jane       Doe       Operations  ft
```

The table is being produced by a program that pulls up employee records based on search criteria. Previously, the records were just printed as colon-separated records without formatting. We just added the routine to print the formatted table, so we know the problem lies somewhere in that routine. We can create a new program file, copy the table printing routine and any others it uses, and copy some database records to use as test data. In particular, we need to use at least the records represented in the faulty table above. We also add some code to create the array to be printed by the routine:

```perl
#!/usr/bin/perl -w
use strict;

chomp( my @data = <DATA> );
@data = map{[split /:/]} @data;
print_table(@data);
```

```perl
sub print_table {
    my @table = @_;
    my @transpose = transpose(@table);
    my @lengths = map{ max_length(@$_) } @transpose;
    for( my $i = 0; $i < @table; $i++ ){
        my $columns = @{$table[$i]};
        for( my $j = 0; $j < $columns; $j++ ) {
            print "$table[$i][$j]  ";
            print " " x ($lengths[$j] - length($table[$i][$j]) );
        }
        print "\n";
    }
}

sub transpose(@) {
    my @mat = @_;
    my @return;
    for(my $i=0;$i<@mat;$i++){
        for(my $j=0;$j<@{$mat[$i]};$j++){
            $return[$j][$i]=$mat[$i][$j];
        }
    }
    return @return;
}

sub max_length {
    my @list = @_;
    my $max = length( shift @list );
    for( my $i = 1; $i < @list; $i++ ) {
        my $length = length( $list[$i] );
        $max = $length if $max < $length;
    }
    return $max;
}

__DATA__
142a13:John:Doe:Sales:pt
119d17:Frank:Cannon:Support:pt
131b21:Christine:Smith:Sales:pt
666s66:Lucy:Kindser:Operations:ft
971a22:Jane:Doe:Operations:ft
```

When we run this we find that we get a properly formatted table like so:

```
142a13  John       Doe      Sales      pt
119d17  Frank      Cannon   Support    pt
666s66  Lucy       Kindser  Operations ft
131b21  Christine  Smith    Sales      pt
971a22  Jane       Doe      Operations ft
```

So the routine appears to be working just as it did when we first created it. The only difference between this table and the faulty table—aside from the bad formatting on the second line of the faulty table—is the order of the data. We change our data to reflect the order given in the faulty table and run it again. This time, we do indeed get incorrect formatting on the second line of the resulting table.

The bad formatting begins after the third field being printed. Everything after that is shifted one character to the right. We also notice that the name in that field, Kindser, is the longest entry in that column. As an experiment, we decide to switch this line of data with the line containing Christine in the second field (Christine represents the longest entry in that column) and rerun our test with the following results:

```
142a13  John    Doe       Sales         pt
131b21  Christine  Smith      Sales          pt
666s66  Lucy    Kindser  Operations  ft
119d17  Frank   Cannon   Support     pt
971a22  Jane    Doe       Operations  ft
```

Now, again, the second line is shifted right, but this time the shift begins at the second field. The line is shifted much farther to the right than previously. In fact, it is shifted right by four characters, exactly the difference in length between Christine and the next longest entry, Frank. We know we have code to determine the longest entry in any column so that our routine can print out the columns appropriately spaced. It appears that our routine is ignoring the second row of data when doing these calculations. Let's look at our max_length() function more closely:

```perl
sub max_length {
    my @list = @_;
    my $max = length( shift @list );
    for( my $i = 1; $i < @list; $i++ ) {
        my $length = length( $list[$i] );
        $max = $length if $max < $length;
    }
    return $max;
}
```

Can you spot the problem in this code? If not, don't worry. It's the kind of mistake that can slip by without noticing. First, let's test our hypothesis. We set up another test program to test just this function, and we insert some print statements to see what's going on:

```perl
#!/usr/bin/perl -w
use strict;
my @words = qw/abc defghi jklm nop/;
my $max = max_length(@words);
print "max length is $max\n";
sub max_length {
    print "Now in max_length sub\n";              #DEBUG
    my @list = @_;
```

```
    print "\twords are: @list\n";                    #DEBUG
    my $max = length( shift @list );
    for( my $i = 1; $i < @list; $i++ ) {
        my $length = length( $list[$i] );
        $max = $length if $max < $length;
        print "\tnow testing: $list[$i]\n";          #DEBUG
    }
    print "Leaving max_length sub\n\n";               #DEBUG
    return $max;
}
```

This gives the following output:

```
Now in max_length sub
        words are: abc defghi jklm nop
        now testing: jklm
        now testing: nop
Leaving max_length sub

max length is 4
```

What's this? We know we are shifting off the first word from the list right away in the program and putting its length in $max. This leaves three elements in the array to which to compare lengths, but we are only testing the last two. The word defghi never gets tested. Looking at the for loop counter variable, we realize that we are looping through the array starting at index 1, thus we never test the string at $list[0].

If this seems like too obvious an error to make, just think about the possible logic while writing the subroutine. The programmer thinks that there are two ways to avoid an unnecessary comparison of the length of the first element in the list with itself: 1) shift the first element and get its length, then compare to the rest of the array, or 2) get the length of the first element (without shifting it off) and compare to the rest of the array starting at the second element (index 1). So, perhaps the programmer wasn't paying enough attention when writing this relatively simple routine and accidently implemented both ideas—thus skipping the comparison with the second element. The routine appeared to work in a few small tests that never happened to have the longest element in the second position.

At any rate, we can correct the subroutine in one of two ways:

```
sub max_length {
    my @list = @_;
    my $max = length( $list[0] );
    for( my $i = 1; $i < @list; $i++ ) {
        my $length = length( $list[$i] );
        $max = $length if $max < $length;
    }
    return $max;
}
```

DEBUGGING BY HAND   *261*

```
sub max_length {
    my @list = @_;
    my $max = length( shift @list );
    foreach my $item ( @list ) {
        my $length = length( $item );
        $max = $length if $max < $length;
    }
    return $max;
}
```

I prefer the second solution because I advocate using a for(;;) loop only when you need to count something or to keep track of the indices of the array. In this case, a foreach loop suffices to iterate through the loop. We fix the routine using the second example and run the corrected program through ALL of the tests with which we originally tested the program, as well as the new test that demonstrated the bug. You always need to ensure that a new version, even with a minor bug correction such as this, passes all the tests you've developed for this program, just in case you introduced a new bug . This is referred to as *regression testing*.

We can summarize the general steps in debugging with the following list:

1 Describe the bug.

2 Reproduce the bug (reliably).

3 Isolate the source of the bug in the code.

4 Understand the root cause of the bug.

5 Correct the bug.

6 Add a new test to the test suite to cover this bug.

7 Fully test the corrected program.

15.2   The Perl debugger

An interactive debugger can be useful tool when your code is giving you problems. The perl binary has such a debugging aid built right in to the program. While I am not a big fan of interactive debuggers, they can be useful. You should know how to use the Perl debugger with your programs.

An interactive debugger is a tool that gives you controls over the execution of your program that include executing it line by line; setting breakpoints to stop execution at a certain line; viewing the current values of variables at a given point in the program; and resuming execution of the program after pausing.

You invoke the Perl debugger by using the -d command line switch when you invoke Perl on your program:

```
$ perl -d programname
```

Before we take a look at the things we can do with the debugger, let's take a look a brief session running the debugger on the following simple script:

```perl
#!/usr/bin/perl -w
use strict;

my $x = 42;
my $y = 2;
print $x / $y, "\n";

my @array = (13,42,2);
my $aref = [ [13,42,2],[11,12,13] ];

foreach my $item ( @array ) {
    print "$item\n";
}
__END__
```

We save this into a file called *blah* for lack of a better name. Sure, I know this program doesn't do much, but it will let us experiment with the debugger. Here is part of a session on this program. I have added line numbers in the left margin to make it easy to refer certain lines in the text that follows:

```
1:    [danger:ajohnson:~]$ perl -d blah
2:
3:    Loading DB routines from perl5db.pl version 1.0401
4:    Emacs support available.
5:
6:    Enter h or 'h h' for help.
7:
8:    main::(blah:4): my $x = 42;
9:      DB<1> s
10:   main::(blah:5): my $y = 2;
11:     DB<1> s
12:   main::(blah:6): print $x / $y, "\n";
13:     DB<1> s
14:   21
15:   main::(blah:8): my @array = (13,42,2);
16:      DB<1> s
17:   main::(blah:9): my $aref = [ [13,42,2],[11,12,13] ];
18:     DB<1> print "@array";
19:   13 42 2
20:     DB<2> x @array
21:   0   13
22:   1   42
23:   2   2
24:     DB<3> s
25:   main::(blah:11):           foreach my $item ( @array ) {
26:     DB<3> print "$aref"
27:   ARRAY(0x8232ccc)
28:     DB<4> x $aref
29:   0   ARRAY(0x8232ccc)
```

```
30:      0   ARRAY(0x8232db0)
31:         0   13
32:         1   42
33:         2   2
34:      1   ARRAY(0x82357e0)
35:         0   11
36:         1   12
37:         2   13
38:    DB<5> q
39:    [danger:ajohnson:~]$
```

The first few lines just provide the version and other configuration information. The real stuff starts on line 8 above. Here the debugger lists the first line of code that will be executed (located in the main package, in file *blah* at line 4). The next line gives us the debugger prompt which looks like DB<1>. The debugger command s tells the debugger to step through and execute the current line of code. We enter this command at the prompt and hit return. Then we see the next line of code to execute and the next prompt. We step through two more lines of code and, when we execute the print statement (at line 13 above), we can see the output of that statement before we see the next line to execute and the next prompt.

After we've stepped through the line of code that initializes the array @array, we enter a regular Perl statement at the prompt. That statement gets executed (see lines 18 and 19 above) without affecting our place in the program. Hence, we can always look at the current value of any variable at any point in the program's execution.

At line 20, we use the debugger's x command, which causes the debugger to output the given variables value in a pretty-printed format, which explicitly lists the array indices and their corresponding values. We do the same thing at line 28 and see the data structure ($aref) printed out in its expanded form. This is convenient for examining nested structures while debugging. Finally, we use the q command to quit the debugger session.

The above might not seem like much, but being able to walk or step through each line of code and examine variable values—or change them—at any given point can be useful when you trying to debug a piece of code. This is like using print statements in the manner of manual debugging, but without having to write them into the code—and without having to locate and delete them later.

The debugger can also do a lot more than just the few commands described above. The *perldebug* pod-page describes all of the commands and actions you can set and perform within the debugger environment. We will discuss only a few of the more commonly used debugging commands shown in table 15.1 on page 265.

Table 15.1 Debugging commands

Command	Description
s	Step through and execute the current statement, including descending into subroutines.
n	Step through and execute current statement; do not descend into subroutines.
c	Continue. Program executes until a breakpoint is hit, a watchpoint is triggered, or the end of the program is encountered.
c line	Program continues until the given line number (or the next breakpoint or watchpoint condition if earlier).
b	Set a breakpoint at the current line.
b line	Set a breakpoint at the given line number.
b condition	Set a breakpoint that will break only if the given condition evaluates to true. Can be combined with line option as in b line condition.
b subname	Set a breakpoint at the first line of the given subroutine. Can be combined with condition.
d	Delete breakpoint at current line.
d line	Delete breakpoint at given line.
D	Delete all breakpoints.
W expr	Add a watch expression.
W	Remove all watch expressions.
L	List all breakpoints and actions.
l	List next few lines.
w	List a window of lines around the given line. (A window of lines is simply a few lines above and below.)
p expr	Print the value of expr, using Perl's print statement.
x expr	Evaluates expr in list context and prints the result in a pretty-printed manner. Prints nested structures.
R	Reload the script and start again.

When you set a breakpoint on a line, you can then use the c (continue) command to run the program and it will halt when it reaches that line—or halt each time it reaches that line if the line is in a loop or subroutine. Setting a condition on a breakpoint allows even finer control. In this case, the program will be halted only if the condition evaluates to a true value.

A watch expression works similarly to a breakpoint, except, instead of halting execution at a given line, a watch expression halts execution whenever the given expression changes. Note, the break will occur when the expression changes—not when it becomes true:

```
#!/usr/bin/perl -w
use strict;
my @array = (12, 7, 3, 11, 9, 14);
my $sum = 0;
foreach my $item (@array) {
    $sum += $item;
}
print "$sum\n";
```

If we save the above code in a file named *blah2*, we can try out some of these commands in a session:

```
[danger:ajohnson:~]$ perl -d blah2

Loading DB routines from perl5db.pl version 1.0401
Emacs support available.

Enter h or 'h h' for help.

main::(blah2:3):          my @array = (12, 7, 3, 11, 9, 14);
  DB<1> l
3==>      my @array = (12, 7, 3, 11, 9, 14);
4:        my $sum = 0;
5:        foreach my $item (@array) {
6:            $sum += $item;
7         }
8:        print "$sum\n";
  DB<1> b 6 $sum == 42
  DB<2> c
main::(blah2:6):              $sum += $item;
  DB<2> print $item
14
```

Here we used the l command to list a few lines of code. The ==> shows the line about to be executed. Next, we set a conditional breakpoint to halt the program at line 6 only when the value of $sum is equal to 42. Then we use the c to continue execution. The program breaks at line 6, before executing it, when that condition is met. We print out the value of the current $item in the array and see that it is 14. We loop through the array until the sum is 42, then stop on the next loop iteration. Here is another session using a watchpoint after reloading the script:

```
  DB<3> R
Warning: some settings and command-line options may be lost!

Loading DB routines from perl5db.pl version 1.0401
Emacs support available.
Enter h or 'h h' for help.

main::(blah2:3):          my @array = (12, 7, 3, 11, 9, 14);
  DB<3> D
```

CHAPTER 15   DEBUGGING

```
Deleting all breakpoints...
  DB<3> s
main::(blah2:4):          my $sum = 0;
  DB<3> s
main::(blah2:5):          foreach my $item (@array) {
  DB<3> W $sum == 42
  DB<4> c
Watchpoint 0:    $sum == 42 changed:
    old value:   ''
    new value:   '1'
main::(blah2:5):          foreach my $item (@array) {
  DB<4> print $item
9
```

Here we used the R command to reload the script and the D command to delete all breakpoints since breakpoints are save across reloaded sessions. Then we step through two lines of code and set a watchpoint to halt execution when $sum is 42. This time, execution halts immediately after the sum becomes 42 and before the next loop assignment is performed. Notice how when the program halts, the value of $item is 9. Execution has halted right after the line in which the watch expression changed. (The watch expression changed from a false value to a true value—but execution would also have halted had we used an expression of $sum != 42, which would have evaluated to true and then changed to false at the same point in the program.)

Getting used to using a command line interactive debugger takes practice. There are many more commands for Perl's debugger than those few shown in table 15.1. (See the *perldebug* pod-page.) Many people are content to debug manually using techniques shown at the beginning of this chapter. In fact, having my editor set up to run the current file's contents as a Perl script, or a selected portion of it, with a simple keystroke and see the output in another window gives me quite a bit of flexibility in debugging without using a debugger. Other options are to use a graphical interface to the Perl debugger. Links to a few such front ends can be found at *http://reference.perl.com/query.cgi?debug*.

The only exercise for debugging is simply to debug. If you are like most programmers, you will have plenty of opportunity to do so on your own projects. Even if you don't think you'd like using the debugger very much you should give it a try—even just to play around with it on working scripts to see what kinds of things are possible. Above all, try to view each debugging experience you go through as an opportunity to learn, not only how to track down errors, but what kind of errors you tend to make. That way you can work harder at preventing them. Debugging is an investigative procedure; the problems are not always readily apparent. Be patient and focus on slowly and systematically narrowing down the scope of the problem by whatever means you can.

And, lastly, remember that the more work you put into up-front design and good programming practices, the less debugging you'll have to do later. So before you start typing code, grab your pencil and paper and map out the design for your solution. I mean that last remark quite literally. Even with today's technology of smart programming editors, debuggers, and whiz bang word processors, I still rely heavily on what I refer to as my "thought processor"—just myself, a pad of graph paper, and my Rotring mechanical pencil (and sometimes a good dark ale doesn't hurt either).

PART IV

Advanced elements

C H A P T E R   1 6

Modular programming

Back in chapter 7, we noted a few reasons for creating and using functions: to hide information; to reduce complexity; and to avoid duplicate code—write it once, use it often. Modular programming is about achieving the same benefits on a wider scale.

We have written a number of little programs in the previous chapters. Until chapter 14 they were all small, self-contained programs. In chapter 14, we made use of modules, written by others, that were external to our programs and provided additional functionality. We reused existing code. In this chapter, we will learn how to create our own modules.

Before we delve into the mechanics of building a module, let's consider a simple case that illustrates how a module helps us reuse our code. Recall the function we wrote in chapter 10 for putting commas in numbers. This is a good little function that does one—and only one—thing. Perhaps we have already reused this function by copying or pasting it into other programs where we needed such a function. Reuse of code is a good thing, but this kind of reuse is problematic. First, when we decide we need that `commify` function, we need to locate one of our previous programs to copy it from. This is not very convenient. Secondly, what if we eventually find that this function has a bug in it and doesn't properly commify a certain numeric input? Now we have to fix this bug and find all the other programs we've written and fix the function there as well. Wouldn't it be better if we could simply write this function in one file and then use it from any other program we create? Well, we can and will do just that.

16.1 Modules and packages

Perl provides a couple of ways for us to use code written in a file other than our main program file. The two common ways involve the `require()` function, or the use statement. We will focus on the latter method, which was introduced with Perl version 5 and has become the most common method for modularization.

As we saw in chapter 14, to use a properly installed Perl module we need only tell Perl we want to use it:

```
use SomeModule;
```

When Perl encounters such a statement it searches through a series of directories (defined when Perl was first compiled) and looks for a file named *SomeModule.pm*. The search path used by Perl is stored in the special array `@INC` (the include array) which you can view by typing `perl -V` on the command line or running the following script:

```
#!/usr/bin/perl -w
use strict;
print join("\n", @INC);
```

The output of the above script produces the following result on my machine:

```
/usr/local/lib/perl5/5.00502/i586-linux
/usr/local/lib/perl5/5.00502
/usr/local/lib/perl5/site_perl/5.005/i586-linux
/usr/local/lib/perl5/site_perl/5.005 .
```

When Perl finds the right file, it compiles and executes it and then continues compiling the rest of our script. The functions defined in the module are then available within our main program either as imported functions, callable simply by name, or as external functions, callable by using the fully qualified *package* syntax, which we will explain directly.

One problem with using one or more modules is that different modules may define functions or variables with the same name. If we use two modules that each define a function called blah(), then which one would get run when we used that function? To avoid such problems, Perl also has a package declaration. The main program is always package main, but other modules can and should be given their own package names. These package names must be the same as the filename without the *.pm* suffix. For example, to make a module named Blah, you could create a file named *Blah.pm* like so:

```
package Blah;

sub blah {
    print "I am blah() from package Blah::\n";
}
1;
```

Note two things about this module: it does not define any import function, and it has a final statement of simply 1;. This last statement is a standard convention. When Perl compiles and executes your included module, the last statement executed must return a true value or Perl will report an error condition.

We can now write a program that uses this module:

```
#!/usr/bin/perl -w
use strict;
use Blah;

Blah::blah(); # fully qualified function call
blah();       # unqualified function call
```

```
sub blah {
    print "I am blah() from package main::\n"
}
```

Now, because the current directory is in the included search path (see output of @INC above), I can run this new script and get the following output:

```
I am blah() from package Blah::
I am blah() from package main::
```

In this way, I have two functions named blah(), one of which is in package main:: and the other in package Blah::. Each function is defined within its own package. A package is simply a different namespace for function and variable definitions. What if we want to import a function into our main namespace so we can call it without using the fully qualified package name every time? In this case, you need to set up an import() function that instructs Perl as to which functions will be imported into the main namespace by default, and which ones can be manually imported. Fortunately, Perl provides us with a tool h2xs and a few other modules that together give us everything we need to create new modules with a minimum of fuss.

16.2 Making a module

Perl comes with a tool called h2xs, which can be used to create a skeleton module that only requires you to fill in the functions and variables and tell it which things you want to export. To create a module named Commify, we simply enter the following command at the command line:

```
h2xs -Xn Commify
```

Running this creates a new directory, Commify, and creates several new files. Here is the output of running this on my machine.

```
[danger:ajohnson:~]$ h2xs -Xn Commify
Writing Commify/Commify.pm
Writing Commify/Makefile.PL
Writing Commify/test.pl
Writing Commify/Changes
Writing Commify/MANIFEST
```

If you run this and then move into the Commify directory, you can open the file *Commify.pm,* which should begin with the following code:

```
package Commify;

use strict;
use vars qw($VERSION @ISA @EXPORT @EXPORT_OK);

require Exporter;
require AutoLoader;

@ISA = qw(Exporter AutoLoader);
# Items to export into callers namespace by default. Note: do not
# export names by default without a very good reason. Use EXPORT_OK
# instead.  Do not simply export all your public
# functions/methods/constants.
@EXPORT = qw(

);
$VERSION = '0.01';

# Preloaded methods go here.

# Autoload methods go after =cut, and are processed by the autosplit
# program.

1;
__END__
```

The use vars statement declares a few global variables we can use without qualification. These are all special variables that Perl's module system knows about. The next two require() lines pull in the library code that is part of Perl's module system: a library module for exporting functions and data, and one for autoloading (which is a topic we do not address in this book). Next, the special @ISA array is populated. All this means is that, if a function is called that does not exist in the current module, the modules listed in this array will be looked at in order to try to find the routine. This is an object-oriented feature called *inheritance* that we will not go into until chapter 18.

Next, an empty @EXPORT array is set up where you can put the names of functions or variables you wish to export by default. Finally, a $VERSION variable is preset with an initial version number for your module.

Some POD documentation is also already inserted at the end of the module. You should, of course, edit this to properly document your modules functionality (see chapter 9), as we will do shortly.

All you need to do at this point is begin defining the functions you wish to include in this module. In our case, we simply add our commify() function definition where it says to put preloaded methods. (A method is just another name for a function, but the term is usually used in object-oriented contexts.)

After defining our function, we need to decide whether we will export it by default, force the calling program to import it explicitly, or not export it at all. To export it by, default we add the function name to the @EXPORT array. To require manual importation, add the function to the @EXPORT_OK array. Do nothing to avoid any importation. We decide to export only if asked by the calling module. Our module now begins as

```perl
package Commify;

use strict;
use vars qw($VERSION @ISA @EXPORT @EXPORT_OK);

require Exporter;
require AutoLoader;

@ISA = qw(Exporter AutoLoader);
# Items to export into callers namespace by default. Note: do not
# export names by default without a very good reason. Use
# EXPORT_OK instead.  Do not simply export all your public
# functions/methods/constants.
@EXPORT = qw(

);
$VERSION = '0.01';

@EXPORT_OK = qw( commify );   # export on demand only

# Preloaded methods go here.

sub commify {
    my $input = shift;
    $input = reverse $input;
    $input =~ s<(\d\d\d)(?=\d)(?!\d*\.)><$1,>g;
    return scalar reverse $input;
}

# Autoload methods go after =cut, and are processed by the
# autosplit program.

1;
__END__
```

Finally, we remember to edit the documentation stub at the bottom of the module. This is a simple example module with only one function so we do not need much in the way of documentation. We may edit the POD as follows:

```
=head1 NAME

Commify - Perl extension for putting commas in numbers

=head1 SYNOPSIS

  use Commify;
  print Commify::commify('3.14159 and 1500 and 4235761.9876');

  use Commify 'commify';
  print commify('3.14159 and 1500 and 4235761.9876');

=head1 DESCRIPTION

This module provides one function that will take a string and
correctly insert commas into any numbers contained therein.

=head1 AUTHOR

Copyright: Andrew Johnson 1999. You may use this module under the
same terms as perl itself.

=head1 SEE ALSO

perl(1), perlfaq5(1).

=cut
```

And that's all there is to creating the module. The other files created by the h2xs tool automate the installation process. To install the module the automated way on Unix, you can simply run the following commands within the modules directory:

```
perl Makefile.PL
make
make test
make install
```

If you have the nmake or dmake tool on a Win32 system, then use that instead of make in the above sequence. If you cannot use either form of make, then copy the file *Commify.pm* into a directory in the @INC path.

You can now write a program that uses this module to get the commify() function. Because the commify() function was not exported by default, the calling program must either call it using a fully qualified name:

```
#!/usr/bin/perl -w
use strict;
use Commify; #imports default functions (none here)

print Commify::commify('3.14159 and 1500 and 42132765.98712');
```

or request that the function be imported by including it in a list of functions to import in the use statement:

```
#!/usr/bin/perl -w
use strict;
use Commify 'commify'; # ask to import 'commify' explicitly

print commify('3.14159 and 1500 and 42132765.98712');
```

As you can see, we can now use this function in any program we write. Should we ever discover an error in the function, we need to fix it only in the one module and reinstall it. On the other hand, a module exists on CPAN called Number::Format that already provides commification and other formatting routines that may be more appropriate to your needs. With so many good modules on CPAN, it is hard to even come up with examples that haven't been done already in one fashion or another: this is generally considered A Good Thing.

16.3   Why make modules?

In the previous section, we took a single function that we thought we might want to reuse and built a module out of it. Most modules are more than a single function. But what exactly is a module? In a general sense, a module is simply a collection of data and routines stored together in one place. However, if you recall chapter 14, or have perused CPAN at all, you have probably already noted that modules are not just willy-nilly collections of any old routines and data. Most modules have some sort of internal consistency about them; they address a particular problem space or provide a related set of data and routines.

Internal consistency or cohesion is an important design component when creating modules. Other components are similar to function design: information hiding and complexity reduction. Let's consider a simple case of a module as a related set of functions. The core Perl language only defines two basic trigonometry functions: sin() and cos(). A module that provides the full suite of trig functions would certainly be convenient. Fortunately, we don't have to create such a module. Since version 5.004, Perl has included a module called Math::Trig that already gives us these functions, as well as a constant for pi and a few other functions for converting between various angle units and coordinate systems.

Another example is the Date::Manip module we looked at in chapter 14. This module provides a large set of routines to compute date-oriented calculations. This module also demonstrates information hiding. Recall the function ParseDate() which could transform dates in several input formats into a particular format used by the other functions in the package. We do not need to know what this internal date representation is or how the transformations and calculations are carried out. We need only concentrate on using the documented functions to obtain the results we want from our input.

Complexity reduction is just the other side of the information coin. Hiding the details of implementation and data formats behind just a few routines in another module, or suite of modules, lets us write less complicated code in our main program. Consider the `LWP::Simple` module: that module uses many other modules in the `LWP` package, yet we need to use only a single function to retrieve the data we want from the web site.

These features of modules can be summarized in one simple statement: a module, like a function, should be like a black box. It operates as advertised in the POD documentation, and you do not need to know anything about how it works on the inside to use it from the outside. You need to keep this in mind when you create your own modules. Your module should not require anyone using it to know how the data is stored or how any routine works. Users should need to know only what data is available, what each function takes for arguments, and what to expect from each function. If you take users' input and store it in a hash, you should provide one or more functions so users can access the needed data. Users shouldn't have to know the data is in a hash, and they shouldn't have to access the hash themselves.

There isn't much more to know about module creation at this point. Making a module containing ten or twenty functions is no different from making a module with a single function. Object-oriented modules will be taken up in chapters 18 and 19. For more information on module use and creation, see the *perlmod* and *perlmodlib* pod pages. For more examples, take a look at some of the standard modules that are already included with your Perl distribution or visit CPAN to find modules that interest you and take a look at their insides to see how they are constructed.

16.4 Exercises

1 Use the `h2xs` tool to create a module. It doesn't matter what you put in it, just that you try out the various features. Export one or more functions by default in the `@EXPORT` array and others by demand in the `@EXPORT_OK` array. Go through the install process and then write a script that uses the module.

C H A P T E R   1 7

Algorithms and data structuring

Many problems you will encounter in your programming career will involve data that needs to be organized and structured in specific ways. Perl's built-in basic data structures—scalars, arrays, and hashes—along with Perl's reference capability allow many complex data structures to be built with relative ease. Occasionally, you will need to build new, more abstract structures out of Perl's basic types. The next three chapters explore this idea and the relationship between how you structure your data and the algorithms you use to accomplish your tasks. Some of what follows is often considered advanced for beginners, but, if you have worked your way through all the previous chapters, you are no longer a beginner, and you have the necessary background to deal with the concepts presented. If you haven't worked through the previous chapters, all bets are off since we will not be explaining any of the basic code in the algorithms that follow, only the algorithms themselves.

In this chapter, we will introduce the notion of imposing structure on your data in the context of discussions of various sorting algorithms. We will start with a few of the basic sorting routines, then introduce a sorting routine that involves a particular data structure called a *heap*. Because Perl has a very good built-in sorting function, learning how to sort isn't something you generally need to worry about when using Perl. But sorting is a well-known problem, one you are likely to be familiar with from everyday life experience.

17.1 Searching

Before we consider sorting routines themselves, let's first look at one problem where having sorted data pays off—searching. Consider the case where we have a collection of data, stored in an array, and we need to search for a particular element of our data—or find out that it doesn't exist in our array. To be more specific, imagine we have an array of employee ID numbers, and we need to know if the array contains ID number 13. If not, we want to add it to the array.

If you immediately thought that we should probably be using a hash to store our ID numbers for easy lookups then congratulations—you are thinking Perlish thoughts. However, for the moment, let's pretend Perl does not have hashes and continue with our discussion.

At first you might consider using the grep() function, which you know takes a list and returns another list containing the things for which some condition is true. In a scalar context, it returns the number of things for which the condition is true:

```
# assume @employees_id is already defined and built
my $id = 13;
unless(grep {$_ == $id} @employees_id) {
    push @employees_id, $id;
}
```

This will push the ID number onto the array unless `grep()` finds at least one element in the array that equals that ID number. Because `grep()` is designed to find all the elements that satisfy the condition, the `grep()` function tests every element in the list even after it has already found an element that satisfies the condition. This is not a very efficient method. A much better solution is to loop through the array and stop when (or if) we find our ID number:

```
my $id = 13;
my $found = 0;
foreach $item (@employees_id){
    if ($item == $id){
        $found = 1;
        last;
    }
}
push @employee_id, $id unless $found;
```

Now we have a simple linear search that progresses from the beginning to the end of our list and stops early if we find what we want. The `grep()` method always tested every element of the list which means it performed N tests in a list of length N. The second method only performs as many tests as required—but how many is that? Well, just one test, if the first element of the list matched the ID number, and N tests if only the last element matched or no elements matched. On average, however, it would do N/2 tests or half as many as the `grep()` method.

How might we improve on this algorithm? If our array was already sorted, we could then perform a binary search to find our ID number. In a binary search, we cut the search space in half at each step in the search. If we have a sorted array of one hundred ID numbers, we could easily search for a given ID number (say ID number = 420). We first examine the value at the midpoint of the array, and if it matches our target, we are done. If the target is smaller than the midpoint, we know we have to search only the lower half of the array or, conversely, the upper half if the target is larger. We then repeat this process on the lower half of the array, checking the midpoint and either finding our value or reducing the search space by half again. This method is much more efficient than a linear search.

In a list of one thousand items, a linear search (with an early stop as in our foreach loop method) would need to check an average of five hundred items, and possibly as many as one thousand if the target matched the last element or didn't exist in the array. A binary search would only have to test ten items in the array, or the number of times you can divide a one-thousand-element list in half, or less. Of course, the efficiency of the binary search comes at a price. You first have to sort the array before you can perform your search, and sorting can be a costly operation. If you will be searching your list many more times than you will be inserting new items into it, a binary search may be a good trade off.

17.2   Sorting

Many different algorithms exist for sorting, ranging from the simple to the complex. Here we will look at three relatively simple routines. Then we'll consider the *heap*—which is another way of thinking about our data—and we'll look at a sorting routine based on structuring our data as a heap. We will build each routine to sort only arrays—not lists in general as the built-in `sort()` routine does—so that Perl can sort the arrays in place. That way we won't have to build a second copy of the list to sort and return.

Probably the simplest sorting routine is called selection sort. This routine involves finding the largest element in the array of length N and swapping it with the last element in the array. This process is repeated on the remaining N - 1 elements of the array. Consider an array of length 5 containing (3, 1, 4, 5, 2). The following list shows the original list and the results of each pass through the list:

```
3 1 4 5 2
3 1 4 2 5     <-- 5 moved to (end)
3 1 2 4 5     <-- 4 moved to (end - 1)
2 1 3 4 5     <-- 3 moved to (end - 2)
1 2 3 4 5     <-- 2 moved to (end - 3)
```

A simple implementation of this routine in Perl is

```
my @array = (3,1,4,5,2);
selection_sort(@array);
print "@array\n";  # prints: 1 2 3 4 5

sub selection_sort {
    return unless @_;
    my $in    = \@_;  # take reference to input array
    my $upper = $#_;  # length of input array
    for(my $i = $upper; $i; $i--){
        my $max = $i;
        for(my $j = 0; $j < $i; $j++){
            $max = $j if $in->[$j] > $in->[$max];
        }
        ($in->[$i], $in->[$max]) = ($in->[$max], $in->[$i]);
    }
}
```

Another simple sorting routine is the insertion sort. Here we take the first element of the array and consider it a sorted list of length 1. We then take the second element in the array and insert it into its correct position in the list comprised of the first two array elements. We leave it where it is if it is larger than element 1, or we put it into position 1 and move element 1 up one position. Similarly, we add the third element by finding its proper position and moving any higher elements up one position. Here are the intermediary results of each pass on the array (3, 1, 4, 5, 2):

```
3 1 4 5 2
1 3 4 5 2    <-- 1 inserted, first 2 elements sorted
1 3 4 5 2    <-- 4 inserted, first 3 elements sorted
1 3 4 5 2    <-- 5 inserted, first 4 elements sorted
1 2 3 4 5    <-- 2 inserted, first N elements sorted

my @array = (3, 1, 4, 5, 2);
insertion_sort(@array);
print "@array\n";    # prints: 1 2 3 4 5

sub insertion_sort {
    return unless @_;
    my $in = \@_;
    for(my $j = 1; $j < @_; $j++){
        my $val = $in->[$j];
        my $i = ($j - 1);
        while($i >= 0 and $in->[$i] > $val){
            $in->[$i+1] = $in->[$i];
            $i = $i - 1;
        }
        $in->[$i + 1] = $val;
    }
}
```

Our final simple sorting algorithm is called the *bubble sort* because larger elements "bubble up" to the top (or end) of the array. In this routine, we step through each element of the array, comparing it with the next element and swapping the two if the first element is larger than the second. In doing so, the largest element is moved to the end of the list and the rest of the array is slightly closer to being sorted. We continue making such passes until we don't make any swaps that indicate that the array is now sorted. Let's consider one pass on our array of (3, 1, 4, 5, 2):

```
3 1 4 5 2
1 3 4 5 2  <-- test 1st and 2nd and swap
1 3 4 5 2  <-- test 2nd and 3rd, no swap
1 3 4 5 2  <-- test 3rd and 4th, no swap
1 3 4 2 5  <-- test 4th and 5th and swap
```

Now, let's look at the results in the array after each pass:

```
3 1 4 5 2
1 3 4 2 5  <-- after first pass
1 3 2 4 5  <-- after second pass
1 2 3 4 5  <-- after third pass
```

A few things can be done to improve this algorithm slightly. As in the selection sort given earlier, after each full pass, the largest element is now in the correct position in the array. So our next pass need only test, and possibly swap, up to the second last element—and so on for each pass. A little less apparent, but more important, is the realization that a large number may move many positions to the right in a given pass. Consider the array (5,3,2,4,1). During the first pass, the number 5 would move all the way to the end of the array. If we provide a reverse test, we can alternate between forward and reverse passes through the array. Here are two lists: one of the array contents after each full pass for a routine that only does the forward pass shown earlier, and one that alternates between forward and reverse passes:

```
forward passes only     alternating passes
5 3 2 4 1                5 3 2 4 1
3 2 4 1 5                3 2 4 1 5     (forward)
2 3 1 4 5                1 3 2 4 5     (reverse)
2 1 3 4 5                1 2 3 4 5     (forward)
1 2 3 4 5
```

One implementation of an alternating pass bubble sort routine is

```perl
my @array = (3, 1, 4, 5, 2);
bubble_sort(@array);
print "@array\n";    # prints: 1 2 3 4 5

sub bubble_sort {
    return unless @_;
    my $in  = \@_;
    my $low = 0;
    my $up  = $#_;
    my $direction = 1;
    my $swaps = 1;
    while($swaps and $low <= $up){
        $swaps = 0;
        if ($direction) {
            for(my $i = 0; $i < $up; $i++){
                if($in->[$i] > $in->[$i+1]){
                    ($in->[$i], $in->[$i+1])
                        = ($in->[$i+1], $in->[$i]);
                    $swaps++;
                }
            }
            $up--;
        } else {
            for(my $i = $up; $i > $low; $i--){
                if($in->[$i] > $in->[$i+1]){
                    ($in->[$i], $in->[$i+1])
                        = ($in->[$i+1], $in->[$i]);
                    $swaps++;
                }
            }
            $low++;
        }
    }
```

```
        if($direction){
            $direction = 0;
        }else{
            $direction = 1;
        }
    }
}
```

All of these routines involve nested loops over the data, which means that, for a given input of size N, the routine will have a worst case running time on the order of N * N (N squared). In other words, we are performing some set of operations on the order of N * N times. The focus here is on the order of growth. When analyzing running times we generally ignore *how much* work is being done, attending instead to *how often* that work is performed. Even if the inner loop executes fewer than N times, if we reduce the upper bound by 1 for each pass for example , we still have a running time based on N * (N + 1)/2, which, as N gets large, is still an N-squared algorithm. The next algorithm we will look at has a considerably lower order of growth of (N * log(base 2) N).

17.3 Heap sort

The previous sorting methods treated the data as a single flat array and operated by iterating through this array comparing and swapping values as necessary. In this section we will consider a method that organizes the data rather differently— although we will still use an array to hold the data.

A heap, actually a binary heap, has what is known as a tree structure—in particular, a binary tree structure. Consider the matrilineal family tree of a Mother (M) who has two daughters (D1 and D2) who each have two daughters (d1 and d2). We could draw a binary tree representing this lineage as shown in figure 17.1.

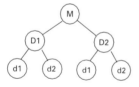

Figure 17.1 Matrilineal binary tree

In computer science, we draw our trees upside down with the root of the tree (M) at the top, and the leaves (each d1 and d2) at the bottom. We generally refer to each branch point—that is, any circle in the diagram shown—as a *node*. The top node is called the *root* node, and any nodes without branches beneath them are called *leaf* nodes. We may also refer to the nodes as *parent* and *children* nodes.

Which are parents and which are children depends on context. In figure 17.1, D2 is both a child and a parent node.

A heap is a particular kind of binary tree—one that satisfies the so-called "heap" property: Any parent node must be greater than its children. Figure 17.2 shows two binary trees, but only one satisfies the heap property throughout.

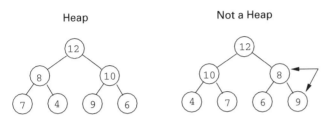

Figure 17.2 Two binary trees: only the left one is a heap

One thing you might notice about the heap is that it is recursive in that, if you have a binary heap, then any parent node and its children also form a heap.

Now, the question is, how might we represent such a structure? One way is to use a simple array with the root node stored in position 1 (not position 0 which is the first position in a Perl array). If you look at the binary heap in figure 17.2 and number each of the nodes, starting with 1 for the root and moving down and left to the right sequentially, you'll have the array indices for each node's position in an array. Figure 17.3 shows us the binary heap and its representation in an array.

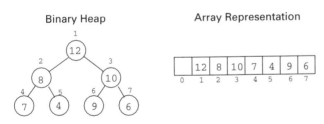

Figure 17.3 A binary heap and its array representation

By sequentially numbering our binary heap in this fashion and using those numbers as indices into an array, we can now write code to easily move through the heap by noting the following properties of the array:

```
If we refer to the node at position i in the array as node(i)
then for any node(i):
    The Parent of node(i)   = node( int(i / 2) )
    Left child of node(i)   = node( i * 2 )
    Right child of node(i)  = node( i * 2 + 1 )
```

A heap itself is not sorted, but it is partially sorted. The largest element is in the root node. Before we consider how we might build a heap from an input array, let's consider how we might produce a sorted array from a heap. The first thing to notice is that the first element of our heap-array is empty (element 0), so we store the size of the heap there. Using the heap in figure 17.3 as an example, we store 7 in element 0 of the array because there are seven elements in the heap. To turn this heap-array into a sorted array, we begin by swapping element 1 with the last element in the heap, thus putting the largest element at the end of the array. We decrease the heap size from 7 to 6 so the last element in the array is no longer considered as part of the heap, even though it is obviously still in the array.

Now we have a new six-element structure that is no longer a heap because the element in the root node is not larger than both of its children. To fix this, we call a routine named pushdown() on element 1 of the heap-array. This routine uses a loop to swap the current element with the largest of its children nodes and set the current element to the node with which it swapped. This loop continues until there are no children nodes to swap with (i.e., the current node is a leaf node) or the current node is larger than its children. When this loop finishes, the heap property is restored on our new smaller six-element heap. We then repeat the entire process on this smaller heap until eventually our heap size is reduced to two elements, and our swap completes the sorting of the array. The action of the pushdown() routine is shown in figure 17.4, where A) shows the initial heap and its array with the heap size stored in position 0; B) shows the result after swapping the root node with the last node and decreasing the heap size by one; C and D) show the new root node being pushed down the heap, restoring the heap property for the new smaller heap.

Let's take a look at what the implementation of the pushdown() routine might look like. To begin with, it needs to be passed two parameters: a reference to the heap-array and the current element to pushdown. We need to pass the current element—rather than just assuming we are starting with the root element— because we will use this same routine when we build the heap in the first place. The size of the heap is at index 0 in the heap array. We only need to continue looping down through the heap while the current element is less than or equal to (size / 2), because any nodes further down the array are leaf nodes. We figure out which child node is greater, then test if the current node is larger than that. If so, we are done. Otherwise, we swap the current node with the largest child node and set the current node position to that child's position in the array:

```
sub pushdown {
    my ($heap, $i) = @_;
    my $size = $heap->[0];
```

```
    while($i <= $size/2){
        my $child = 2 * $i;
        if ($child < $size and $heap->[$child] < $heap->[$child+1]){
            $child++;
        }
        if ($heap->[$i] >= $heap->[$child]) { last }
        ($heap->[$i], $heap->[$child])
            = ($heap->[$child], $heap->[$i]);
        $i = $child;
    }
}
```

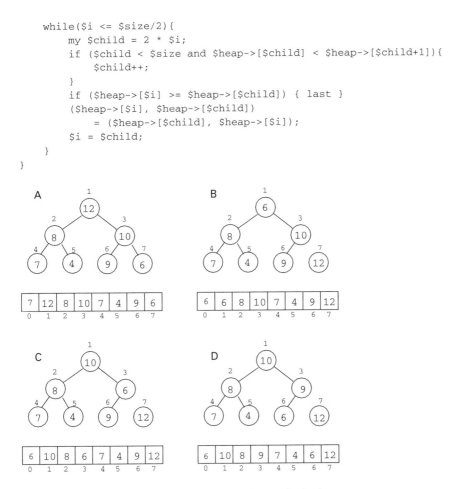

Figure 17.4   The action of pushing down an element in the heap

Now that we know how we will sort the heap-array once it's built, we need to figure out how we will build a heap-array from an ordinary array. To do this, we take our ordinary array, unshift() its size into its first element (element 0), and build it into a heap from the bottom up. Let's consider an array containing (4, 9, 7, 10, 8, 12, 6). Figure 17.5 shows this array in binary tree form and in array form after unshifting the size onto the array.

Obviously, this binary tree does not satisfy the heap property. But you'll note that if we call pushdown() on node 3, the last parent node in the structure, this causes the 7 and the 12 to be swapped. Node 3 along with its children is now a small heap. Similarly, calling pushdown() on node 2 causes the 9 and the 10 to be swapped turning that subtree into a proper heap. Finally, calling pushdown on node 1, the root node, works as it did in our previous example: the 4 in node 1 is

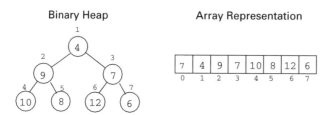

Figure 17.5 Ordinary array shown in heap and array form

swapped with the 12 now in node 3; node 3 is tested; the 4 we just put in node 3 is swapped with the 7 in node 6; and we have created a heap from our original array.

Finally, we can construct a heap sort algorithm that sorts an array in place by, first, using one loop to build the heap from the bottom up. Then we use a second loop to swap the first and last nodes of the heap, to reduce the heap size, and to restore the heap property on the new smaller heap that remains. The algorithm, which calls the pushdown() routine shown above, is

```
sub heap_sort {
    my $heap = \@_;
    unshift @$heap, scalar @_;
    for(my $i = int($heap->[0] / 2); $i >= 1; $i--) {
        pushdown($heap, $i);
    }
    for(my $i = $heap->[0]; $i >= 2; $i--){
        ($heap->[1], $heap->[$i]) = ($heap->[$i], $heap->[1]);
        $heap->[0]--;
        pushdown($heap, 1);
    }
    shift @$heap;
}
```

Earlier I said that this sorting routine has a running time based on (N * log(base2) N). Well, log(base 2) N is roughly the height of the heap, so we can say it runs in N * h time, where h is the height of the heap. You'll notice that the height of the heap grows slowly relative to N. For N = 1000, h is 10, and for N = 1,000,000, h is only 20. Thus, it is easy to see that even if the heap sort is doing more underlying work than other routines, as N grows large, the heap sort is certainly not doing it as often: 1000 * 1000 is far more than 1000 * 10. A quick series of benchmarks for various sizes of arrays of random numbers produced the following rough timings:

```
         N = 50                          N = 100
Bubble Took:   0.05 seconds    Bubble Took:   0.18 seconds
Insert Took:   0.02 seconds    Insert Took:   0.06 seconds
Select Took:   0.01 seconds    Select Took:   0.06 seconds
Heap Took:     0.03 seconds    Heap Took:     0.05 seconds


         N = 500                         N = 1000
Bubble Took:   4.79 seconds    Bubble Took:   19.27 seconds
Insert Took:   1.21 seconds    Insert Took:   4.84 seconds
Select Took:   1.31 seconds    Select Took:   5.26 seconds
Heap Took:     0.34 seconds    Heap Took:     0.76 seconds


         N = 5000
Bubble Took:   (way too long)
Insert Took:   122.11 seconds
Select Took:   132.48 seconds
Heap Took:     4.43 seconds
```

Of course, the goal here was not to create the fastest sort routine in Perl code. The built-in sort() function can sort a good deal faster than any of the routines shown here. (For example, the built-in sort routine sorts a list of size 5000 in about 0.29 seconds on the same machine that produced the above timings.)

No, the goal of this chapter was to use sorting algorithms as a context to introduce you to alternate ways of structuring your data that can lead to improved algorithms. We have also touched upon some basic terminology you will encounter in further studies of abstract data structures—nodes, trees, binary trees, heaps—as well as an informal introduction to comparing the order of growth of running times in different algorithms. We will encounter some of these concepts again in the following chapters.

17.4 Exercises

1   Rewrite the pushdown() routine to use recursion rather than a while loop to push an element down the heap. Will this help or hurt the running time of the heap sort or make little difference?

2   An alternate way to build a heap is by insertion—recall how insertion sort built its sorted list. Write a routine that builds a heap by insertion. This will work in a bottom up fashion.

3   Can you think of other problems besides sorting where a heap or heap-like structure might be useful?

CHAPTER 18

Object-oriented programming and abstract data structures

Perhaps you've heard of object-oriented programming (OOP) sometime during the past decade. You might have heard that it is just a bunch of horse hooey, or perhaps that it is the greatest productivity advancement since caffeine. OOP does indeed have its share of vocal proponents and detractors. Fortunately, we can happily ignore the extremists and make up our own minds.

This chapter will begin with a brief overview of OOP in general, to give you a feel for the subject and to introduce a few new fancy terms to your vocabulary. We will settle right down into using Perl's OOP features to begin building classes and objects and using them in our programs. Then we'll use classes and objects to create a few well-known abstract data structures.

If you are already familiar with the concepts and terminology of OOP programming, you may want to skip the next section and jump straight to section 18.2 on Perl OOP (straight to the POOP as it were). Perl's OOP capability makes use of references, so, if you had any trouble understanding references, you might want to review chapter 8 and the *perlref* pod-page. In recent releases of Perl, version 5.00503, there is also a *perlreftut,* which provides a short tutorial on Perl's references.

18.1   What is OOP?

Entire books could be written about object-oriented programming and how one might use it effectively. In fact, a great many such books have been written. Indeed, the publisher of the book you are now reading is also publishing a book on object-oriented programming using Perl that should come out around the same time as this book. I tell you this only so you understand that I can only present a rather abbreviated and informal introduction to OOP here—enough to get you started, but not the whole messy enchilada.

To begin with, let's take a look at some the terminology that is commonly used in OOP-speak: *abstraction, encapsulation, inheritance,* and *polymorphism.* Big words, but not difficult to grasp. We've already touched upon the first two back when we discussed functions and subroutines in chapter 7. We will discuss each in turn as they come up again in the following discussions.

Typically—at least so far in this book—we approach a programming problem from a perspective we can call procedural or one of algorithmic decomposition—that is, identifying the tasks that need to be accomplished to solve the problem. If we are given a problem, we tend to focus on the *verbs* in the problem statement—in other words, the actions that need to be performed on the data.

In some cases, as with the heap sort routine in the previous chapter, we may look more closely at the data to consider how it might be organized or structured before we decide on a processing approach.

In an OOP approach to a problem, dividing and structuring the data space is a central concern. We want to identify the things with which we will be working. In this case, we tend to focus on the *nouns* in the problem statement and how we might model them using different data structures and functions.

Let's take a trip back to our childhood and use a few well-known sentences from children's book to illustrate the OO approach. Let's begin with "See Spot run." For those who don't remember, or who never read this particular series of books, you should know that Spot is a dog). Now let's say that we want to write a program to do animation for an online version of this book.

In a traditional approach, we might immediately start sketching out a `run()` procedure that would move a picture of Spot around the screen while animating Spot's legs. Obviously, this subroutine would need to know quite a lot about how Spot is represented graphically. Consider that the next page of our story says, "See Dick run" (Dick is a human). Our `run()` won't work with Dick because he has only two legs to animate while Spot has four. Now we need either two subroutines— `spot_run()` and `dick_run()`—or one big `run()` subroutine called as `run(dick)` or `run(spot)` that contains the code to do either animation. Things would get messier still if we had other creatures that were going to run.

Looking at this from an OOP perspective, we might first identify the nouns, Spot and Dick, and their behaviors. In figure 18.1, we show one way we might begin to think about our data types. Notice that in this diagram we have also added category names, "human" and "dog."

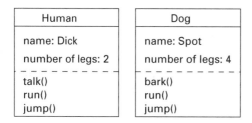

Figure 18.1 Modeling Dick and Spot

If we have modules that define such data types, then in our main book animation program, we need only use these modules to create a Spot object and a Dick object. Then we can ask each object to run on the appropriate pages of the book.

What we have done is created abstractions for our data—humans and dogs. We call these abstractions *classes*. When we use an abstraction to create a specific instance of a thing—for example, creating an instance of a Dog, called Spot—we call that instance an object. We have also used encapsulation here. Each class encapsulates the data and the behaviors of the objects it defines. We usually refer to the data as the attributes or properties of the object, and the behaviors as *methods*. The latter are really just ordinary functions.

We could have created a more general class called Mammals that just contained the "name" and "number of legs" attributes and a `run()` method. Then we could have defined the other two classes as special types of Mammals. This approach would use *inheritance*—that is, each special subtype inherits the properties of its *parent class*. This approach would also involve polymorphism because each subtype's `run()` method would have to be redefined for that particular subtype. *Polymorphism* means that children classes can alter their properties and methods so they are not identical to their parents.

You can't really appreciate OOP until you actually start doing it, so without further ado, let's get back to programming.

18.2   OOP in Perl

By creating a class, you are defining a whole new data type to use in your programs. This class defines how the data is stored, how it is accessed, and what functions (i.e., methods) this data type can perform. Think of the array data type—you know how to assign data to particular places in the array and how to access their values again later using array indices. You also know several functions defined to work on arrays: `shift`, `push`, `pop`, `unshift`, `splice`. Similarly, you know how to assign key/value pairs to a hash and access those values later. You also know how to use several functions defined to work on hashes: `exists`, `each`, `keys`, `values`. And you already know how important and useful these data types can be for many purposes.

18.2.1   The basics

So, how do we create a class in Perl? We begin by using the `package` declaration to define a new namespace, the same way we did when building an ordinary module. This package/module will contain the definition of our class. We will store all this in a file of the same name as the package but with a `.pm` extension added, just as we did for ordinary modules.

```
package Student;
```

Here we have started the definition of a class named Student. This will provide us with a Student data type. We do not have to worry about any exporting when making classes because OOP modules should not export anything.

The first thing this class has to define is a method of creating a new Student object that we can use in our programs. Such a method is called a *constructor* method. We can name this method anything we want, but most people prefer to call it `new()`. This method will return a reference to the underlying data structure it creates. Not just any reference, but a reference that has been specially tagged by Perl's bless() function. This *blessing* mechanism is at the heart of Perl's OOP capability.

```
sub new {
    my $class = shift;
    my $self  = {};
    $self->{name}    = undef;
    $self->{courses} = [];
    bless $self, $class;
    return $self;
}
```

When a constructor is invoked using an arrow syntax that you'll soon be very familiar with— (Student->new('arg1', 'arg2'))— the package name before the arrow is actually passed to the function as the first argument, moving the given arguments back one position in the argument list. In the constructor above, we have shifted off the class name, created a reference to a new anonymous hash, provided a couple of initial values for a name and course key in this hash, blessed this hash reference, and returned it. By blessing it, Perl will always know that this particular hash reference belongs to the package Student—it is now a Student object. If you leave off the second argument to the bless() function, it will default to the current package/class, but using the second argument leaves room for other benefits, as we will see shortly.

We said that a class also defines the behaviors of the object in question, so let's give our Student object the ability to tell us who it is and what course it is taking. The following two functions go in the Student package:

```
sub name {
    my $self = shift;
    $self->{name} = shift if @_;
    return $self->{name};
}

sub courses {
    my $self = shift;
    @{$self->{courses}} = @_ if @_;
    return @{$self->{courses}};
}
```

In Perl, when you call an object's method, using the arrow syntax shown above for the constructor, the object reference itself is automatically passed as the first argument to the function. So, in the two functions above, we shift off the first argument into a variable that we usually name $self but could call anything we wanted. That variable now holds the reference to the hash. We can access any value in this hash reference in the usual ways. Above, we set the values for these fields if the functions are passed arguments, or we just return the values if no arguments were passed. Some people prefer to create separate functions for setting and retrieving object attributes.

If we have the above package saved in a file named *Student.pm* and included a final statement of just `1;` to return a true value as we did with our modules in chapter 16, we can use this new data type in a program:

```
#!/usr/bin/perl -w
use strict;
use Student;
my $student = Student->new();
$student->name('Bill Jones');
$student->courses('Math', 'English');
print $student->name(), "\n";                    # prints: Bill Jones
print join(' ', $student->courses()), "\n";      # prints: Math English
```

We could have also accessed the name or courses of the student directly because we know that a student is just a hash reference. We could have said `print $student->{name}` to get the student's name, but this is not a good practice. When you use an object, you should access it only through its documented functions. This way, the underlying structure of the object can be changed in the future without affecting your program. Perhaps in the future we will decide to change the Student class to use an array reference rather than a hash reference. We will change its methods accordingly:

```
package Student;
sub new {
    my $class = shift;
    my $self  = [];
    $self->[0] = undef;
    $self->[1] = [];
    bless $self, $class;
    return $self;
}

sub name {
    my $self = shift;
    $self->[0] = shift if @_;
    return $self->[0];
}

sub course {
    my $self = shift;
    @{$self->[1]} = @_ if @_;
    return @{$self->[1]};
}
1;
```

If our programs had been accessing the name and courses of the student objects by directly accessing the hash keys, the programs would no longer work. However, by only using the documented accessor functions, our programs can continue to work correctly regardless of how we change the underlying data structure in the class:

```
print $student->{name}, "\n";  # no longer works
print $student->name(), "\n";  # still works as advertised
```

Notice one additional thing about using objects that can be demontrated with a simple script using our original, hash-based Student class above:

```
#!/usr/bin/perl -w
use strict;
use Student;
my $student = Student->new();
$student->name('Bill Jones');
$student->courses('Math', 'English');
my $h_ref = {name => 'Bill Jones', course => 'English'};

print "$student\n";          # prints: Student=HASH(0x80c44cc)
print ref($student), "\n";   # prints: Student
print "$h_ref\n";            # prints: HASH(0x80d1bb0)
print ref($h_ref), "\n";     # prints: HASH
```

You can see that although we know the underlying data structure of a Student class is a hash reference, we also know that it is not just an ordinary hash reference—it's a hash reference that also knows what class (package) it belongs. The ref() function returns the type of reference for an ordinary reference as well as the class-name of a blessed reference (i.e., an object). We can use this information to create more general constructor functions:

```
package Student;
sub new {
    my $type  = shift;
    my $class = ref($type) || $type;
    my $self = { name    => undef,
                 courses => [],
               };
    return bless $self, $class;
}
# other methods...
1;
```

We can call this constructor in the normal fashion or as an object method using an existing object:

```
my $student1 = Student->new();
$student1->name('Bill Jones');
my $student2 = $student1->new();
```

It is important to realize that $student2 in the above example is not a copy of $student1. It is a completely new (and empty) Student object of its own. The $student1 object was only used to access the constructor method. It does not provide any additional parameters to the constructor. The constructor method now tests whether it was called using the class name or if it was called from an existing object. If it was called from an object, it gets the class name by using the ref() function.

18.2.2 Inheritance

If you have a general class such as our Student class above, you can derive more specific classes directly from it using inheritance. This means you do not have to create entire new classes that duplicate parts of existing classes. Let's say that we also want a special type of Student to represent a part-time student. This student can only be registered for a maximum of three courses.

In Perl, we implement inheritance using a special array called the @ISA array. This array must be a package global variable, not a lexical variable so, if you are using the strict pragma inside your class modules, you will have to declare this variable using the use vars pragma (see below). The @ISA array holds the names of the classes from which you want to inherit. When an object of your derived class calls a method and that method does not exist in that object's package, then Perl searches the classes within the @ISA array to try to locate that method. Perl will also search any classes listed in those packages' @ISA arrays as well.

To start our new Student class definition, we can simply inherit everything from the parent class:

```
package PT_Student;
use strict;
use Student;
use vars '@ISA';
@ISA = qw(Student);
1;
```

We now have a new class called PT_Student that is exactly the same as our Student class. Because this class does not define any methods, Perl searches the classes listed in the @ISA to find method calls:

```
#!/usr/bin/perl -w
use strict;
use PT_Student;
my $pt_stud = PT_Student->new();
```

```
$pt_stud->name('John Smith');
$pt_stud->courses(qw/Math English Biology Chemistry/);
print join(' ',$pt_stud->courses()), "\n";
```

You can see that this PT_Student class behaves just the same as our Student class, and we didn't have to rewrite all the code in this new class. This is inheritance—in other words, the PT_Student class inherits its functionality from its parent class. But, we don't want our PT_Student class to be exactly the same as its parent; we want to allow a part-time student to have at most three courses in its course list. We can do this by creating a new `courses()` function for the part time student.

```
sub courses {
    my $self = shift;
    if (@_ > 3) {
        die "part time students can only have 3 courses.\n";
    }else{
        @{$self->{course}} = @_ if @_;
    }
    return @{$self->{courses}};
}
```

Now everything about part-time students is the same as that for regular students, except that if you try to set the course list to more than three courses, the part-time student will `die` with an error message. You might want to do something other than having the student die just for trying to take more courses. Perhaps you would only want to issue a warning message and return a false value.

By redefining the `courses()` function, we have used polymorphism—our derived class has a slightly different shape, or functionality, than its parent class.

Figure 18.2 shows the relation between the Student and PT_Student classes. A PT_Student IS A Student with a modified `courses()` method.

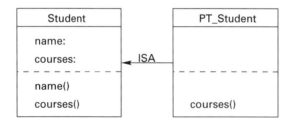

Figure 18.2 Relation between Student and PT_Student

18.3 Abstract data structures

In the last chapter and the previous sections, you've learned a little about how to think about your data in a more abstract way (heaps, trees, students) and about representing your data as objects with behaviors. In this section, we will continue our practice with *OOP* techniques while exploring basic abstract data structures further.

18.4 Stacks, queues, and linked lists

Virtually any programming book that even mentions abstract data structures will almost always give examples of *stacks* and *queues*. This book is no exception. Stacks and queues are elementary data structures. Even though their functionality is largely built into Perl, both are useful to know so you can see examples of building simple objects and better appreciate what Perl gives for free.

18.4.1 Stacks

A stack data structure in computer programming is much the same as a stack in your everyday life. Perhaps you have a stack of books lying next to your desk, and perhaps you took this very book off the top of that stack. When you take a break from reading, you might place this book back on top of the stack. This describes the fundamental property of a stack—you only add and remove things from the top. In real life, you might try slipping a book out of the stack from the bottom, or lifting several books at a time off the top, but you risk toppling your stack or injuring your back or both. A stack in the programming world limits you to placing or removing single items from only the top of the stack.

We generally refer to the operation of adding to a stack as *pushing* an element onto a stack, and the removal operation as *popping* an element from the stack. We also give a name to this ordering of placement and removal with a stack: Last In, First Out (LIFO). Figure 18.3 depicts the basic stack and its operations.

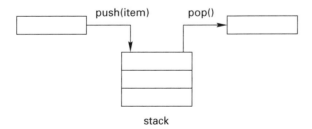

Figure 18.3   Graphic representation of a stack and its operations

Stacks are useful anytime you want to save the last things you were doing or had calculated, then later retrieve these "last things" in order from last to first. Consider reversing a string of characters: you could read the characters one-by-one pushing them onto a stack. When you reach the end of the string, you could just pop each character off the top of the stack and print or concatenate them together.

Another use for a stack would be for saving states in a parser. Imaging writing a tool that read a plain text file that contained certain markup tags to change the character formatting—perhaps tags to begin and end emphasized text (italics), strong text (bold), and headline text (larger font). If your job is to write a program that sends the file to a printer with the proper printer font commands, you could make use of a stack to save the current state while you switch to a new state (i.e., new character type). Imagine some text such as

```
Here is some plain text, now <em> some in italics <:em> now back to
plain, now <strong> some bold <em> and bold italic <:em> text
<:strong>. And lastly, <em> here is emphasized text <em> containing
<:em> even more emphasized text<:em>, in which case you would
probably want the word containing in the previous phrase to be in
plain fonts again.
```

If you were parsing such text, you would not want to simply switch states when you hit a tag. What would you do when you hit the ending tag? What state would you switch to? You need to be able to remember earlier states as you move into nested states and work your way back out again. With a stack, you can keep pushing any new state you enter onto the stack. Whenever you hit an end tag, you can simply pop the current state off the stack. Whatever is left on the top of the stack is now your current state.

You may suddenly wonder what all this fuss is about. Don't Perl's arrays already allow this kind of behavior? You are right; they do. But arrays in a great many languages are nothing at all like Perl arrays. Usually, all you can do with arrays in other languages is allocate a size for the array, then store and retrieve values using array indices only (no pushing, popping, splicing, or dicing). Perl's arrays are different and convenient because they can grow or shrink on demand, and they have the functionality of stacks built right in as well as and the functionality of queues, as you will see shortly.

So do we need to bother with creating our own stacks in Perl? Not often, but it is easy to do and, by doing so, we can add a little extra functionality, such as providing a size limit to the stack if desired and automatically producing warnings if we reach the bottom or top of the stack. Besides, creating stacks gives us a chance to demonstrate the use of inheritance when we create our queue object.

To keep things simple, we use Perl's arrays to implement our stack on the inside, but on the outside we just have a stack object that might have an optional size limit and provides only the following functions: push, pop, top, is_empty, and is_full. The top function merely returns the top element in the stack without removing it. This is useful when you want to compare the current state with the previous state without having to pop the previous state off the stack, compare them, and push it back on again.

We use another module in our stack object, the Carp module that comes as part of the Perl distribution. This module allows us to issue warnings using the carp() function—or errors using the croak() function—from inside our object's methods. These warnings point to the line in our main program that called these methods, as you'll see shortly. To begin with, we start our package and create a simple constructor to return a reference to an anonymous array as the blessed object:

```
package Stack;
use Carp;
sub new {
    my $type = shift;
    my $class = ref($type) || $type;
    my $max_size = shift;
    my $self = [$max_size];
    return bless $self, $class;
}
```

We now have an anonymous array as an object with a maximum size attribute stored in its first position. We can construct our two test methods to test if the stack is empty or full. We assume that, if the maximum size is 0 (no size was given when the object was created), we want a limitless stack so the full test should always fail in that case.

```
# $stack->is_empty(); returns true if stack is empty
sub is_empty {
    my $self = shift;
    return !$#$self;
}

# $stack->is_full(); returns true if stack is full
sub is_full {
    my $self = shift;
    return 0 unless $self->[0];
    return ($#$self == $self->[0]);
}
```

What the heck is !$#$self? Well, ! is just the logical not operator, $#, which, when used on an array, gives us the index of the last element of that array. $self, our object, is a reference to an array. Thus, is_empty() simply returns the logical negation of the last index of the array—that is, if the last index is 0 (a false value), !0 returns true. Similarly, if the last index is greater than 0, then it is a true value and !true return false.

With these simple tests in place, we can now implement our remaining functions easily by first testing our stack for the appropriate condition, then using the features already built into Perl's arrays to do the rest. The rest of module looks like this:

```perl
# $stack->push($item); pushes $item onto stack if stack not full
sub push {
    my $self = shift;
    my $item = shift;
    if($self->is_full()){
        carp "Stack is full:";
        return;
    }
    push @$self, $item;
}.

# $stack->pop(); pops the top item from the stack if not empty
sub pop {
    my $self = shift;
    if($self->is_empty()){
        carp "Stack is empty:";
        return;
    }
    return pop @$self;
}

# $stack->top(); returns the value of the top element if not empty
sub top {
    my $self = shift;
    if($self->is_empty()){
        carp "Stack is empty:";
        return;
    }
    return $self->[$#$self];
}
1;
__END__
```

Now we save this in a file named *Stack.pm,* and we write a simple little script to test its functionality:

```perl
#!/usr/bin/perl -w
use strict;
use Stack;
my $st = Stack->new(4);
#test push() to overflow
for(3,5,2,9,11){
    print "pushing: $_\n" if $st->push($_);
}
```

```
print "popped: 9\n"    if $st->pop(),"\n";
print "pushed: 42\n" if $st->push(42);
print 'top is: ', $st->top(),"\n";

#test pop to underflow
for(1..5){
    print 'popped: ',$st->pop(),"\n";
}
print $st->top(),"\n";
```

This script produces the following output:

```
$ perl stack.pl
pushing: 3
pushing: 5
pushing: 2
pushing: 9
Stack is full: at stack.pl line 7
popped: 9
pushed: 42
top is: 42
popped: 42
Popped: 2
popped: 5
popped: 3
Stack is empty: at stack.pl line 16
Popped:
Stack is empty: at stack.pl line 18
```

Now, notice how the carp() messages point to the line in the script we are running? Had we used ordinary warn() calls, the first message would have been

```
Stack is full: at Stack.pm line 26.
```

which wouldn't help us locate the problem in our script, which is where the problem lies because that's where we are attempting to overflow the stack. The Carp modules' croak() function provides a similar alternative to Perl's die() function.

While we won't write a full parser here, we can give an example of using a stack that is a little less trivial than our test script. Consider a program that accepts, parses, and then evaluates simple mathematical expressions involving basic arithmetic. Further, let's assume that this program allows two kinds of parentheses, round and square, to be used—presumably so that the person entering the expression can alternate between brace types to help keep them from mis-entering equations. One of things you might want to do as a first test for a valid equation is to check for mismatched braces:

```
3 + [ ( 4 * [ 9 - 2 ] - 1 ) / 2 ]    is correctly nested
3 + [ ( 4 * [ 9 - 2 ) - 1 ] / 2 )    is incorrectly nested
```

A simple subroutine using a stack can be used to work through each token in the statement and push any opening brackets (left brackets) encountered onto the stack. When a closing bracket is encountered, it can pop the last opening bracket from the stack to see if it is of the correct type. Such a routine also catches instances of missing brackets. For readability, these equations are nicely spaced out, but we will split on nothing to allow for equations that are not spaced out. The following script provides the subroutine plus a helper routine for printing errors:

```perl
#!/usr/bin/perl -w

use strict;
use Stack;

my $expression1 = '3 + [ ( 4 * [ 9 - 2 ] - 1 ) / 2 ] ';
my $expression2 = '3 + [ ( 4 * [ 9 - 2 ) - 1 ] / 2 )';

check_braces($expression1);
check_braces($expression2);

sub check_braces {
    my $expr = shift
    my $st = Stack->new();
    my $pos = 0
    my $valid = 1; #assume validity
    my $token;
    foreach $token (split //, $expr){
        if($token =~ m/\(|\[/){
            $st->push($token);
        }elsif($token =~ m/\)|\]/){
            die not_valid($token,$expr, $pos) if $st->is_empty();
            my $prev = $st->pop();
            unless( $token eq ')' && $prev eq '(' or
                    $token eq ']' && $prev eq '[' ){
                die not_valid($token,$expr, $pos)
            }
        }
        $pos++;
    }
    $token = $st->top();
    die not_valid($token,$expr, $pos) if not $st->is_empty();
    return 1;
}

sub not_valid {
    my ($token,$expr,$pos) = @_;
    my $ptr = ' ' x 19 . ' ' x $pos .'^';
    return <<ERROR;
Mismatched '$token' in: $expr
$ptr
ERROR
}
```

which produces the following output:

```
Stack is empty: at chkeq.pl line 32
Mismatched ')' in: 3 + [ ( 4 * [ 9 - 2 ) - 1 ] / 2 )
                                    ^
```

18.4.2 Queues

A queue is similar to a stack in that you can only add and remove single elements at a time, but in a queue the ordering is altered. In a queue, the first element entered into the queue will be the first element taken out of the queue. A queue is like a line-up of people at the movie theater—in fact, in many countries people don't stand in "line," they wait in the "queue"—hoping to get a ticket to see the next film that features Perl (such as the movie "Sphere," which apparently featured a brief snippet of Perl code flashing by on a console). Generally, the people who are first in line are the first to get their tickets—barring some rude exceptions we won't allow in our queues.

As with all new concepts in computer science, there are terms for everything including entering a queue (*enqueuing*), exiting a queue (*dequeuing*), and the processing order of a queue (First In, First Out—FIFO).

As I alluded earlier, Perl's arrays also have queue-like functionality using the shift() function to remove elements from a queue. You can push elements onto the end of the array, and shift them off the front, or you could unshift() onto the front of the array and pop them off the back. With Perl, you can use arrays as stacks or queues in either direction.

To build our queue class, we need methods for enqueuing and dequeuing. We also need methods for peeking at the front element as well as testing if the queue is empty or full. (We might as well allow for limits on our queue just as with our stacks.)

We have already provided some of this functionality in our Stack class, haven't we? It has a constructor that returns an anonymous array, which is what our queue will use, it can test that array for being empty or full; and its push mechanism is just our enqueue function under a different name. All we need to do is provide the dequeuing method as well as a method for peeking at the front operations. We should also rename the enqueuing function for consistency.

To make use of Stack's existing functionality we use inheritance. Our Queue class inherits any functionality it doesn't define itself from the Stack class. We also use the Carp module again.

To make Queue a *child class*, or derived class, of Stack, we need only use the module in our new class and tell Perl we want to inherit from that module. We tell Perl this by creating a special package global array—not a my() variable—called

@ISA in our Queue class and storing the names of any parent classes from which we want to inherit inside this array. Our Queue package begins

```
package Queue;
use strict;
use Carp;
use Stack;
use vars '@ISA';  # declare @ISA as package global
@ISA = qw(Stack); # inherit from Stack
```

Now that we are inheriting from the Stack class, we need only define what we need that the Stack class doesn't provide:

```
# inherited functions:
#     $queue = Queue->new()
#     $queue->is_empty()
#     $queue->is_full()

# $queue->enqueue($item); shoves $item into queue
# we are merely renaming Stacks push() function rather
# than inheriting it:
sub enqueue {
    shift->push(shift);
}

#$queue->dequeue(); removes and returns front of queue
sub dequeue {
    my $self = shift;
    if($self->is_empty()){
        carp ref($self)," is empty:";
        return;
    }
    return splice(@$self,1,1);
}

# $queue->front(); returns front of queue (doesn't remove)
sub front {
    my $self = shift;
    if($self->is_empty()){
        carp ref($self)," is empty:";
        return;
    }
    return $self->[1];
}
1;
__END__
```

The only thing really different here is the carp() statement. Rather than saying "Queue is empty", it says ref($self) is empty. Remember that the ref() function on an object returns the object's class name. We have to go back to the

Stack module and change those `carp()` statements to also use this technique instead of hard-coding in the word `stack` in the messages because sometimes the `$self` being used in Stack's functions is no longer a `Stack` but a `Queue`. After saving the example above in *Queue.pm* and making the minor changes to the Stack classes `carp()` statement, we can now run the following test script:

```
#!/usr/bin/perl -w
use strict;
use Queue;

my $q = Queue->new(4);
for(3,2,4,9,11){
    $q->enqueue($_);
}

print $q->dequeue(),"***\n";
$q->senqueue(42);
print $q->front(),"***\n";

for(1..5){
    print $q->dequeue()," *\n";
}
print $q->front();
```

which produces the following output (the asterisks are only to help differentiate different print statements):

```
Queue is full: at queue.pl line 7
3***
2***
2 *
4 *
9 *
42 *
Queue is empty: at queue.pl line 15
 *
Queue is empty: at queue.pl line 17
```

18.4.3 Linked lists

It is hard to appreciate all that Perl gives you for free with its built-in data types. Linked lists are another freebie. In many languages, structures such as arrays are static in nature. You state at the beginning of the program how big you want your array and that's the only array you get to use. What if you aren't sure how big your array will need to be? In Perl, this isn't a problem because Perl itself takes care of this for you by providing you with a dynamic array that can grow and shrink as needed—at least within the memory limits of your computer.

As long as the language is able allocate new memory on demand, linked lists can be used to solve such dynamic problems by providing a way of pointing to this new memory. Obviously, Perl can allocate new memory on demand during runtime. You can always create new variables in Perl, and Perl can point to this new memory through references to new variables, or anonymous structures. So, while not often needed in most Perl programs, you can create linked lists in Perl readily. Also, while the linked list structure may not be that useful, the same techniques can be used to create other structures such as trees.

So what is a linked list? Consider that you have to read in a variable number of simple inventory records (part-number:name:quantity) and you want to be able to search the list for certain fields. Easy, right? Well, let's say that now you have to do it without using an array or hash to hold the entire list although you can still use small anonymous arrays or hashes to hold individual records as in

```
    record as hash      or    record as array
{                       #     [
    p_num => 144,       #         144,
    name  => pencil,    #         'pencil',
    quantity => 7,      #         7,
}                       #     ]
```

Graphically these records could be represented as in figure 18.4, where we simply assume you have some storage device with slots you can use to hold the different fields, regardless of whether you also store the field names [keys] along with them.

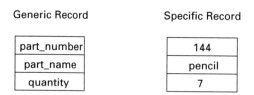

Figure 18.4 Graphical representation of inventory record

The slots that contain the field data could hold any scalar data. A reference to one of these structures is just a scalar value. So, if we can have three fields in each structure, why not another, or even two more?

In figure 18.5, each structure holds two additional fields, one containing a reference to the next structure (if any) and one containing a reference to the previous structure (if any). The small black circles are just our reference depiction from chapter 8, and the arrows are meant to point to the whole next (or previous) structure, not just one field. Each node, or individual record-structure, contains a "link" (a reference) to its next node and its previous node.

Generic Record

Specific Records

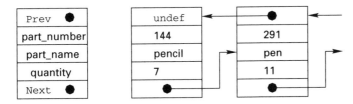

Figure 18.5 **Records with additional pointer fields**

If we had a reference to the first node, perhaps stored in a variable, then we have access to this node and, by reference, its next node, and that node's next-node, and so on, until we hit a node whose "next" field is undefined. We could also work backwards following the references in each node's "previous" field. The only thing holding the different records together as a list are the references that link them. Hence, this is called a linked list. Actually, this is a double-linked list because it has links in each direction.

In the above description, I've only described creating a linked list of structures that contain the data itself. A more general approach would be to use a key field—to hold just a key you associate with your data, as with a hash—and a data field— which would hold your data, most likely as an anonymous hash or array representing your record. The key field is then your search field when looking for particular items in the list:

```
    A node in the linked list
{
    previous => (reference to previous item),
    key      => (your key),
    data     => (your data),
    next     => (reference to next item),
}
```

In some cases, the key itself might be the only data, but in many cases, you will have a key *and* a record to go with it. Such a record is called the *satellite data* for the key. Satellite data was not pertinent previously because our stacks and queues did not need to support a search operation.

The following package is a partial implementation of a linked list supporting methods to insert new nodes into the list, search the list for a given key, test for emptiness, and return the list of the stored records (i.e., dump the list). Since we do not need to traverse the list in both directions, this package just implements a singly linked list. Each node knows the next node, but no node knows its previous node—say that five times fast.

```
package Llist;

sub new {
    my $type = shift;
    my $class = ref($type) || $type;
    my $self = {};
    return bless $self, $class;
}
```

All our new function does is create a completely empty node, which we are representing with an anonymous hash. This node (i.e., anonymous hash) is blessed and returned and will be the base node for our list.

The real work is done by the insert() method. One line in our insertion routine here that you haven't seen before looks like this:

```
my $data = defined($_[0]) ? $_[0] : $key;
```

This ?: operator is called the ternary operator and operates rather like an if/ else clause in an expression. Its general form is

```
(condition) ? (this expression) : (that expression)
returns: this expression if condition was true
returns: that expression if condition was false
```

The above line of code tests if $_[0] is defined. If so, we assign that value to $data. If not, we assign $key to $data instead. We do not simply use

```
my $data = shift || $key;
```

because it is possible that the value we are shifting is 0, which would evaluate as false, and we would wind up assigning $key instead of the perfectly valid data value of 0. In the ternary conditional, we test to see if the argument is defined, not to see if it is true. Thus we avoid this potential problem.

To do our insertion, we need to consider two cases: Our first node, self, is empty—and, thus, the list is empty, and we need only copy our key and data into it—or our first node is not empty. In the second case, we insert by creating a new node and copy the first nodes data and next pointer into this new node. Then, we add our new key and data into the first node and stick the new node into our first node's next field. In this way, the list grows like a reversed stack, with new elements being pushed onto the front of the list. Each node actually contains its next node object:

```
sub insert {
    my $self = shift;
    my $key  = shift;
    my $data = defined($_[0]) ? shift : $key;
```

```
    if ($self->is_empty()){
        $self->{key}  = $key;
        $self->{data} = $data;
        $self->{next} = undef;
    }else{
        $node = $self->new();
        $node->{key}  = $self->{key};
        $node->{data} = $self->{data};
        $node->{next} = $self->{next};

        $self->{key}  = $key;
        $self->{data} = $data;
        $self->{next} = $node;
    }
    return 1;
}
```

Testing if the list is empty requires only that we test if the first node is empty. We do this by testing to see if the key field is not defined.

```
sub is_empty {
    return !defined shift->{key};
}
```

The search and dump-list methods are similar because they both must be able to traverse the list. The difference between the two methods is that the search will end and return the data associated with that key if it finds the key for which it is looking. The dump method must continue through the whole list:

```
sub search {
    my $self = shift;
    my $key  = shift;
    return 0 unless defined $key;
    while(1){
        return $self->{data} if $self->{key} eq $key;
        last unless defined $self->{next};
        $self = $self->{next};
    }
    return 0;
}

sub dump_list {
    my $self = shift;
    my @list = ($self->{data});
    while(1){
        last unless $self->{next};
        $self = $self->{next};
        push @list,$self->{data};
    }
    return @list;
}
1;
__END__
```

Notice that, unlike with a hash, there is nothing preventing us from sticking in new data with keys we have already used. Our search method will only return the first found item. We could change our insert routine to disallow identical keys—by first searching to see if the key already exists—or to replace the data of the key if that key already exists in the list rather than adding a new node. (Again, we would have to search the list to find the right node, if any.)

The following exercises allow you to add further functionality to this object.

18.5 Exercises

1 Use `perldoc perltoot` to read Tom Christiansen's excellent tutorial on object-oriented programming with Perl (or view the HTML page if that's what you prefer to use to read the documentation).

2 Also take a look at the *perlobj* and *perlbot* pod-pages.

3 The linked list object could benefit from a method that dumps the keys of the list rather than the values. Add a `dump_keys()` method to this object.

4 The main thing missing from our linked list is a method to delete a node. For this, you first need to search the list to find the node. Then you must splice it out of the list. This requires that you keep track of the previous node because to splice the current node you need to set the previous node's next field to the current node's next field.

C H A P T E R   1 9

More OOP examples

In this chapter, we begin by returning to our heap data structure and implement a heap class, and discuss some of it applications. We then turn to a more practical example of creating a few classes. From these classes, we can revisit and extend the example we used at the beginning of chapter 8, building a system to query and make reports from a data base of student assignment and exam grades.

19.1 The heap as an abstract data structure

Before tackling this section, you may wish to familiarize yourself with the heap structure and the algorithms we used in chapter 17 to create a heap and pull items off the top of the heap.

For our Heap class, we will again use an array to store our heap. We will also use the first element of the array to store additional information—in this case, the size of the heap, as well as an anonymous subroutine we can use to compare two keys in the heap. We begin by defining our package and setting up a private hash of comparison functions.

```
package Heap;
use strict;

my %comp = ( str  => sub {return $_[0] cmp $_[1]},
             rstr => sub {return $_[1] cmp $_[0]},
             num  => sub {return $_[0] <=> $_[1]},
             rnum => sub {return $_[1] <=> $_[0]},
           );
```

This hash is private to the Heap package, no other package can access it. We expect the caller of our new() constructor to supply an argument indicating which comparison routine to use. str and rstr are for string comparisons in normal and reverse sorted order, similarly for num and rnum. If no routine is specified, we default to using numeric comparisons:

```
sub new {
    my $this = shift;
    my $class = ref($this)||$this;
    my $comp = ( shift || 'num' );
    my $self = [ { size  => 0,
                   comp  => $comp{$comp},
                 },
               ];
    return bless $self,$class;
}
```

This constructor has set up our initial empty heap as an anonymous array with a hash reference in its first position. This hash reference contains the size of the heap and a reference to the anonymous subroutine for comparisons.

Unlike our heap model in chapter 17, we wish to be able to insert items into the heap on demand rather than building a heap out of an existing list of items. We will first create a node out of the arguments passed in—a key and a data element—and then call another method to do the actual insertion:

```
sub insert {
    my $self = shift;
    my $key  = shift;
    my $data = defined($_[0])? shift : $key;
    my $node = { key  => $key,
                 data => $data,
               };
    $self->_insert_node($node);
}
```

Using an underscore is just a convention to mark some functions as private to the class. Such methods should never be called from outside the package. Our method to do the actual insertion works as follows. We first increase the size of the heap, which has the effect of adding a new leaf onto to our binary tree. We then start moving up the tree from this final node, copying each parent node down one element if it is smaller than the current key. When the next parent node is larger than the current node, we have found the place in the heap to insert the node, which we do.

```
sub _insert_node {
    my ($self, $node) = @_;
    my $i = ++$self->[0]{size};
    my $comp = $self->[0]{comp};
    while ( $i > 1 and
            $comp->($self->[parent($i)]{key}, $node->{key})<=0 ) {
        $self->[$i] = $self->[parent($i)];
        $i = parent($i);
    }
    $self->[$i] = $node;
}
```

In figure 19.1 on page 318, we show the steps such an insertion method would go through on an example heap. In this figure, we are adding an element with a key of 15 to an existing heap of eight elements. In A, we add an empty element to our existing heap. In B, we move the parent of our empty element into the empty element because it is smaller than our new key, leaving the node that held key 8 empty. In C, we compare our key with the parent of the new empty node and, because it is also smaller, we move that parent into this empty node. In D, the parent of the empty node is greater than our key so we insert our key into this empty node.

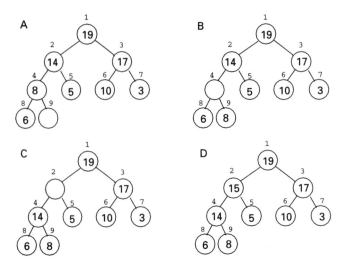

Figure 19.1 Inserting an element into a heap

The code shown on page 317 uses another routine `parent()`, which returns the parent index of the index passed to it. This is just a regular function, not an object method; such functions are simply considered class methods. We will define this function, and the related `left()` and `right()` functions later, but you already know how to calculate these indices from our discussion in chapter 17.

A method that returns the top element without extracting it requires only that we return the data portion of whatever is at index 1 of our heap-array:

```
sub top {
    my $self = shift;
    if ($self->[0]{size} < 1) {
        return;
    }
    return $self->[1]{data};
}
```

To extract the top item from the heap, we do the same things we did in our heap-sort routine in chapter 17, except that we don't put the top element at the end of the array. We only return it. We still need to put something in the top position, so we take the last element of the heap and push it down using the push-down() algorithm from chapter 17.

```
sub extract_top {
    my $self = shift;
    if ($self->[0]{size} < 1) {
        return;
    }
```

```
        my $top = $self->[1]{data};
        my $node = pop @$self;
        $self->[0]{size}--;
        if ($self->[0]{size} > 0) {
            $self->[1] = $node;
            $self->_pushdown(1);
        }
        return $top;
    }
```

The routine to push an element down the heap is the same as we used in chapter 17, only modified to use the comparison routine.

```
sub _pushdown {
    my ($self, $i) = @_;
    my $size = $self->[0]{size};
    my $comp = $self->[0]{comp};
    while( $i <= $size/2 ) {
        my $kid = left($i);
        if ( $kid < $size and
             $comp->($self->[$kid]{key},$self->[$kid +1]{key}) < 0)
          {
            $kid++;
          }
        last if $comp->($self->[$i]{key},$self->[$kid]{key}) >= 0;
        ($self->[$i],$self->[$kid]) = ($self->[$kid], $self->[$i]);
        $i = $kid;
    }

}
```

The three class methods we use to return the parent, left, and right indices are all extremely simple one-line functions:

```
sub parent { return int($_[0] / 2) }
sub left   { return $_[0] * 2 }
sub right  { return $_[0] * 2 + 1 }

1;
__END__
```

The following is a simple test script to read in a few lines of colon-separated data and insert anonymous hashes of these records into a heap using the name field as the key. We want to process these records in alphabetical order, so we pass the heap constructor the string rstr to tell it to compare using reverse alphabetical order. Our heap normally puts the largest element on the top, so we need to reverse this idea and put the smallest element on top to get proper alphabetical ordering:

```perl
#!/usr/bin/perl -w
use strict;
use Heap;

my $heap = Heap->new('rstr');

while(<DATA>){
    chomp;
    my($name,$age,$beer) = split /:/;
    $heap->insert($name,{name => $name,
                         age  => $age,
                         beer => $beer,
                        });
}
while($_ = $heap->extract_top()){
    foreach my $key (keys %$_){
        print "$key:$_->{$key}\n";
    }
    print "----\n";
}

__DATA__
Brad:37:ale
Andrew:35:ale
Susanna:40:lager
John:33:stout
```

A heap can be used to implement what is known as a priority queue, where you can store a list of things to process according to their priority. These queues are usually dynamic; new elements are inserted while elements from the queue are processed. In the real world, you could consider a hospital emergency room as using a priority queue to process patients. Patients are not treated in order of arrival, but according to the severity of their physical condition. In the computing world, you may have heard of priority queues being used to manage job scheduling on a multi-user computer or as the means of holding jobs in a printer queue. Different users may have different priorities on the system, and their tasks are entered into the queues based on their priority level.

19.2 Grades: an object example

In this section, we will no longer be dealing with standard computer science types of data structures. Instead, we will formulate our own structures to use as objects for a more familiar kind of data processing task.

Recall the problem given at the beginning of chapter 8. We needed to create a report of assignment grades for each student in a class. Here we will consider a more generalized version of the same problem. We want to be able to store grades for students in a given course and retrieve current summary information for each student in the course. As before, we just want to be able to enter a student's score for a particular assignment in a plain text file as these assignments come in and are graded. (Perhaps the exams are performed on the web and automatically graded and appended to this file.) We also want to be able to use our program for more than one course. In this example, we consider two courses: Math-101 and Math-201.

To begin, we define a configuration file format that can be used for each course. The format will specify the total score possible for each assignment and the value of each assignment's contribution to the final course grade. For example, in our Math-101 course, we may decide that we will give three assignments, each scored out of 50, but counting for only 25 percent of the final mark; and one exam marked out of 75 and counting for 25 percent of the final mark. We create our configuration file *math-101.cfg* as colon-separated records, one for each type of graded work. Each record contains fields for the type of graded work (Assign or Exam), the assignment or exam number, the raw score it is marked out of, and the amount it contributes toward the final grade (expressed simply as a number out of 100). Thus, our *math-101.cfg* file looks like this:

```
Assign:1:50:25
Assign:2:50:25
Assign:3:50:25
Exam:1:75:25
```

When we record the grades in our grade file for the course—named here *math-101*—we need to record the student name, the assignment number (1, 2, or 3 for assignments, or E1 for the 1st exam), and the raw score the student obtained. So part of the data file for this class might look like this:

```
Bill Jones:2:35
Anne Smith:3:41
Sara Tims:2:45
Sara Tims:3:39
Bill Jones:1:42
Bill Jones:E1:72
Anne Smith:1:42
Sara Tims:1:41
Anne Smith:2:47
Bill Jones:3:41
Anne Smith:E1:69
```

Now, let's look at the types of things we have in our problem statement—we have courses, students, and assignments (or exams). Let's consider the most general category first, the course category. A given course has a course name, and it contains a list of its students. Thus, we also create a file. with a .std extension.

containing all the names of the students in a given class. So, for our Math-101 course, we have the file *math-101.std* containing

```
Bill Jones
Anne Smith
Sara Tims
Frank Worza
```

So, how might we want to use this course class in our reporting program? Well, keeping things simple and assuming we just want to create a report for the whole class, we can imagine a program that is invoked with the course name as an argument:

```
#!/usr/bin/perl -w
use strict;
use Course;
@ARGV || die "You must supply a course name.\n";
my $class = Course->new($ARGV[0]);
while(<>){
    chomp;
    $class->add_student_record(split /:/);
}
$class->print_report();
__END__
```

Remember, our data file of grades has the same name as the course, so the data file is in $ARGV[0] when the program is called. This program creates a new course, iterates through the data file adding student records to the course, and then prints out a report of the course grades. Presumably, the Course class knows how to add student records and print the report. We make our Course class use a Student class and have it store a list of student objects—one for each name in the class list. Let's begin building our Course class:

```
package Course;
use Student;
use strict;

sub new {
    my $type  = shift;
    my $class = ref($type)||$type;
    my $course = shift;
    my $self = { course   => $course,
                 number   => 0,
                 students => {},
               };
    bless $self, $class;
    $self->_configure_course();
    return $self;
}
```

This constructor creates a Course object that contains fields for the name of the course, and the number of students as well as a field that contains an empty hash reference that holds a hash of student names and the student objects. Much of the real work is done within the configuration routine we call near the end of the constructor. This routine is responsible for reading in the configuration file and the student list for the given course name. It builds a configuration hash that holds the information about each assignment or exam. Thus the routine reads the student list and creates a new student object for each student in the list.

```
sub _configure_course {
    my $self = shift;
    my $cfg_file = $self->{course} . '.cfg';
    my %cfg;
    open(CFG,$cfg_file)||die "can't open $cfg_file: $!";
    while(<CFG>){
        chomp;
        my ($type, @data) = split /:/;
        $cfg{$type}[$data[0]] = [ @data[1,2] ];
        $cfg{"$type".'_no'}++;
    }
    close CFG;
    my $stud_file = $self->{course} . '.std';
    open(STD,$stud_file) || die "can't open $stud_file: $!";
    while(<STD>){
        chomp(my $name = $_);
        $self->{students}{$name} = Student->new(\%cfg,$name);
        $self->{number}++;
    }
    close STD;
}
```

We can now add a few accessor type functions to retrieve the data in our course object. These are pretty straightforward:

```
# course(): returns the course name
sub course {
    my $self = shift;
    return $self->{course};
}

# number(): returns the number of students in the course
sub number {
    my $self = shift;
    return $self->{number};
}

# student(name): returns the student object associated with
# the given name
```

```
sub student {
    my $self = shift;
    my $name = shift;
    return $self->{students}{$name} || undef;
}

# list(): returns the sorted list of student names
sub list {
    my $self = shift;
    my @list = map { $_->[0] }
                sort{ $a->[2] cmp $b->[2] }
                map { [$_,split] } keys %{$self->{students}};
    return @list;
}
```

We need to add the functionality we saw in our main program—namely, we need to be able to add student records and print a class report. For these functions, we assume that the student objects themselves have functions for adding assignments and printing their own reports:

```
sub add_student_record {
    my $self = shift;
    my $name = shift;
    my $student = $self->student($name);
    $student->add_assignment(@_);
}
sub print_report {
    my $self = shift;
    my $course = $self->course();
    my $number = $self->number();
    print "Class Report: course = $course: students = $number\n";
    foreach my $name ( $self->list() ){
        $self->student($name)->print_report();
    }
}

1;
__END__
```

Don't forget to end your class module with a true statement such as the 1; shown above. At this point, we know that we will be passing the configuration hash to the Student constructor, and we know that class will need a method for adding assignments to the student and printing a report on the student. Just as our Course class used the Student class, our Student class makes use of an Assignment class we will define later:

```
package Student;
use Assignment;
use strict;
```

```
sub new {
    my $type  = shift;
    my $class = ref($type)||$type;
    my $cfg   = shift;
    my $name  = shift;
    my $self  = {config      => $cfg,
                 name        => $name,
                 assignments => 0,
                };
    bless $self, $class;
    return $self;
}
```

There is nothing much new in this constructor; we have fields for a reference to the configuration hash and the students' names passed when each new student is created. We also have a field to hold the number of assignments this student has completed.

The method to add an assignment creates new fields in the object; one holding an anonymous array of assignments, and the other holding an anonymous array of exams. These arrays are populated with new Assignment objects, and the assignment count incremented:

```
sub add_assignment {
    my $self = shift;
    my($num, $score) = @_;
    my $cfg = $self->{config};
    my $type;
    if($num =~ s/^E//){
        $type = 'Exam';
    } else {
        $type = 'Assign';
    }
    $self->{$type}[$num] = Assignment->new($cfg,$type,$num,$score);
    $self->{assignments}++;
}
```

We also add a couple of accessor functions to this class to return lists of assignment objects (either assignments or exams). We use the grep() function to discard possibly empty elements in either array:

```
sub get_assigns {
    my $self = shift;
    return grep{$_} @{$self->{Assign}};
}

sub get_exams {
    my $self = shift;
    return grep{$_} @{$self->{Exam}};
}
```

Our function for printing a student's report is longer, but not complicated. It assumes that a given assignment knows how to print its own report and only needs to maintain a running total of each assignments contribution toward the final mark—$fscore:

```perl
sub print_report {
    my $self = shift;
    my $cfg  = $self->{config};
    print $self->{name},":\n";

    unless($self->get_assigns()||$self->get_exams()){
        print "\tNo records for this student\n";
        return;
    }

    my ($ftotal,$a_count,$e_count) = (0,0,0);
    foreach my $assign ($self->get_assigns()){
        print "\t";
        $assign->print_report();
        $ftotal += $assign->fscore();
        $a_count++;
    }

    foreach my $assign ($self->get_exams()){
        print "\t";
        $assign->print_report();
        $ftotal += $assign->fscore();
        $e_count++;
    }

    if($cfg->{Assign_no} == $a_count and
       $cfg->{Exam_no}   == $e_count){
        print "\tFinal Course Grade: $ftotal/100\n";
    }else{
        print "\tIncomplete Record\n";
    }
    print "\n";
}
1;
__END__
```

Finally, we have our Assignment class. The constructor for this class is fairly simple, passing off the hard work to its own _assign() function:

```perl
package Assignment;

sub new {
    my $type = shift;
    my $class = ref($type)||$type;
    my $cfg = shift;
    my $self = {config => $cfg};
    bless $self, $class;
```

```
    $self->_assign(@_);
    return $self;
}
```

The `assign` method is responsible for checking that the assignment or exam number is valid (as per the configuration file), and calculating and formatting the adjusted score for the assignment (the `$fscore`). This is another long method, but again, not a complicated one :

```
sub _assign {
    my $self = shift;
    my $cfg = $self->{config};
    my ($type, $num, $score) = @_;
    my ($raw, $final, $fscore);

    $type =~ m/^(Assign|Exam)$/ or
        die "unknown assignment type: $type\n";

    $cfg->{$type}[$num] or
        die "Unrecognized $type number: $num\n";

    ($raw, $final) = @{$cfg->{$type}[$num]};
    if($type eq 'Assign'){
        $type = "Assignment $num";
    } else {
        $type = "Exam $num";
    }
    $fscore = sprintf("%.2f",$score /($raw/$final));
    $self->{type}   = $type;
    $self->{score}  = $score;
    $self->{raw}    = $raw;
    $self->{fscore} = $fscore;
    $self->{final}  = $final;
}
```

To these we add one accessor function to return the final score and one method to print out a report of the assignment:

```
sub fscore {
    my $self = shift;
    return $self->{fscore};
}

sub print_report {
    my $self = shift;
    print $self->{type},": raw = ";
    print $self->{score}, "/",$self->{raw}," : Adjusted = ";
    print $self->{fscore}, "/",$self->{final},"\n";
}

1;
__END__
```

Now we can run our original program given at the start of this section and pass it the name of our course, Math-101. We already have the data file of the same name as well as the math-101.cfg and the *math-101.std* files created. We assume we save the program in a file named *report.pl,* and we have all three modules and data files in the same directory as our program:

```
$ perl report.pl math-101
Class Report: course = math-101: students = 4
Frank Howza:
        No records for this student
Bill Jones:
        Assignment 1: raw = 42/50 : Adjusted = 21.00/25
        Assignment 2: raw = 35/50 : Adjusted = 17.50/25
        Assignment 3: raw = 41/50 : Adjusted = 20.50/25
        Exam 1: raw = 72/75 : Adjusted = 24.00/25
        Final Course Grade: 83/100
Anne Smith:
        Assignment 1: raw = 42/50 : Adjusted = 21.00/25
        Assignment 2: raw = 47/50 : Adjusted = 23.50/25
        Assignment 3: raw = 41/50 : Adjusted = 20.50/25
        Exam 1: raw = 69/75 : Adjusted = 23.00/25
        Final Course Grade: 88/100
Sara Tims:
        Assignment 1: raw = 41/50 : Adjusted = 20.50/25
        Assignment 2: raw = 45/50 : Adjusted = 22.50/25
        Assignment 3: raw = 39/50 : Adjusted = 19.50/25
        Incomplete Record
```

You'll notice that the student name Frank Howza has no records. He appears in our class list file, but there were no assignments or exams for him in the data file. Similarly, Sara Tims has no record for her exam, so her report is marked as incomplete.

If we had another course with a completely different set of assignments (and perhaps different students), we could simply create a new configuration file and class list file for that course's data and run the same program on it. For example, our Math-201 course might have only two assignments, both out of 50 points, but with the first one making up 25 percent and the second only 10 percent of the final grade. There are also two exams, both out of 75, with the first contributing 20 percent and the second exam contributing 45 percent to the final grade. The configuration file would look like this:

```
Assign:1:50:25
Assign:2:50:10
Exam:1:75:20
Exam:2:75:45
```

For simplicity's sake, we assume the same class list applies. The data file of grades now appears as

```
Bill Jones:1:43
Sara Tims:2:32
Sara Tims:1:44
Anne Smith:1:44
Anne Smith:2:39
Bill Jones:E1:75
Sara Tims:E1:69
Anne Smith:E1:70
Bill Jones:2:40
Bill Jones:E2:75
Sara Tims:E2:69
Anne Smith:E2:70
```

Running our same program with an argument of math-201 now produces a full report for this new course:

```
$ perl report.pl math-201
Frank Howza:
        No records for this student
Bill Jones:
        Assignment 1: raw = 43/50 : Adjusted = 21.50/25
        Assignment 2: raw = 40/50 : Adjusted = 8.00/10
        Exam 1: raw = 75/75 : Adjusted = 20.00/20
        Exam 2: raw = 75/75 : Adjusted = 45.00/45
        Final Course Grade: 94.5/100
Anne Smith:
        Assignment 1: raw = 44/50 : Adjusted = 22.00/25
        Assignment 2: raw = 39/50 : Adjusted = 7.80/10
        Exam 1: raw = 70/75 : Adjusted = 18.67/20
        Exam 2: raw = 70/75 : Adjusted = 42.00/45
        Final Course Grade: 90.47/100
Sara Tims:
        Assignment 1: raw = 44/50 : Adjusted = 22.00/25
        Assignment 2: raw = 32/50 : Adjusted = 6.40/10
        Exam 1: raw = 69/75 : Adjusted = 18.40/20
        Exam 2: raw = 69/75 : Adjusted = 41.40/45
        Final Course Grade: 88.2/100
```

Because the reporting functionality is built into the objects themselves, we can modify the program to provide an interactive query for individual students— or even individual assignments—if we desired. Here is a version that allows you to query the data for individual student reports:

```
#!/usr/bin/perl -w
use strict;
use Course;

@ARGV || die "You must supply a course name.\n";
```

```
my $class = Course->new($ARGV[0]);
while(<>){
    chomp;
    $class->add_student_record(split /:/);
}

while(1){
    print "Enter a student name [or 'l' for list; 'q' to quit]: ";
    chomp(my $name = <STDIN>);
    last if $name =~ m/^q$/;
    print join("\n",$class->list()),"\n" and next if $name eq 'l';
    if($class->student($name)){
        $class->student($name)->print_report();
    }else{
        print "no student by that name\n";
    }
}
```

By using a configuration file to define the marking scheme for the assignments and exams, rather than hard-coding them into a script, we not only achieve the generality to use these programs with other courses, but to change our course configuration as well. Occasionally, a teacher will decide that a particular assignment shouldn't count for as much as originally intended. With this system, the teacher can simply reduce the final contribution amount for that assignment and increase the values of one or more of the others respectively in the configuration file. The teacher can then simply rerun the reporting program to see the new results.

19.3 Exercises

1 Another handy feature to have in our grade-tracking system would be the ability to read in data on multiple courses and then query the data base to retrieve and print a record for a given student for all the courses in which that student is registered. Try adding this feature.

2 Examine any programs you may have written while working through this book to see if your data could be modeled in a more object-oriented fashion. Create classes to represent the data and behaviors, and rewrite your program to use these objects.

CHAPTER 19 MORE OOP EXAMPLES

C H A P T E R   2 0

What's left?

What's left? A lot! You have nearly reached the end of this book, but you're not at the end of the road by any means. As Larry Wall quotes in Perl's own source code, "The road goes ever on and on...."

As I stated in the introductory chapter, Perl is a large language, and although we have covered a great deal in a short space, there is quite a bit more Perl to discover.

One thing we never discussed is how to use Perl as a command line tool. But we haven't left that out altogether. Appendix A provides a brief overview of some of the more common command line switches with a few examples of running Perl from the command line. Appendix B provides a brief reference on a few of Perl's special built-in variables. (See the *perlvar* pod-page for a complete listing.)

We did a little bit of network programming using the `LWP::Simple` module in chapter 14. Perl has low-level socket programming with the `socket()` function and several other network related functions, as well as a more convenient socket programming interface via the `IO::Socket` module. To find out more about network programming, you can see the *perlipc* pod-page (ipc for inter-process communication).

Did you ever want to have your program read in raw source code during runtime and then execute it within your program? Perl's `eval()` function can be used to do this sort of thing. It can also be used to trap errors raised by other subroutines. Read about `eval()` in the *perlfunc* pod-page. *Advanced Perl Programming* by Sriram Srinivasan[1] has a very good chapter on the uses of `eval()` as well.

Perl can also do more than just open read and close files and directories—you can `rename()` and `unlink()` (delete) files, change their permissions (`chmod()`) and ownership (`chown()`), and create and remove directories (`mkdir()`, and `rmdir()`).

With Perl, you can also `fork()` children processes (if your system supports forking), use DBM databases (several different flavors), and even more yet. And, as I keep stressing, CPAN contains hundreds of additional modules providing all manners of additional functionality—never be afraid to look to CPAN for easy solutions. Indeed, if I tried to catalogue everything you can do with Perl, the list would be notable only for what it left out.

Larry Wall once said while writing about the natural language aspect of Perl, "You don't learn a natural language even once, in the sense that you never stop learning it." To help you further your learning, Appendix C provides a brief list of other Perl resources. This is not an exhaustive list, merely a few signposts in a vast landscape that I hope you will enjoy exploring as much as I do.

My original plan was to leave off by reviewing some of what I think are important rules or guidelines in the design, style, and coding of your programs. But Perl isn't about following the rules and rigidly adhering to the conventions of others—and I know I've broken a few rules in this book that others might consider sacred. So if I have any wisdom at all to impart in my final remarks, it is just to do whatever works for you—and to have fun doing it.

---

1 Srinivasan, Sriram. *Advanced Perl Programming.* Sebastopol, CA: O'Reilly and Associates, 1997.

A P P E N D I X   A

Command line switches

You are already familiar with the most important command line switch, the -w switch, which turns on warnings. Quite a few additional command line switches exist, many of which are designed to facilitate using Perl as a command line tool. By command line tool, I mean invoking Perl directly from the command line of the shell and supplying one or more statements to perform. Consider the following one liner:

```
perl -pi.bak -e 's/red/blue/g' filenames
```

This combines several switches and takes all the filenames given and replaces every occurrence of red with blue. It also saves the original files with a .bak extension. In this appendix, we will briefly describe the most useful command line switches. (See perldoc perlrun for additional switches and further information.)

-c

When used, Perl will compile the script and check the syntax, but will not run the program. This is a useful first step in testing your program for syntax errors without actually running it.

```
$ perl -c programname
```

-e commandline

Takes `commandline`, which may be several statements, as the script to run.

```
$ perl -e '$blah = shift @ARGV; print "$blah\n"' argument
argument
```

-p

This switch causes Perl to construct the following loop around your script (whether your script is in a file or given in a -e argument):

```
while (<>) {
    # your script
} continue {
    print;
}
```

Hence, the following three examples are all the same:

```
$ perl -p -e 's/red/blue/g' filename
```

```
#!/usr/bin/perl -p
s/red/blue/g;
```

```
#!/usr/bin/perl
while (<>) {
    s/red/blue/g;
}
continue {
    print;
}
```

-n

Like -p except without the continue block.

```
$ perl -n -e 'print if m/foo/' filename
```

This prints all lines containing the pattern `foo` in the file *filename*

-i[.extension]

This means that all the files given on the command line are to be edited in place. In other words, changes are written to the files themselves. If given the optional extension, then the original files are saved with that extension:

```
$ perl -p -i.bak -e 's/red/blue/g' filenames
```

or with the switches combined:

```
$ perl -pi.bak -e 's/red/blue/g' filenames
```

-a

Used with -n or -p to turn on autosplit mode. This causes a split (' ') to be performed as the first statement in the implied loop, and the results of the split are assigned to the array @F. The following three examples are equivalent and will print the second field in each line of data in the given file:

```
$ perl -a -n -e 'print "$F[1]\n"' filename
$ perl -ane 'print "$F[1]\n"' filename

#!/usr/bin/perl
while (<>) {
    @F = split ' ';
    print "$F[1]\n";
}
```

-Fpattern

Allows you to supply an alternate pattern to split on in autosplit mode (when using -a). To split each line on colons instead of the default whitespace:

```
perl -an -F/:/ -e 'print "$F[1]\n"' filename
```

-d

This invokes the Perl debugger on the script (see chapter 15).

-Mmodule

Allows you to use a module from the command line:

```
$ perl -MCPAN -e 'shell'
```

Invokes Perl and calls use CPAN; before executing the statement shell, which, under the CPAN.pm module, puts you into an interactive shell mode.

-v

Prints the Perl version information.

-V

Prints a detailed summary of the configuration details used when compiling Perl and prints out the value of the @INC array.

A P P E N D I X   B

Special variables

You have already seen many of Perl's special built-in variables (such as the $_ variable). Table B.1 is a partial list of the most common such variables. (See `perldoc perlvar` for further information.)

Table B.1   Special variables

Variable	Description
$_	Default variable for input and pattern matching.
$.	The current line number of the current or last file handle read.
$/	Input record separator. Default is a newline.
$\	Output record separator. Default is a newline.
$"	List separator. Value printed between items in an array when it is interpolated in a double-quoted string. Default is a space.
$0	The current program name.
$^W	Current warning value. You can set this within a script to turn warnings off and on for particular blocks of code.
$ARGV	Current file being read from <ARGV>.
@ARGV	Command line arguments.

Table B.1   Special variables (continued)

Variable	Description
@INC	Search paths for use and require statements.
@F	The autosplit array.
%ENV	Hash of current environment variables, may be set to change the environment for spawned processes.
%SIG	Hash of signal handlers. (See perldoc perlipc.)
ARGV	File handle that iterates over @ARGV, also specified with the empty input operator: <>
STDIN	Standand input file handle.
STDOUT	Standard output file handle.
DATA	Special file handle referring to data following an __END__ or __DATA__ token.

APPENDIX C

Additional resources

Your first line of investigation should be the documentation and FAQs that are included with your distribution of Perl, but here are a few additional resources for learning more about Perl.

Newsgroups

comp.lang.perl.misc. The primary forum for discussions and questions regarding the Perl language.

comp.lang.perl.modules. A forum for discussions and questions relating to the copious existing modules as well as issues surrounding creating your own modules.

comp.lang.perl.moderated. A moderated forum for Perl discussions.

comp.lang.perl.tk. Discussions involving using Perl with the Tk graphical interface.

comp.lang.perl.announce. Announcements relevant to the Perl community.

Web pages

www.perl.com. Your starting place for exploring the world of Perl. From here you can find links to the Perl documentation, CPAN, and lists of other resources.

reference.perl.com. A reference list of modules, tutorials and other Perl-related things.

www.perl.org. The Perl Institute's homepage, another good place to find Perl news and information. At the time of this writing, the Perl Institute had just dissolved and was being passed on to the Perl Mongers, but the web address will probably remain the same. (If not, check the Perl Mongers page given below.)

theory.uwinnipeg.ca/search/cpan-search.html. A search engine for searching the CPAN archives.

www.pm.org. The Perl Mongers homepage. Visit here to find a Perl Mongers group in your area or to start your own if one doesn't exist near you.

Books and magazines

Christiansen, Tom, Randal Schwartz, and Larry Wall. *Programming Perl, 2nd ed.* Sebastopol, CA: O'Reilly and Associates, 1996. Also known as "the camel book" (because of the animal on the cover), this book is *the* reference book on the Perl language. It is somewhat out of date (current to Perl version 5.003), and much of the text is duplicated in the included documentation.

Christiansen, Tom, and Nathan Torkington. *The Perl Cookbook.* Sebastopol, CA: O'Reilly and Associates, 1998. This book is chock-full of recipes and examples and is an asset for any Perl programmer's library.

Cormen, Thomas, Charles Leiserson, and Ronald Rivest. *Introduction to Algorithms.* Cambridge, MA: MIT Press, 1990. This is an outstanding introduction to algorithms and data structures. If you aren't interested in the analysis of algorithms, the data structures presented later are still easily understood.

The Perl Journal. This quarterly journal is an excellent resource with articles ranging from beginner to advanced to the simply whimsical. See *http://tpj.com/* for subscription details and contents of pervious issues.

APPENDIX D

Numeric formats

Our standard number system uses base-10 numbers. If you consider a number such as 42, it really means 4 tens and 2 ones. The rightmost position counts ones and each position leftward in a number counts units 10 times (or base times) greater than the previous position. Thus, 342 is 3 hundreds and 4 tens and 2 ones. There are three other common bases used for numeric data in computer science: binary, octal, and hexidecimal (usually just called hex). These represent base 2, base 8, and base 16, respectively. Hexidecimal is a little odd because we cannot count up to 15 using single digits, so we use letters instead—the letters "a" to "f" stand for the numbers 10 to 15. The following table shows several numbers written in each of these base formats.

Table D.1 Numeric formats

Decimal (base 10)	Binary (base 2)	Octal (base 8)	Hex (base 16)
0	0	0	0
1	1	1	1
2	10	2	2
3	11	3	3
4	100	4	4
5	101	5	5
6	110	6	6
7	111	7	7
8	1000	10	8
9	1001	11	9
10	1010	12	a
11	1011	13	b
12	1100	14	c
13	1101	15	d
14	1110	16	e
15	1111	17	f
16	10000	20	10
17	10001	21	11
…	…	…	…
32	100000	40	20
42	101100	52	2a

glossary

absolute path. The full, unadulterated directory path to a file, beginning with the root of the file system.

alias. When one variable represents another variable, it is said to be an alias for that variable.

anchor. In regular expressions, an anchor is a special character, or metacharacter, that matches a particular *location* in a string as opposed to matching a particular *character*.

argument. What you give your spouse (or child, or parent) when telling that person what to do. Similarly, an argument is data that you give to a program or subroutine that tells the program or subroutine what to work with and how to proceed.

array. A type of variable that holds an ordered list of data.

autovivification. When something comes into existence automatically just by being used as if it has always been there. For example:

```
my $foo;
$foo->{bar} ='baz';
```

In the second statement, $foo is used as if it holds a reference to a hash. Since it did not, an anonymous hash is automatically created and stored in $foo so that we can assign a key and value in that hash.

backreference. Used within a regular expression, a backreference is a special sequence consisting of a backslash followed by an integer that stands for the text matched by a preceding set of capturing parentheses of the same number.

bless.   More like a baptism really, blessing is the act of dubbing a reference as belonging to a particular package, providing a basis for Perl's object-oriented capabilities.

block.   A structural segment of a program consisting of one or more statements that are delimited in Perl by curly braces.

Boolean.   A two-valued (usually true or false) property or variable. Perl does not have Boolean variables, but it does evaluate some expressions (such as conditional expressions) in a Boolean context. This means that, while Perl evaluates the expression to its real value, the condition itself is concerned with only whether the expression is true or false.

byte offset.   As used with the `seek( )` and `tell( )` functions, a position in a file measured in bytes relative to another position in the file (often the beginning or the previous position). A byte is an 8-bit piece of binary data, often representing a character in the ASCII character set.

child class.   Also called a derived class, this is a class that inherits some or all of its functionality from a parent class.

chunk.   Hardcore technical jargon from the `noweb` literate programming tool. Documentation and code are presented in relatively small segments—usually a paragraph or two, or a handful of lines of code—called chunks.

class.   A module that defines data and methods that can be used as an object.

closure.   An anonymous subroutine that is deeply bound to the lexical environment in which it was generated.

command line argument.   Data explicitly passed to a program when it is invoked from the command line

concatenation.   Joining two or more things, usually strings or files.

constructor.   Something used to build or create something else. A class method used to create and return an object is called a constructor. The `[ ]` and `{}` used to create anonymous arrays and hashes can be called constructors (or composers).

coupling.   The degree of interdependency among components (data structures, functions) within a program and/or its modules.

debug. De Volkswagen Beetle is sometimes called de bug. In programming, errors in syntax or logic are referred to as bugs. Debugging is the task of isolating the problems and fixing the code.

declare/declaration. Telling the compiler/interpreter about something—such as a variable or subroutine—rather than telling it to do something (as with a statement).

delimiter. Something—usually a character or string—that demarks the beginning and end of something else, such as a record, a field, or a string. The quotation marks you use around a string in Perl are that string's delimiters.

dereference. To undo the reference in order to follow it to where it points.

dispatch table. A hash table of subroutine references that can be called upon (i.e., dispatched) when the corresponding key is used.

encapsulation. Wrapping up data and functions (or methods) into a neat little package that has a simple interface compared with the code that actually does the work.

evaluate. The act of computing the result of an expression.

expression. Any literal, variable, subroutine, operator, or combination of these that evaluates to a value.

flag. A marker or switch that can be set to cause different actions to take place depending on its value.

function. A named piece of code defined in one place that can be called from someplace else (or many places) in the program. Also called subroutines, especially if the code in question isn't used for its return value.

hash. A type of variable that holds an unordered list of key/value pairs.

heap. A data structure that dynamically maintains a partial ordering of the data it contains.

here-document (here-doc). A form of quoting large, multi-line blocks of text.

inheritance. In object-oriented programming, acquiring characteristics (data and/or methods) from a parent class.

initialize. The act of giving an initial value to a variable.

input. Data that comes into a program or subroutine.

interpolate. Replacing a variable with its value within double-quoted strings.

interpret. In terms of programs, an interpreter reads a program (or a compiled form of a program) and executes the statements contained therein. In terms of creating strings, backslash interpretation is the act of reading certain special sequences of characters as standing for some other (usually non printable) character.

iterate. To sequentially step through a list of values (or a list of key/value pairs).

key. In a hash, the key is what you use to look up values.

keyword. Any built-in function name (such as `print`, `index`, `open`) or other named language construct (such as `while` or `if`) in the Perl language.

literate programming (LP). A method or style of programming that places emphasis on source code documentation. Various tools exist to assist an author in writing more human readable programs.

method. A function that is part of a class.

loop. A flow of control construct which can cause a statement or series of statements (i.e., a block) to be repeated some number of times.

module. A package, defined in its own file, that provides data or functions (or objects and methods) to a program that uses it.

operator. A built-in function, often represented by one or more special symbols.

output. The data that comes out of a program or function.

package. A namespace where you can define variables and functions that won't interfere with the main:: program's namespace or other packages/modules that it uses.

parameter. See argument.

parent class. A class, usually designed to be general in form, that provides basic functionality to its children classes.

POD. The standard markup syntax for embedding documentation within Perl programs, POD stands for plain old documentation.

polymorphism. The ability to be different. Child classes can redefine behaviors inherited from a parent class. Thus, a parent class can have children of many different shapes (i.e., they are polymorphic).

quantifier.   A regular expression term referring to the special symbols that denote some number (possibly zero) of occurrences of the previous character or subexpression.

queue.   A data structure providing a first-in, first-out (FIFO) processing order, rather like a line at the DMV, except you'll want to process your queue faster than that.

recursion.   If defining something in terms of itself makes for a circular definition, then recursion should be thought of as a spiral definition. Defining something recursively means to first rigidly define at least one special case and then a mechanism that can be repeatedly applied to turn other cases into one of the special cases.

reference.   A pointer to the real data. Or the address where some piece of data is stored in memory.

regular expression.   A way of specifying a set of strings (or substrings) by using a variety of pattern-describing symbols and text.

return value.   The final resulting value of an expression or function.

satellite data.   The organization of chunks of data is often based on just a small segment or piece of data called a key. The remaining chunk of data may be referred to as the satellite data for that key.

scalar.   A type of value that is singular in nature, like a single number, a single string, or a single character. A type of variable in Perl that holds a scalar value.

scope.   The range or limits within which a variable is active (i.e., exists). Also referred to as the visibility of the variable.

sentinel value.   A value used as a flag or switch that can be used to determine when a process or loop should stop iterating.

shebang.   Common name for the #! character pair, also called pound bang. The first line of a Perl script—or shell script and many other interpreted scripts—that contains the path to the executable interpreter is often referred to as the shebang line.

slice.   A (possibly non-contiguous) subset of a list of values.

stack.   A data structure providing first-in last-out processing order, like a stack of dishes next to your sink. Presumably they were stacked there one at a time on top of each other, and you will then wash them one at a time starting from the top of the pile. If you are like me however, your dishwashing structure may resemble something more like a heap or just a pile.

standard input.   The input stream for a program, accessible in Perl via the STDIN file handle.

standard output.   The output stream for a program, accessible in Perl via the STDOUT file handle.

statement.   Telling the computer to do something, such as add two numbers, compare two values, or print a string.

string.   A sequence of character data, possibly empty (e.g., the null string).

subroutine.   See function.

subscript.   A syntactic construct for accessing or referring to elements of an array or hash. `$array[2]` uses a subscript of 2 to refer the value stored in the third element of the array (subscripts count from zero). `$hash{key}` uses a subscript of key to refer to the value stored under that key in the hash.

substitution operator.   Like the match operator but also able to replace matched portions of the target string with replacement text.

syntax.   How various symbols can be legitimately put together in a given language.

tangle.   In literate programming, this is the process of extracting and assembling the program code into a format ready to be compiled and/or interpreted.

variable.   A named location of memory where data may stored and retrieved by name.

weave.   In literate programming, this is the process of creating the formal typeset program documentation including any cross reference information specified in the source file.

index